SAUCES
DRESSINGS & MARINADES

Cecilia Norman

SAUCES
DRESSINGS & MARINADES

Macdonald

A Macdonald BOOK
© Cecilia Norman 1985

First published in Great Britain in 1985
by Macdonald & Co (Publishers) Ltd
London & Sydney

A member of BPCC plc

British Library Cataloguing in Publication Data
Norman, Cecilia
    Sauces, dressings and marinades.
    1. Sauces
    I. Title
    641.8'14   TX819.A1

    ISBN 0-356-10662-4

Filmset by Text Filmsetters Ltd, London SE1
Printed and bound in Italy by Tipolitografia
G. Canale & C. S.p.A – Turin

Editor: Julie Dufour
Designer: Sally Downes
Production: John Moulder
Cover Photography: Peter Myers
Food Photography: Peter Chadwick
Stylist: Dawn Lane
Indexer: Michèle Clarke

Macdonald & Co (Publishers) Ltd
Maxwell House
74 Worship Street
London EC2A 2EN

Acknowledgements

The publishers would like to thank the
following for the loan of props:

NEFF (UK) Limited

Way-in Living at Harrods, London
Fortnum and Mason, London
David Mellor, London
Elizabeth David, London

Contents

Foreword

When I first thought about writing a book on sauces I planned a serious work, taking the reader through the various cooking processes for all the traditional sauces made in the old-fashioned way. On reflection, I decided this would never be read except for reference or specific research and would spend most of its time on the shelf gathering dust. Although sauces are greatly improved if they are made from scratch – almost to the point of 'catching your ox to get the bones' – there is a happy medium between spending hours and hours on preparation and whipping up a quick flavourless sauce in no time at all.

A practical book that combined both the traditional and the modern is what I was looking for, so I have devised a work which, though still including those traditional recipes of the likes of Escoffier and the modern, yet still complex, methods of Michel Guérard, has a solid core of practical 1980s recipes. These are all possible, practical and workable.

I hope you will find the layout of the book easy to follow: just look up under the food you are going to serve and you will find a selection of suitable recipes plus some serving suggestions. At the top of each recipe it will tell you whether it is easy to cook, whether you can cook it by microwave, or partially by microwave, whether it will freeze, and any other tips or hints for success.

Salad dressings and marinades have a chapter to themselves, so do try out these very varying recipes. They can make all the difference to the flavour of meat, fish, poultry and even vegetables.

My publisher has given me unstinting help and encouragement and has made it possible for me to include a large number of colour illustrations to make the book so much more enjoyable.

This book assumes that all fruit and vegetables have been washed prior to use and that all spoons are level. Butter or margarine may be used unless otherwise stated, although butter gives a better flavour. Metric, Imperial and American measures are not interchangeable. Use only one type of measurement in each recipe.

Opposite title page: Ice cream sundaes made with *(left)* Melba Sauce *(see page 120)*, *(centre)* Fudge Sauce *(see page 115)* and *(right)* Butterscotch Sauce *(see page 121)*

Opposite: Cream Cheese, Parmesan and Nutmeg Sauce with colourful pasta spirals *(see page 96)*

Introduction

Why Sauces?

There are not many savoury foods that are eaten without some kind of sauce, be it tomato sauce with a burger or simply prepared mustard for serving with steak. Vinegar is frequently sprinkled over fried fish and mayonnaise and salad dressings are an accepted part of our diet. Good food should not need a sauce to disguise it, but a sauce invariably adds interest to ordinary food and, when used judiciously, improves and aids the digestion.

The History of Sauces

Sauce making started with the ancient Egyptians – their national dish was roast goose with beer – and, by the time of ancient Rome, sauce making had established itself as a special branch of cookery. The upper classes in Rome never ate anything that was not sauced or dressed in some way and they made use of all the then-known herbs and spices. Sauce making was an acknowledged art, as is apparent from the large number of sauce recipes given by Apicius, the only Roman cookery writer whose books have survived. Although many oriental spices were imported, the Romans made considerable use of dill, mint, thyme, savory, cumin, borage and oregano, all of which could have been grown in their local gardens. They also used mustard seed to make into a sauce with vinegar: the forerunner of our vinaigrette.

During many of the ancient civilizations a standard sauce was made from a basic condiment called 'garum'. Although the exact composition of this is a mystery, it is understood that it was made from the entrails of fish such as anchovies, sprats and small mackerel, which were put into pots with salt. These pots were then left out in the sun for a few months and subsequently the liquid was strained off and stored in jars. Although it can be traced back to the Greeks in the 4th century BC it was not introduced until much later in Italy; but soon appeared there in every recipe, where wine vinegar and spices were the main additional components. A small bottle of strained *liquamen*, the other name for garum, was even found in the ruins of Pompeii. It was Alexis Soyer, the 19th-century chef, who suggested that it must have had a shrimp base because of the derivation of the word.

In ancient China, because of deaths from food poisoning, fermented food sauce was frowned upon, but nowadays in Nordic countries herrings are often left to ferment before serving – although, obviously, the conditions in which this is done are properly controlled.

Whereas the basis of Roman sauces was garum, the basis of sauces for mediaeval food and cookery was fruit. These sauces were made from grapes that were never quite ripened and was called verjuice. To make this nowadays, it is better to use underripe apples rather than grapes, as our grapes are much too sweet.

Sauce making in mediaeval Paris was the prerogative of special guilds. In the time of Louis XII, these guilds were given the exclusive privilege of making and selling sauces. A statute in 1394 mentions cameline, which was made of cinnamon, cloves, ginger, breadcrumbs and vinegar and included grains of paradise which are similar to allspice. It also mentions tence which was made of almonds, ginger wine and verjuice, and some other sauces, including *le saupiquet, le mortechan, la galatine, la sauce à l'alose, au moût*, milk, garlic and green sauces. Most of these sauces were sweet but peppery.

The early mediaeval sauce 'gramose' was a custard sauce made from eggs, still cider, stock and vinegar. A sauce for boiled fowl consisted of stock with pounded sweet spices plus, in winter, hyssop, sage and parsley and, in summer, green sorrel. The mediaeval French also made a white sauce with almonds instead of walnuts and added a little sugar to this. For roast fowl, they would serve a garlic sauce with almonds and sweet wine and in winter they would use the grape juice (verjuice). At least one sauce, Sauce Robert, went on being made for centuries – though no doubt with some changes – and was still being made by Louis XIV's cook, François Pierre de la Varenne.

Nineteenth-century sauces are very much associated with clubs. It was the height of fame for a club to have one of its sauces pass into current use bearing its name. At such a club, a customer might be expected to be charged more for the sauce than for the dish. There was quite an array of famous sauces created at this time including Reform, Prince Regent's, Alboni, Benton, Cambridge, Cumberland and Dr. Kitchener's. The Prince Regent's sauce served with roast chicken was made of butter, ham, shallots, wine, chicken stock and brown sauce. Reform sauce, which was invented by Alexis Soyer for the club, consisted of espagnole sauce, jellied brown sauce, lemon juice, redcurrant jelly, red wine, cayenne pepper, black pepper, tomato purée, hard-boiled egg in strips, sautéed mushrooms and cooked ham. Béchamel was prepared for Marquis Béchamel, Lord Steward to Louis XIV, and Escoffier made his béchamel sauce with seasonings and raw cubed veal, cooking the veal until it was tender to extract the flavour. Today we make béchamel using stock because it is so much cheaper than spending a large amount of money on meat that may not subsequently be eaten.

According to Dickens, sauces were very varied and he writes of many that are still in use to this day, such as bread sauce. Sauces seem to have been to the middle class what gravy was to humbler diners, who consumed it in enormous quantities.

Alexander Dumas said 'No cook can be a good cook until he has mastered the art of sauce making'. Indeed in every hotel the sauce chef is especially respected.

Modern Days

We are now accustomed to having sauces with our food even though we may resort to packets or cans of sauces. The cans of sauce that you actually cook the food in are at best undetectable and at worst unacceptable. The problem is that there is not sufficient variety and that is where the home cook scores, for, at the drop of a spoon, you can add a little mustard or tomato purée or sprig of fresh herbs of whatever variety is growing in the garden. So sauce making can become positive fun and, if you don't enjoy cooking something, you won't enjoy eating it either.

The Functions of Sauces

There are three main functions of a sauce – to enhance flavour, to mask lack of flavour and to act as a binder.

The simplest savoury sauce could be just melted butter perhaps seasoned with a little salt, lemon juice and herbs. And a dry pudding is much improved when custard is poured over it, or a melted ice cream can simply be poured over a dessert in place of cream.

A sauce is any liquid or semi-liquid adjunct that complements a dish. It can be thick, medium or thin and made with a variety of simple ingredients. A sauce does not necessarily have to be cooked separately; many are cooked in with the main food ingredients so that the juices and flavours of both the food and the added ingredients can intermingle. Included among these are Boeuf Bourguignon, Coq au Vin, and Sole à la Bonne Femme.

A sauce will give moisture or richness to a plain or dry dish, will enhance its appearance and may even add to the nutritional value. A sauce is sometimes used to contrast with the food it is to accompany: for example, pork with apple sauce, duck with orange sauce, or fish with tartare sauce. On other occasions, a sauce can be used as a coating to improve the appearance of food that might otherwise be somewhat uninspiring: *chaud-froid* is a combination of a mayonnaise set with gelatine and sometimes aspic jelly, which gives sauce a very glossy appearance.

Sauces do not have to be runny; they can be hard, such as a mixture of butter and brandy with sugar to give a brandy sauce. Nor does a sauce have to be cloyingly sweet or even rich; a simple fruit sauce can be made by puréeing soft fruits such as raspberries and strawberries.

The number of sauces that you can make is endless. The main thing to remember is not to serve too many sauces at any one meal.

Thickenings

More often than not a sauce is thickened in some way and this thickening is known as a liaison. Its purpose is to prevent the separation of the liquids and solids. A liaison or thickening agent may be cornflour (cornstarch), arrowroot, flour, potato flour, rice flour, barley flour, eggs and cream, or blood, and these are all added to the sauce in some way to make it thick. However, some sauces are thickened merely by reduction, that is cooking for a long time until most of the liquid has evaporated. Methods of thickening depend upon the type of sauce you are making.

Roux

A roux is the most common thickening and this is a mixture of melted fat with an equal quantity of flour. The roux is usually cooked for a few moments to prevent the sauce from having a raw flavour but, in sauces that are being cooked for several minutes, this may not be necessary as prolonged heating helps to cook the flour. A roux sauce does not have to be white, it may be blond – that is a kind of biscuit colour – or the roux may be cooked for a much longer time over a very low heat so that the mixture becomes almost chestnut in colour. This would then be the basis for a brown sauce.

Beurre Manié

This is an equal volume of fat and flour that is mixed together to form a paste. It is then added in small pats to the boiling liquid towards the end of the cooking period and each pat should be whisked in vigorously.

Fécule

These are farinaceous ingredients, such as cornflour (cornstarch) or arrowroot, which are mixed with a small quantity of cold liquid before being stirred into the boiling sauce.

Eggs

Whole eggs or yolks only are beaten with a small quantity of the sauce before adding to the pan. The sauce is then cooked over a gentle heat until it thickens. Eggs are also used for making custards.

Eggs and Butter

These are used in combination for making hollandaise and Béarnaise sauces and are sometimes called emulsified sauces. To make these the butter is melted, then eggs and other ingredients, such as lemon juice, salt, pepper and seasonings, are added and the sauces are cooked over a gentle heat until they thicken.

Blood

One of the few accepted recipes where blood is used as a thickener is Jugged Hare.

Classification of Sauces

Sauces may be classified in many ways although there are a large number of recipes where there is an overlap. The main divisions are:
White sauces which include béchamel, velouté, allemande.
Brown sauces of which the best known is espagnole.
Cold Sauces which include mayonnaise and *chaud-froid*.
Sweet hot sauces encompassing egg custards and sabayon.
Sweet cold sauces which might include chocolate sauce and butterscotch sauce.
Hard sauces of which the best known is brandy butter.
Miscellaneous where you would expect to find horseradish, apple sauce, curry sauce and mint sauce.

Salad dressings and gravies are also considered to be sauces and many marinades are used in sauce making, but perhaps the most important ingredient in sauce making is the liquid that is used. This is frequently a stock, which may either be made from the long slow cooking of bones and skin or the use of water and a stock cube.

All kinds of sauces are included in this book, some are complicated, many are easy and most are capable of adaptation.

Notes on Sauce Making

Here is a collection of tips and hints that I have found most useful.

Heavy-based saucepans are the best to use as they heat up more slowly and more evenly.

There is now a machine called a saucemaker on the market. This may be useful for making some of these sauces, but do read the instructions carefully before use.

When cooking a roux sauce, you will find that it thickens as soon as the liquid boils and then, as you continue cooking, the sauce will thin and lighten.

When sauce ingredients are added to fish or meat for casserole cooking, the food is usually first coated with flour. This flour should be part of the measured flour and not additional to the recipe.

Do not heat sauces thickened with egg yolks beyond 160°F/70°C or the sauces will curdle.

When using a double saucepan, only put 1 in/2.5 cm of hot water in the base as, if the bottom of the top half of the saucepan touches the water, the sauce will curdle. If it is necessary to top up during cooking because of evaporation, the added water must be very hot.

To lighten a sauce, whisk 2 egg yolks with 3 tablespoons of cold water until foamy, then whisk into the boiling sauce. The quantity can be increased and will give added volume.

When sauces thickened with *beurre manié* are boiled fiercely, they become less creamy but do look glossier.

Crème fraîche gives a light creamy texture to a sauce. Mix the *crème fraîche* into the sauce and bring to the boil, then continue cooking to reduce the sauce to the amount you require.

The addition of finely puréed cooked vegetables will thicken and enrich a fish or meat sauce. Sometimes you can cook the fish or meat with the vegetables, then remove and purée the vegetables before pouring back over the fish or meat.

Flat tasteless sauces are improved by the addition of a little lemon juice or wine vinegar.

A sauce that is tart or bitter after cooking can be improved by adding sugar, fortified wine or cream.

Sauces lacking character or poor colour can be improved by the addition of a little demi-glace or espagnole sauce or jellied fish stock. Freshly ground black pepper or a few drops of brandy also help.

It is usually better to boil wine first to decrease the volume and evaporate the alcohol before using it in a sauce. In white wine this reduces the acidity, and in red wine the bouquet becomes more concentrated. Wine has a tendency to make sauces thin on prolonged cooking and this is particularly true of roux-based sauces. Boiling the wine first should overcome this.

Do not use metal whisks in metal saucepans when making pale sauces or the colour will be affected.

When a sauce is made with both milk and an acid ingredient, such as tomatoes, lemon juice or wine, there is always a danger of curdling. The milk proteins separate into curds and whey when there is too much heat and any acid ingredient. To overcome this, add the acid ingredients a little at a time, beating vigorously after the milk-based sauce is cooked and thickened.

Sauces are always better when cooked over a gentle heat.

Many sauces are cooked in with the main food so that the juices and flavours of both the food and the added ingredients can intermingle. Stews and casseroles of red meat will thicken further due to the blood content in the meat. If you are going to reheat these dishes, it is better to reduce the quantity of flour.

Opposite: Basic Mayonnaise *(see page 140)*

It is not always possible to regulate the heat under the saucepan and sauces may therefore turn out to be too thick or too thin. To thin down sauces, either reduce the cooking time or add stock or boiled milk. Thin sauces may be reduced for longer and this must be done before adding a liaison such as eggs, cream or yogurt.

Egg yolks should always be beaten first with a little cool liquid before adding to the boiling sauce.

For special brown sauces, you can bake the flour until it is a chestnut brown colour. Do this in a slow oven, then use this browned flour when making a roux.

Always add sauces towards the end of the cooking time because they become stronger in flavour as they are reduced.

The base for a white roux sauce may be milk, thin cream or a mixture of milk and water. Sometimes veal, chicken or fish stock are used but beef stock is usually used for darker heavier sauces.

Evaporated milk, because it is concentrated, produces richer sauces.

When a sauce requires to be reduced, do not imagine that the results will be just as good if you cut down the initial quantity of liquid. The flavours are concentrated by reduction.

Using the microwave
Timings will be shortened by about three-quarters when adapting recipes from conventional instructions. As this is primarily a conventional cook book the term 'Microwave' simply indicates that the sauce could be successfully prepared by using the microwave oven.

To brown mince in the microwave, cook on Full Power, breaking up the lumps frequently, and drain before use. The microwave leeches fat, separating it from the meat.

To reduce sauces in the microwave, cook on Full Power in an uncovered bowl and stir occasionally to prevent overthickening round the outside edge. Sauces take longer to reduce in the microwave.

When adding an egg/cream liaison to sauces that are cooked in the microwave, always add these last and then heat on Defrost.

Use the microwave oven to regenerate butter/egg emulsion sauces, such as hollandaise. Use the Defrost setting and whisk the sauce frequently.

When sautéeing vegetables, it is usual to reduce the oil or fat as these are not absorbed when cooking by microwave.

There is less moisture loss when cooking by microwave, so sauces requiring long cooking will require less liquid.

When converting delicate sauces normally cooked in a double saucepan to the microwave, the Defrost setting should be used.

All dishes and bowls used in microwave cookery must be made of suitably acceptable materials.

Freezing
Sauces that can be frozen will usually keep for three months. However, spicy sauces should be used within two months. If sauces thicken during freezing, add extra liquid when thawing and reheating.

Thaw sauces in the refrigerator or in a double saucepan or in the microwave. If the recipe includes cream or eggs, only add these once the sauce has completely thawed.

Do not freeze mayonnaise-type sauces.

Only freeze hollandaise if you have a microwave oven. Bring it back in the microwave on Defrost setting, beating frequently.

White, blonde or brown roux can be made up in large quantities and will keep in the freezer for three to four months. Freeze them in ice-cube sections and drop these into hot liquid as you would *beurre manié*.

Sometimes sauces appear grainy after thawing. To bring them back to perfect condition, blend them in the liquidizer. Starch-based sauces, whether hot or cold, will also regain their texture better when reheated and then left to cool if necessary. Liquidizing also lightens the colour.

To prevent skin forming on sauces the following methods may be found helpful:
1 Pour a thin layer of milk over the cooked sauce, mixing it in just before reheating or serving.
2 Draw a teaspoon of butter over the hot sauce immediately after cooking and stir in as above.
3 Cover the sauce with a piece of plastic cling film, but inevitably a little of the sauce will be lost where it adheres to the plastic cling film.
4 Dampen a piece of wax or greaseproof paper on one side only, place the wet side directly in contact with the surface of the cooked sauce and remove just before reheating or serving.

Master Recipes

Although there are many different types of sauces, the main savoury sauces fall into the following categories:

a) *Roux-based sauces* where flour and butter are cooked together, then liquid is added and the sauce is completed by heating until it thickens.

There are three main sauces in this category, white sauce, blond sauce (velouté) and brown sauce (espagnole). The difference between them is the colour of the butter and flour mixture before the liquid is added.

To make a white sauce there needs to be a white roux, where the butter is melted, the flour is stirred in and both are cooked together for 1-2 minutes, just enough to cook the flour and remove any raw taste but not to colour it.

To make a blond or pale roux for a velouté sauce, cooking is continued for up to 5 minutes after the flour is added to the melted butter and this mixture is cooked until it is a pale biscuit colour.

To make a brown sauce, the flour is added to the sautéed vegetables and is then cooked for up to 10 minutes or until the mixture is a nut brown colour.

These are the bases for the grand sauces (*les grandes sauces*), béchamel, velouté and espagnole, and are also often known as mother sauces.

Sauces based on a white roux cooked with water and extra butter are flavoured in various ways to produce derivative sauces.

The liquid used in preparing the three roux-based sauces influences the flavour and kind of sauce being made. Thus a fish stock would be used for a fish dish, a chicken stock for a chicken dish and so on, but the white sauces nearly all include milk. Recipes for suitable stocks (*fonds de cuisine*) will be found in the chapter on Stocks.

The proportions of fat and flour to liquid determine how thick the finished sauce will be. As a rule of thumb, a pouring sauce requires 1oz/25 g/¼ cup flour and 1 oz/25 g/2 tbsp butter to 1 pt/600 ml/2½ cups liquid.

For a creamy pouring sauce, use 1 oz/25 g/¼ cup flour and 1 oz/25 g/ 2 tbsp butter to ¾ pt/450 ml/2 cups liquid.

For a coating sauce, use 1 oz/25 g/¼ cup flour and 1 oz/25 g/2 tbsp butter to ½pt/300 ml/1¼ cups liquid.

For a very thick sauce or *panada*, use 1oz/25 g/¼ cup flour and 1 oz/ 25 g/ 2 tbsp butter to ¼ pt/150 ml/⅔ cup liquid.

The recipes can, of course, be easily increased.

b) *Emulsified sauces* contain no starch and are thickened by the addition of eggs. There are two main sauces in this category. The warm, butter and egg emulsion known as hollandaise requires cooking, and mayonnaise, which is an oil and egg emulsion, requires no cooking and is a cold sauce.

c) *Tomato sauce* is also known as a *grande sauce* because it can be used in so many sauces and other dishes, but the method of making it is different and the thickness is obtained by reduction, that is to say simmering until much of the liquid has been evaporated.

d) Other master sauces are *vinaigrette*, which comes into the category of salad dressings, and *savoury butters*, which are chilled and sliced and served as toppings to add flavour and moistness.

The methods of making the main categories are set out in a step-by-step form in this section. The recipes and other sauces based on these methods are in the main recipe chapters. Sauces derived from the mother sauces are known as *sauces composées* or compound sauces and are sometimes called daughter sauces.

You will also find in this section instructions for making *beurre manié*, to use for thickening sauces, and three methods for making clarified butter, which is good for frying or to seal pâtés to prevent them from becoming dry.

Mayonnaise (*Egg/oil emulsion*)

To make a fairly solid mayonnaise use 1 egg yolk to ¼ pt/150 ml/⅔ cup salad oil and flavour it with a pinch of mustard powder, salt and pepper to taste and 1-2 tablespoons vinegar or lemon juice. However, 1 egg yolk will hold up to 6 fl oz/175 ml/¾ cup oil. The oil and eggs must be at a similar temperature to avoid curdling (a curdle resembles tiny hard pieces floating in a clear liquid and no amount of beating will bring it together). To resuscitate a curdled mayonnaise, beat 2 more egg yolks together thoroughly, then gradually whisk in the curdled mixture. Sometimes a teaspoon of hot water beaten into the yolks before the oil is added will lessen the chances of curdling.

1 Combine the egg yolks and seasonings in a bowl and beat until the yolks thicken. Beat in the oil drop by drop until the sauce begins to thicken.

2 When the sauce has thickened, add the oil in a fine steady stream, beating continuously. Once all the oil has been incorporated, mix in the vinegar or lemon juice and add seasonings to taste.

Tomato Sauce

There are a large number of tomato sauces that can be used to give flavour to other sauces. Choose a recipe that includes sautéed diced bacon and sautéed chopped onions and carrots. Use ripe red tomatoes or, if these are not available or are very expensive, substitute with canned tomatoes. If the sauce lacks flavour, add a tablespoon or so of tomato purée and sprinkle in a few herbs – many herbs combine well with tomatoes and basil is particularly good.

Once the ingredients are cooked, simmer the sauce until it is reduced by one-third to one-half. The sauce should then be puréed in a liquidizer or blender or pressed through a fine sieve before using.

Clarified Butter

Clarified butter is used for frying because it has a higher smoking temperature due to the salts and milk solids having been removed. It is also used for coating pâtés to keep them moist and exclude the air. There are three basic methods of clarifying butter:

1 Put the butter in a saucepan and place over moderate heat until the butter bubbles. Leave for a few moments, then strain through muslin or a clean white kitchen cloth. A small quantity can be strained through a tea strainer, first lining it with a piece of absorbent kitchen paper towel. Discard the solids and use the butter as required. When set, clarified butter regains its colour but the texture is more like solid fat.

2 To make in the microwave, place the butter in a large jug or bowl and cover the top with plastic cling film to prevent the butter from spattering. Remove from the microwave as soon as the butter is fast bubbling. Do not remove the cover until 1 minute has elapsed to prevent residual heat from causing spattering. Strain as above.

3 Put the butter in a small saucepan, just cover with cold water, then bring to the boil over moderate heat. Pour into a narrow jug, refrigerate or freeze until set firm, then lift the disc of butter out of the jug and scrape away any sediment from the underside. Pat the solid butter dry with kitchen paper towel, then wrap in plastic cling film and cover with foil. Store in the refrigerator or freezer and use as required.

Basic White Sauce (*Roux blanc*)

A white sauce can be sweet or savoury and if it has to be kept waiting either cover the sauce with a piece of damp wax or greaseproof paper, the damp side against the sauce, or pour a tablespoon of milk over the surface, or draw a teaspoon of butter over the hot sauce, allowing it to melt over the surface. Stir in the milk or butter just before serving or reheating.

The best known derivative of the white sauce is béchamel in which the milk is heated to steaming point with herbs and vegetables. This is left to infuse for 15-30 minutes and then the milk is strained and used as the liquid in the recipe.

1   Melt the butter in a heavy-based saucepan over moderate heat. Add the flour, then stir in using a wooden spoon – make sure that every particle of flour is mixed in.

2   Reduce the heat to minimum and cook for 1 minute, stirring constantly.

3   Remove the pan from the heat and gradually stir in the cold liquid. OR Leave the pan over moderate heat and add cold liquid all at once. OR Leave the pan on the heat and add hot liquid gradually.

4   Cook over low heat, stirring continuously with a wooden spoon, until the sauce thickens. Add seasoning or flavouring. Continue cooking for 1-2 minutes, stirring continuously. Add any other seasonings you like that require no further cooking (e.g. cheese).

Velouté Sauce (*Roux blond*)

A velouté sauce is made with either veal, chicken or fish stock and the roux is cooked until it is golden. It is sometimes used in allemande, aurore and supreme sauces.

1   Bring he stock to the boil. Melt the butter or margarine in a heavy-based saucepan over moderate heat. Stir in the flour using a wooden spoon – make sure that every particle of flour is mixed in.

2   Reduce the heat to minimum and cook for 3-4 minutes, stirring continuously, until the paste begins to change colour. Remove the pan from the heat and leave for 1-2 minutes for the roux to cool a little.

3   Gradually beat in the hot stock using a wooden spoon. Replace the pan over moderate heat and bring the sauce to the boil, skimming if necessary. Add seasonings.

4   Reduce the heat and simmer in the uncovered pan, stirring occasionally, until the volume is reduced by one-third. Strain before use.

Basic Brown Sauce (*Roux brun*)

The basic brown sauce is sometimes known as espagnole. It can be cooked by other methods but it is always essential to brown the flour. One small onion and 1 small carrot, finely chopped, are sufficient to add flavour but mushrooms or mushroom peelings can also be included when adding the stock. If you like, 1 or 2 rashers of trimmed finely chopped bacon may be cooked in with the vegetables. Allow 1 tablespoon tomato purée to each ¼ pt/150 ml/⅔ cup stock. The stock must be a good quality brown meat stock.

Espagnole sauce may be used on its own or with the addition of other ingredients or sauces for derivative or daughter sauces, such as ambassadrice, Italian or Madeira sauces.

1 Peel and finely chop the vegetables.

2 Melt the butter, margarine or dripping in a heavy-based saucepan. Stir in the vegetables and cook until tender.

3 Stir in the flour and cook, stirring continuously, until the mixture is a hazelnut brown colour and a nutty odour can be detected. (Do not overcook or the sauce will taste bitter.)

4 Gradually add the stock, stirring continuously, and bring to the boil. Stir in the tomato purée and reduce the heat to minimum. Half-cover the pan with the lid and cook gently, stirring occasionally, allowing 15 minutes cooking time for each ¼ pt/150 ml/⅔ cup stock. Purée, then strain back into the saucepan. Season to taste and reheat.

Hollandaise Sauce (*Butter/egg emulsion*)

There are various methods of making hollandaise sauce. A little of the butter is sometimes melted first before beating in the eggs, then the remaining butter is added as shown below. The sauce may also be made in a bowl over a pan of gently steaming water instead of a double saucepan, but it is inadvisable to use a single saucepan as there is a great risk of curdling.

To make a basic hollandaise sauce use 2 egg yolks, 1½ teaspoons water and 4 oz/100 g/½ cup unsalted butter. Season with salt and pepper and add either 1½ tablespoons vinegar or lemon juice to flavour it. If the recipe calls for the liquid to be reduced, put the liquid in a saucepan and boil until reduced to the specified amount, then cool slightly.

1 Beat the egg yolks and reduced liquid and strain into the top half of a double saucepan.

2 Put 1 in/2.5 cm of hot water in the base and place over minimum heat. Place the top part of the saucepan in position.

3 Stir the egg yolk mixture continuously until it thickens. Add the seasonings.

4 Cut the butter into small pieces. Add the butter a piece at a time, beating each in thoroughly until it has all been incorporated and the sauce is thick and the consistency of mayonnaise. Remove the pan from the heat and lift the top section away from the base. Add extra lemon juice or vinegar and more salt and pepper to taste.

To make hollandaise sauce in a liquidizer:
1 Put the egg yolks, salt and pepper in the liquidizer and blend until thick.

2 Heat the butter in a small saucepan until it is fast bubbling, then switch on the motor and pour the hot butter through the feed tube in a steady stream. Finally, add the vinegar or lemon juice.

To make hollandaise sauce in a microwave:
1 Put the butter in a bowl, place in the microwave oven and switch on at Full Power until the butter is thoroughly melted.

2 Blend seasonings and lemon juice together with the eggs and beat thoroughly. Strain into the hot melted butter and beat thoroughly. Replace the bowl in the microwave oven set on Defrost or Full Power and beat every 15 seconds until the sauce thickens. Immediately remove the bowl from the microwave and beat thoroughly as the sauce cools. The sauce will thicken considerably on cooling.

To reconstitute hollandaise in the microwave:
1 Put the block of sauce in a glass bowl and place the bowl in the microwave oven. Close the door.

2 Set on Defrost 35% or Full Power No. 3 and switch on for 20 seconds or until the block begins to melt around the sides.

3 Stir the sauce thoroughly, return to the microwave oven if lumps still remain. Switch on for a further 10 seconds, remove from the cabinet and beat thoroughly. Repeat as necessary.

Vinaigrette (French Dressing)

1 Put about 1 in/2.5 cm vinegar or lemon juice into an empty jar or vinegar bottle.

2 Top up with 2-3 in/5-7.5 cm oil.

3 Add seasonings. Close the jar or cork the bottle and shake thoroughly.

This is an easy way of measuring, but you can also mix all the ingredients together in a jar or bowl using a tablespoon or measuring jug to obtain the correct proportions you require (see Salad Dressings).

Savoury Butters

1 Beat the butter in a bowl until it is softened.

2 Beat in the flavourings or seasonings.

3 Shape the butter into a cylindrical block. Roll up in a wax or greaseproof paper and cover with foil, folding in the ends securely.

4 Freeze until firm, then unwrap and slice into pats or grate coarsely, first chilling the grater.

5 Store in the freezer in layers interleaved with wax or greaseproof paper or packed loosely in a sealed container until required.

Beurre Manié (*For thickening sauces*)

1 Measure out an equal volume (not weight) of butter and flour. Place the butter in a small bowl and beat until soft. Gradually stir in the flour until a smooth paste is formed.

2 Bring the liquid in the saucepan to the boil. Add a small piece of butter paste, sliding it down the side of the pan and, without removing the pan from the heat, whisk in thoroughly. Add more pieces of butter paste in the same way.

The sauce will begin to thicken as soon as you add the first piece of butter paste and the more butter paste you add, the thicker the sauce will become.

Beurre manié may be made up in a large quantity to be frozen in tiny pats. There is no need to thaw these pats of butter paste before adding to the boiling liquid.

Beurre manié will not keep in the refrigerator.

Stocks

Stocks are used for making soups and sauces and to improve the flavour in combination dishes where the meat, poultry or vegetables are cooked in a sauce. Stocks have little nutritional value, but the flavour of a dish incorporating a properly-made stock is vastly different from the results obtained when using stock cubes or beef or yeast extracts. Commercial preparations do not vary much in their flavour and cannot give the gelatinous texture that a home-made meat or fish stock produces.

A stock is very similar to a clear soup so that you do not necessarily need a stock to produce a good soup. A few raw bones added to the liquid and other ingredients when making a soup will be sufficient to add body. Be sure to retrieve the bones before serving the soup. Use a light hand with seasonings when making a stock as the flavours intensify when the liquid is reduced. The longer the liquid simmers, the stronger the stock will be and also the more gelatinous. A stock however *is* desirable in sauce making and becomes a valuable *glace de viande* or meat glaze when it is reduced over a long period to a mere tablespoonful of concentrate.

The basic *fonds de cuisine* or stocks are:
White stock – made from veal bones
Chicken stock – similar in colour but with a more definite flavour
Brown stock – a richer colour made from beef meat and bones
Fish stock – which is extremely gelatinous.

A sixth stock, vegetable stock, is useful where no animal derivative or pronounced animal flavour is desired or permitted. Vegetable stocks do not have a sticky texture.

If you are feeling really lazy and do not want to follow a recipe for a stock, all you have to do is to put the bones in a pan with a few flavouring ingredients, cover with cold water, then bring to the boil. Immediately reduce the heat and simmer for some considerable time (with the exception of course of fish stocks which require only a short length of cooking time). Skim frequently during cooking, strain after use, cool rapidly and remove the fat.

The fact that stocks take quite a long time to cook presents few problems, but the odour created can permeate the whole house. Try to have some ventilation in the kitchen which will also reduce the problem of condensation. These are the main reasons why cooks are often discouraged from making stocks. Beef and lamb stocks should really be made conventionally, but chicken, game, fish and vegetable stocks all cook well and comparatively quickly in the microwave oven and the odours are trapped inside the cabinet. Any condensation can easily be wiped up afterwards. If you are a microwave cook, you will have discovered that poultry skins do not soften very well in roasting or casseroling and, because fat is trapped under the skin, dishes containing them often require skimming. However, these skins come in very handy for making stocks and should not be thrown away. To cook poultry stock in the microwave oven, put bones and skin in a 5-pint/2.8-litre/6-pint bowl, add seasonings and flavourings, three-quarters cover the top of the bowl and cook for 35-40 minutes on Maximum setting. Cook fish stocks in a bowl or jug that is really much larger than you think it needs to be, as fish stocks tend to boil up and over. As soon as the stock has reached boiling point, reduce the setting from Maximum to Defrost 35% and every alarming boil-up will be followed by a quiet period which prevents an overspill. Fish stocks are best when they are cooked uncovered.

Stocks should never be boiled, so it is imperative to reduce the temperature to simmering as soon as the liquid reaches boiling point.

Boiling will spoil the flavour and the texture of meat stocks and cause fish stocks to become bitter.

Chop bones into small pieces to enable the maximum extraction of calcium and gelatine and skim stocks frequently during cooking. Stocks should be cooled rapidly after cooking and preferably chilled so that every vestige of fat can be removed, which reduces the likelihood of rancidity. Strain after use, cool rapidly and remove the fat. The fat from meat and poultry stocks, although flavoured, need not be discarded. Scrape any sediment away from the underside and use as dripping when roasting meat.

In meat and fish stocks, the vegetables are used solely for flavour and should not be left in the stock after cooking because they will absorb the flavour and mineral salts from the liquid making the stock poorer. Potatoes and peas are generally unsuitable for use in stock making as they not only produce clouding but also impair the keeping qualities. It is tempting to throw in scraps and peelings from any leftover ingredients, but if these have no food or flavouring value there is little point in adding them.

Stocks do not keep well. You must be careful to store them in a cool place and, excepting fish stocks, bring them to the boil every 24 hours. Never add fresh ingredients to a warm stock and then leave it without any further cooking as this will make it sour. Although raw bones produce the best flavour and texture, you can use well-washed cooked meat bones or a carcass from a roast chicken.

The most economical way to store stocks is to boil them down until they are highly concentrated and then freeze in quantities you are likely to require. It is often convenient to do this in an ice cube tray. Use meat stocks for meat dishes, chicken stocks for chicken dishes and fish stocks for fish dishes.

When making poultry stocks from giblets, the giblets must be cleaned properly. Slit the gizzard round the outside edge and scrape out any bits and pieces from the inner sack. If the gall bladder has not been removed from the liver, take it away, but if it has been ruptured in the process of trussing, scrape away any yellow stains which will cause bitterness. The heart should be properly cleaned, removing blood clots in cold salted water. To achieve a good giblet stock, three or four chickens are required but it is sometimes possible to buy giblets separately.

To clear and clarify cloudy stock, beat 1 crushed egg shell and 1 egg white into each 2 pt/1.2 litres/5 cups cold strained meat or chicken stock, bring the liquid to the boil over moderate heat and whisk continuously until the mixture boils. Cook for a further 5-10 minutes without stirring, remove the pan from the heat and leave for about 20 minutes, then strain through a double thickness of muslin. The egg white and egg shell will have attracted all the solids, leaving the stock completely clear.

When using cubes for stock making, make sure that they are completely dissolved in hot water and take particular care with stale stock cubes which tend to dry up and become grainy. If you are using stock cubes in a stock or sauce that is to be reduced, use only half the quantity recommended on the packet. Canned consommé is often a better substitute than stock cubes and it is sometimes possible to obtain consommé powder which you can mix up to a strength to suit yourself. A packet of powdered clear chicken soup or beef broth is a useful standby and a small quantity of meat extract will perk up a flavourless stock. For quickly-made vegetable stock, use either a teaspoon of yeast extract to add flavour or vegetable stock cubes which are also available.

1

Aspic Jelly

*Requires some expertise and an hour to drip through the jelly
bag · Do not microwave · Freeze · Use for glazing canapés or in chaud-
froid · Makes 1½ pt/900 ml/3¾ cups but do not make a smaller quantity
unless you are certain that you have sufficient*

1½ pt/900 ml/ 3¾ cups stock or water ¼ pt/150 ml/⅔ cup sherry 5 tbsp tarragon vinegar 5 tbsp malt vinegar Juice and grated rind of 1 lemon 12-16 black peppercorns 1 tsp salt	Combine in a large saucepan.
1 small carrot 1 small onion 1 stick celery	Peel and slice the carrot and onion and slice the celery and add to the saucepan.
2 egg whites Shells of 2 eggs	Whisk the egg whites into the cold liquid. Crush the shells and stir in.
2 oz/50 g powdered gelatine	Add to the pan. Heat gently, stirring constantly until the liquid is warm and the gelatine begins to dissolve. Using a wire whisk, beat until the mixture is frothy. Remove the whisk and bring to a full boil. Move the pan away from the heat and whisk once more. Bring back to the boil, then strain through a jelly bag over a deep bowl. If the jelly begins to set in the bag before it has all dripped through, return the mixture to the saucepan, whisking as before. To use, place the bowl of jellied aspic over a saucepan of gently simmering water and stir to bring the aspic back to the correct consistency. To aid and hasten setting, the bowl of cool aspic can be placed over a bowl of ice cubes.

Note: The colour of the aspic will depend on
the stock you use.

2

Chicken Stock

*Easy to cook · A pressure cooker can be used · Microwave – excellent
but requires a 5-pt/2.8-litre/6-pt bowl and takes about 40
minutes · Freeze · Yield depends upon the quantity being cooked – in
the microwave the maximum yield is about 1½ pt/900 ml/3¾ cups*

Chicken bones, carcass, skin and cleaned giblets 1 large carrot, scraped and cut into chunks 1 medium onion, quartered 1 stick celery, cut into chunks 1 bay leaf 1 sprig parsley 1 sprig rosemary 1 sprig thyme	Combine in a heavy-based saucepan. **Note:** Use fresh chicken bones and skin or the carcass from a roast chicken. Add giblets which must be carefully washed first. Giblets must be cut before being used in the microwave oven.
Cold water	Add sufficient water to cover the vegetables and bones. Bring to the boil over moderate heat, skimming frequently. Cover, reduce the heat and simmer for 1 hour. Remove the lid and simmer for a further 30 minutes. Strain, cool rapidly, then refrigerate or chill in the freezer until a layer of fat settles on the top. Remove the fat.
Salt Pepper	Reheat and season to taste. Use as a basis for soups or sauces.

Note: When cooking in the microwave oven
the stock should be three-quarters covered
with plastic cling film during cooking and
skimming will not be necessary.

3

Rich Brown Stock

Easy to cook · Do not microwave . Freeze · After using to make stock, the meat has lost practically all its goodness and so is not really suitable to eat · The recipe can be made with just bones · Makes about 1¾ pt/ 1 litre/4½ cups of liquid or half the quantity of jellied stock.

1 lb/450 g cheap minced or ground beef	Place in a large saucepan and cook over a moderate heat, stirring continuously, until the mince is browned. Drain away the fat.
1 marrowbone, broken into pieces	Add to the beef.
3 pt/1.7 litres/7½ cups cold water	Add to the bones and meat.
Bouquet garni	Add to the saucepan. Bring to the boil over moderate heat, then reduce to simmering and cook with the lid on for 3 hours. Top up with boiling water if the liquid reduces beyond the level of the meat and bones.
1 onion, unpeeled and coarsely chopped *1 large carrot, scraped and sliced* *1 stick celery, coarsely cut* *1 tsp salt*	Stir into the pan and simmer for 1 hour. Remove the lid and simmer for a further hour. Skim the stock from time to time during cooking. Strain the cooked stock and adjust the seasoning. Cool rapidly and use as required.

4

Economical Court Bouillon

Easy to prepare · Microwave – reduce setting once boiling point is reached · Freeze · Increase or decrease the quantity of vinegar and water but always keep them in the same ratio and cook for longer if a stronger Court Bouillon is required · Use a ratio of 6 parts water to 1 part vinegar · Yield according to the quantity used

¼ pt/150 ml/⅔ cup white vinegar *1½ pt/900 ml/3¾ cups cold water* *1 small onion, peeled and halved* *1 stick celery, coarsely cut* *1 small carrot, peeled and sliced* *5 white peppercorns* *1 bay leaf* *3 sprigs parsley* *½ tsp tarragon leaves or pinch dried tarragon*	Combine all the ingredients in a large saucepan and bring to the boil over moderate heat. Reduce the heat and simmer for 5 minutes, leave the mixture to cool, then strain and use as required.
Salt *Pepper*	Season to taste before using.

Above: Aspic Jelly

1 Assemble the necessary ingredients before you start.
2 Whisk the egg whites into the cold liquid.
3 Strain through a jelly bag over a deep bowl.
4 Use for glazing and decorating canapés.

Fish Fumet

Easy to prepare but must be skimmed to prevent boiling over ·
Microwave – switch to Defrost setting after liquid boils · Use hot or start
from cold · Makes 6 fl oz/175 ml/³⁄₄ cup

1½ lb/700 g fish bones, trimmings and skins 1½ pt/900 ml/3¾ cups cold water	Combine in a large saucepan, making sure that there is enough water to cover the fish.
12 peppercorns 1 stick celery, roughly chopped 2 sprigs parsley 1 bay leaf 1 sprig thyme 1 carrot, peeled and sliced 1 large onion, peeled and roughly chopped ½ tsp salt 1 tbsp white wine vinegar 7 fl oz/200 ml/⁷⁄₈ cup dry white wine (use leftover wine)	Add to the pan, bring to the boil, then remove the scum. Reduce the heat, cover with a lid and simmer for 30 minutes. Strain through muslin or a fine nylon sieve. Return to the saucepan and boil vigorously without a lid until the liquid is reduced by one-third. Use as required

Poultry or Game Stock

Easy to cook · The flavour of the stock depends on the poultry or game
used · Microwave · Freeze · Yield will be small unless several carcasses
are available

Carcasses, feet, giblets, etc. from the poultry or game	Rinse and clean where necessary and place in a large saucepan.
Cold water	Add sufficient to just cover the bones
1 small onion 6 white peppercorns	Peel and slice the onion and put both into the saucepan.
6 black peppercorns 2-3 tbsp red wine 2 mushrooms 1 bay leaf	Add to the pan and bring to the boil over minimum heat. Reduce to simmering and cook for at least 2 hours in the covered pan. Remove the lid and cook for a further 30 minutes. Strain.
Salt Pepper	Season to taste, reheat and use as required.
	The stock may be cooked in the microwave oven for about 40 minutes in a large bowl three-quarters covered with plastic cling film. The bones should be stirred once during cooking but the stock will not be as strong as when prepared in a saucepan.

Vegetable Stock (1)

Easy to cook · Microwave · Freeze · Makes approximately 2½ pt/
1.5 litres/6¼ cups

8 oz/225 g carrots, peeled and thinly sliced 8 oz/225 g onions, peeled and sliced 3 sticks celery, sliced 2 tbsp vegetable oil	Combine in a heavy-based saucepan and cook over moderate heat until the vegetables brown.
3 pt/1.7 litres/7½ cups boiling water 6 tbsp tomato purée 6 white peppercorns 1 bay leaf 2 sprigs parsley ½ tsp lemon juice 1 tsp yeast extract	Stir into the vegetables, bring to the boil, then reduce the heat and simmer covered for 45 minutes.
4 cabbage leaves, shredded	Add to the pan and cook for a further 10 minutes. Strain and use as required. If you wish to turn this into a vegetable sauce, replace the carrots, onions and celery and purée in a liquidizer or blender. Return the stock and vegetables to the saucepan and boil until the mixture is thick.
Salt Pepper	Season to taste.

Vegetable Stock (2)

Easy to cook · Microwave – use half quantity of liquid and make up with
boiling water after cooking. Three-quarters cover bowl and stir
occasionally · Freeze · Refrigerate – will only keep 24 hours · Makes
1½ pt/900 ml/3¾ cups

8 oz/225 g carrots, peeled and thinly sliced 8 oz/225 g onions, peeled and finely chopped 2 sticks celery, finely sliced 2 oz/50 g spinach, shredded 1 medium leek, trimmed, washed and finely sliced 1 bay leaf 1 blade mace 6 sprigs parsley 6 chives 2 oz/50 g swede, diced (if available) 1¾ pt/1 litre/4½ cups cold water	Combine in a large saucepan and bring to the boil. Reduce the heat and simmer in the pan for 30-40 minutes. Remove the pan from the heat, leave for 15 minutes, then strain into another saucepan.
Salt Pepper	Add seasoning to taste and reheat until boiling. Use as required.

Court Bouillon

Easy to cook · Microwave · Freeze · The quantity of liquid may be increased or decreased using the same amount of herbs and vegetables · One quantity of Court Bouillon can be used at least once more to cook similar fish · Makes 2 pt/1.2 litres/5 cups

1 pt/600 ml/2½ cups cold water	Combine all the ingredients in a large saucepan, bring to the boil over minimum heat, then simmer for 30 minutes. Strain into a bowl or saucepan.
1 pt/600 ml/2½ cups white wine	
6 sprigs parsley	
1 tsp chopped thyme leaves	
1 bay leaf	
6 peppercorns	
2 cloves	
1 small onion, sliced	
1 small carrot, thinly sliced	
Salt Pepper	Season to taste and use as required.

Ordinary Brown Stock

Fairly easy to cook · Do not microwave · Freeze · Makes about 1¾ pt/ 1 litre/4½ cups

2 lb/1 kg beef bones, chopped into small pieces	Combine in a roasting tin and bake at 375°F/ 190°C/Gas Mark 5 for 45 minutes, stirring the mixture occasionally, until the bones are golden brown. Transfer the mixture to a large saucepan, add 3½ pt/2 litres/4½ pt water, gradually bring to the boil over medium heat, skimming once or twice.
4 oz/100 g bacon rinds	
2 medium carrots, peeled and sliced	
2 medium onions, peeled and sliced	
Bouquet garni	Add to the pan and simmer the stock, without covering, for 2 hours or until the liquid is reduced by half. If before the 2 hours is passed the liquid reaches a lower level, add boiling water.
Salt Pepper	Season to taste with salt and pepper. Strain and reheat as required.

Marrowbone Stock

Easy to cook · Do not microwave · Freeze · The yield depends upon the amount of bones and water that you use

Chopped marrowbones, well washed	Place in a large saucepan.
Cold water	Add sufficient water to cover the bones. Bring to the boil, then reduce the heat and simmer in the pan without covering for about 2 hours. Skim frequently.

Brown Stock

Requires some attention but is not difficult to cook · Freeze · Refrigerate – the stock must be boiled up every 24 hours · Makes about 3 pt/1·7 litres 7½ cups

2 lb/1 kg beef or lamb bones	Put into a roasting tin in a hot oven, 425°F/ 220°C/Gas Mark 7. Roast for 30 minutes, turning the bones frequently until they are brown.
1 carrot	Prepare and coarsely chop and combine with the bones in a large saucepan.
1 onion	
1 stick celery	
4 pt/2.3 litres/5 pt water	Pour over the bones and vegetables and, without covering, bring to the boil over moderate heat. Skim.
1 tsp salt	Add to the pan, then cover with the lid. Reduce the heat and simmer for 3 hours. Strain into a large bowl and use as required.

Leftovers Stock

Easy and quick to cook · Rinse the bones before using · Microwave · Do not freeze · The stock should be used as soon as possible · Yield depends upon quantity of bones and vegetables used

Meat or chicken bones, either raw or from cooked roasts or grilled or broiled chops	Combine in a large saucepan
Fresh or cooked leftover vegetables, including onions, carrots, leeks, cabbage, parsnips, beans, tomatoes but not potatoes	
Cold water	Add sufficient water to cover, bring to the boil, then reduce the heat and simmer in the pan without a lid for 50-60 minutes, skimming when necessary. Strain.
Salt Pepper	Reheat, seasoning to taste.

Crab Liquor

Fairly easy to prepare · If you have no secateurs, use a mallet and strong chopping board · Microwave – reduce the setting as soon as the liquor boils · Freeze · Refrigerate for 24 hours only · Reboil stock every 24 hours if required to keep for longer, adding a few tablespoons of cold water at each reboil · Use in soups or sauces · Makes ½ pt/300 ml/1¼ cups

1 medium crab, claws, shell and legs	Crush thoroughly and place in a large saucepan.
1½ pt/900 ml/3¾ cups water	Pour into the saucepan, bring to the boil, then reduce the heat and simmer for 20 minutes. Strain into another saucepan and continue cooking until only ½ pt/300 ml/1¼ cups of liquor remains.
Salt Pepper	Season to taste.

1

Light Beef Stock

Very easy to cook · Use a very large pan · Do not microwave · Freeze · Refrigerate – stock must be reboiled every 24 hours or it will become sour · Makes about 3 pt/1.7 litres/7½ cups

About 5 lb/2.25 kg beef shin and veal knuckle bones chopped into several pieces
5 pt/2.8 litres/6 pt cold water

Place in a very large saucepan and bring to the boil slowly, removing the scum as it appears on the surface. Reduce the heat and continue simmering in the pan without a lid for a minimum of 4 hours, skimming frequently. Leave until cold, then chill and remove the fat layer from the surface.

8 oz/225 g carrots
1 medium onion stuck with 4 cloves
1 bay leaf
2 or 3 sprigs parsley
3 sticks celery, roughly cut
Salt
Pepper

Return the stock to the pan, add the vegetables and season to taste. Bring back to the boil, reduce the heat and simmer for 1 hour. Strain to remove the vegetables and use as required.

2

Simple Fish Stock

Easy to prepare · You can use skins only but the addition of bones produces a more glutinous stock · Microwave – reduce setting to Defrost when stock boils up and use large container · Freeze – it loses its texture but it recovers when reheated · Refrigerate – it becomes rancid after a couple of days · The recipe may be increased but cooking time remains the same · Use as the basis for fish soup or in sauces · Makes about 6 fl oz/175 ml/¾ cup

8 oz/225 g fish trimmings
1 strip lemon peel
1 tsp dried fennel

Combine in a large saucepan, cover the fish trimmings with cold water, bring to the boil, then reduce the heat and simmer for 10 minutes. Strain into a bowl.

Salt
Pepper

Season to taste and use as required.

White Stock

Easy to prepare · Requires a large saucepan · Takes about 3 hours · Do not microwave · Freeze · Refrigerate – stock must be boiled up every 24 hours · Makes 3 pt/1.7 litres/7½ cups

2 lb/1 kg veal bones

Scrape away fat and wipe the bones thoroughly. Put into a large saucepan.

1 tsp salt
4 pt/2.25 litres/5 pt cold water

Add to the bones and leave to stand for 30 minutes.
Bring to the boil over low heat, then simmer without covering for 1 hour.

1 tbsp white vinegar
1 onion, peeled
1 stick celery, broken
8 white peppercorns
1 strip lemon rind
1 bay leaf

Add to the pan. There is no need to chop the vegetables. Cover and simmer for 3 hours, checking that the liquid does not reduce to less than half. Strain into a bowl and use as required.

Above: Light Beef Stock

1 Remove the scum as it appears on the surface.
2 Leave until cold, then chill and remove the fat layer from the surface.
3 Add the chopped vegetables to the stock.
4 Strain the stock to remove the vegetables and use as required.

3

Rich Fish Stock

Easy to cook · Microwave · Freeze as cubes or in the quantities required · Makes 2 pt/1.2 litres/5 cups

1 oz/25 g/2 tbsp butter or margarine	Place in a large saucepan and melt over gentle heat.
8 oz/225 g onions, peeled and finely sliced	Stir into the melted butter and sauté until the onions are soft but not coloured.
Handful sprigs parsley, rinsed *1 lb/450 g fish bones and trimmings from white fish, coarsely chopped* *1 tbsp fresh lemon juice* *8 fl oz/250 ml/1 cup dry white wine*	Stir into the sautéed onion mixture and cook for 5 minutes or until the stock comes to the boil.
2 pt/1.2 litres/5 cups water	Stir into the stock. Bring back to the boil, then reduce the heat and simmer without covering for 20 minutes. Strain through muslin or a fine nylon sieve.
Salt *Pepper*	Add seasoning to taste. Stir before using.

4

Lamb Stock

Easy to cook · Do not microwave . Freeze · Makes 1³/₄ pt/1 litre/4¹/₂ cups

3 lb/1.5 kg shoulder or leg of lamb bones, including a little of the meat but not the fat	Place in a roasting dish and cook at 400°F/ 200°C/Gas Mark 6 for 30 minutes, turning the bones over once during roasting. Transfer the bones to a large saucepan.
2 bay leaves *2 sprigs parsley* *1 sprig thyme* *6 black peppercorns* *Small piece onion* *Small piece celery* *1 rasher bacon* *2 ripe tomatoes, coarsely chopped*	Add to the pan.
Cold water	Cover the bones, herbs and vegetables with cold water. Bring to the boil over moderate heat, then reduce the temperature and simmer in the pan without a lid for 2 hours, skimming when necessary, until the liquid is reduced to about half. Strain into a bowl, then refrigerate or chill in the freezer until a layer of fat settles at the top. Remove the fat, reheat.
Salt *Pepper*	Season to taste and use as required.

Gravies

A roast is rarely served without gravy and the sediment and juices are vital to produce a well-flavoured gravy to complement freshly-cooked sliced meat and poultry. Roasts, by their very nature and the method of cooking, tend to be on the plain side and are a little dense in texture. The gravy adds just that extra touch of moisture and flavour which makes the food more appetizing and at the same time stimulates the gastric juices. When a roast is to be reheated and served on the following day, it is unlikely that there will be any gravy left over, so gravy must be made from scratch. There are recipes in this chapter to cover both eventualities.

Gravies can be served unthickened and indeed some people prefer just to have the meat juices served straight from the roasting pan, but it is more usual to thicken gravies and this is done with flour or cornflour (cornstarch). If you want a thin gravy, simply remove all the fat from the roasting dish and sprinkle a minimal amount of flour over the residual juices, then add the stock or vegetable water. For a thicker gravy you will need about ½ pt/ 300 ml/1¼ cups liquid to 1 tablespoon flour and about 1 tablespoon of the fat. To make a basic gravy, remove the surplus fat from the roasting pan after the joint has been removed, place the pan on the hob or if you prefer pour the juices into a saucepan, stir in the flour, add stock or water and cook, stirring continuously, until the gravy boils and thickens. Blot away any fat that comes to the surface using a wad of absorbent kitchen paper towel, then season the gravy to taste, adding colouring if you wish. Do not strain unless the gravy is particularly lumpy as there are bound to be some meat or poultry solids left in the sediment and these are a valuable ingredient. If you prefer a thick gravy, it is better to boil it for longer and reduce the liquid rather than to add extra flour or cornflour (cornstarch). Cornflour (cornstarch) tends to produce a thicker smoother gravy, while flour gives a softer texture. The flavour may also be improved if the flour has been pre-browned. You will need more of this than uncooked flour as part of the starch is broken down during the browning process. To brown flour, either put it in a roasting dish set in a cool oven or put it in a frying pan over minimum heat and cook, stirring frequently, until the flour is a nutty brown colour. This flour can be kept for a short time in a sealed container.

Browned flour will also give extra colour to the gravy. Other ways of improving the colour are to use dark stock cubes, wine, canned consommé or beef or yeast extracts, but these do have a flavour of their own. You can buy bottled gravy browning which lasts for ever, but you can also make it yourself by simply heating granulated sugar with water and caramel (see recipe, page 151). This will keep in a screw-top jar or bottle for up to six months. If you wish to go one step further, you can flavour the liquid caramel by adding 1 tablespoon Worcestershire sauce, 1 teaspoon tomato purée, ½ teaspoon sweet paprika, ¼ teaspoon ground turmeric, ½ teaspoon salt, ½ teaspoon freshly ground black pepper and 1 teaspoon dried mixed herbs. Remember to shake the bottle or jar before using.

Gravy powder is readily obtainable and is easy to use as it is a combination of thickener, colouring and spices. It will however always give the same flavour.

Never overseason with salt as the saltiness becomes more pronounced during cooking. It is always possible to add a little more salt afterwards. Monosodium glutamate (MSG), used in most Chinese dishes, also brings out the flavour and adds a touch of saltiness, but some people find that it upsets their stomachs.

As a rule, poultry juices produce a much more gelatinous texture than meat juices and a good sticky stock can do wonders when making a gravy without sediment from the roast. To make a meat glaze, all you have to do is to cook stock very very slowly over minimum heat for several hours until 1 pt/600 ml/2½ cups is reduced to a mere tablespoon. One teaspoon of this enriches and turns an ordinary gravy into an *haute-cuisine* experience.

Gravy (1)

Very easy to prepare · Microwave · Serve hot · Makes 1 pt/600 ml/ 2½ cups

2 tbsp fat and all residual meat juices from the roasting pan 2 tbsp cornflour (cornstarch)	Blend together in the roasting pan, saucepan or jug, if using the microwave.
1 chicken or beef stock cube (optional) 1 pt/600 ml/2½ cups stock or cold water	Crumble the cube into the cornflour mixture and stir in the water. Bring to the boil, then cook for 3 minutes, stirring continuously.
Few drops gravy browning	Add to give extra colour.

Milk Gravy

Very easy to cook · Microwave · Do not freeze · Serve hot · Makes 6 fl oz/175 ml/¾ cup

2 oz/50 g/¼ cup unsalted butter ¼ pt/150 ml/⅔ cup milk	Put into a small saucepan and heat gently until the butter is melted. Stir briskly.
Salt Pepper	Add seasoning to taste. Bring to steaming but not boiling point and use immediately.

Giblet Gravy

Fairly easy to prepare but time-consuming · Do not microwave · Freeze · Serve hot · Makes 1 pt/600 ml/2½ cups

Turkey or chicken giblets	Rinse and clean thoroughly and place in a large heavy-based saucepan.
2 x 10 oz/285 g/1¼ cup cans condensed chicken soup 1 pt/600 ml/2½ cups water 1 onion, peeled and quartered 1 carrot, scraped and sliced 1 stick celery, sliced 6 black peppercorns, crushed 1 bay leaf 1 blade mace	Add to the giblets in the saucepan, bring to the boil over moderate heat, then skim if necessary. Reduce the heat, place the lid on the pan and simmer for about 2 hours. Strain and measure the liquid and make up to 1 pt/ 600 ml/2½ cups with water.
1 oz/25 g/¼ cup flour 2 oz/50 g/¼ cup butter	Blend together in a small bowl. Bring the gravy back to the boil and add the butter paste in small pieces whisking continuously until the gravy thickens.

Soured Cream Gravy

Easy to cook · Requires sediment and juices from the roast · Do not microwave · Makes about 1 pt/600 ml/2½ cups

Sediment, juices and 4 tbsp fat left in the pan after roasting	Leave in roasting pan or transfer to saucepan on the hob.
4 tbsp cornflour (cornstarch) 6 tbsp red wine	Blend together in a small bowl. Stir into the pan juices and fat and cook over moderate heat for 4 minutes, stirring continuously.
¾ pt/450 ml/2 cups water	Stir into the flour mixture.
1 dark beef stock cube	Crumble into the liquid and cook, stirring, until the gravy has thickened.
Salt Pepper	Season to taste.
¼ pt/150 ml/⅔ cup soured cream	Stir into the gravy just before serving.

Wine Gravy

Easy to cook · Do not microwave · Freeze · Makes 1 pt/600 ml/2½ cups

1 oz/25 g/2 tbsp beef dripping	Melt in a pan over moderate heat.
1 oz/25 g/¼ cup flour	Stir into the melted dripping. Cook, stirring continuously, until the flour browns.
¾ pt/450 ml/2 cups boiling water	Gradually stir into the flour mixture and bring back to the boil, whisking continuously.
1 beef stock cube	Crumble into the boiling sauce.
¼ pt/150 ml/⅔ cup medium red wine	Pour into the sauce and cook for 1 minute.
Salt Freshly ground black pepper	Add seasoning to taste.

Gravy (2)

Easy to cook · Microwave · Serve hot · Makes 8 fl oz/250 ml/1 cup

2 tbsp fat plus 5 tbsp residual meat juices from a roast, pot roast or casserole 2 tbsp flour	Combine in a roasting pan or saucepan and whisk thoroughly until well blended. Cook over gentle heat, without stirring, until the flour browns.
8 fl oz/250 ml/1 cup boiling water	Stir into the browned flour.
1 beef stock cube	Crumble into the mixture in the pan. Stir vigorously until the gravy thickens.
Salt Freshly ground black pepper	Add seasoning to taste.
1 tsp dry sherry	Stir in just before serving.

Chicken Liver Gravy

Easy to cook · Make sure that the chicken livers are rinsed, trimmed and halved before cooking · Microwave · Freeze · Serve hot · Makes 1 pt/ 600 ml/2½ cups

6 chicken livers (weighing about 8 oz/ 225 g in total), rinsed, trimmed and halved 2 tbsp dripping or oil	Cook gently in a saucepan, stirring frequently, until the chicken livers are opaque.
1 tbsp flour	Stir into the chicken livers and cook for 1 minute, stirring continuously.
¾ pt/450 ml/2 cups thin chicken stock	Gradually mix into the chicken livers, stirring continuously until the gravy thickens slightly. Purée in a liquidizer or blender, strain back into the saucepan.
Salt Pepper	Season to taste. Reheat.
1 tsp butter	Stir into the gravy just before serving.

Rich Pork Gravy

Easy to prepare · Do not microwave · Freeze · Serve hot · Makes 1 pt/ 600 ml/2½ cups

8 oz/225 g lean pork	Dice or chop finely.
1 oz/25 g/2 tbsp lard	Melt in a heavy-based pan.
1 oz/25 g/¼ cup flour	Heat the lard until smoking, then stir in the flour and cook, stirring continuously, until the flour browns. Stir in the diced pork.
1 pt/600 ml/2½ cups boiling water ¼ chicken stock cube	Stir into the pork mixture, making sure that the stock cube dissolves. Cook over moderate heat for 15 minutes.
Salt Freshly ground black pepper	Season the sauce to taste, then cook without covering for 15 minutes. Purée in a liquidizer or food processor. Pour back into the saucepan and reheat.

Cider Gravy

Easy to cook · Microwave · Freeze · Serve hot · Makes ¾ pt/450 ml/ 2 cups

1 oz/25 g/2 tbsp lard	Place in a saucepan and melt over gentle heat.
1 oz/25 g/¼ cup cornflour (cornstarch)	Stir into the melted fat. Remove the pan from the heat.
12 fl oz/350 ml/1½ cups dry cider ¼ pt/150 ml/⅔ cup water	Gradually blend into the cornflour mixture. Place the pan over moderate heat and bring to the boil, whisking continuously
¼ chicken stock cube	Crumble into the sauce and mix until well blended.
Salt Freshly ground black pepper	Season to taste Pour the sauce through a strainer and reheat.

Gravy (2) *(see page 25)*

1 Take the roasting pan out of the oven and put the meat on a plate.
2 Stir the flour into the pan juices until well blended and cook over a gentle heat until the flour browns.

3 Stir the boiling water into the browned flour. Add the crumbled stock cube and stir vigorously until the gravy thickens.
4 Add seasoning to taste and the sherry and pour into a gravy boat.

Savoury Sauces

MEAT

Beef

Allemande
Beef and
    Mushroom
Chilli Tomato
Cranberrry
Espagnole 1
Espagnole 2
Italian
Madeira 1
Madeira 2
Miroton
Piquante
Piquant Pepper
Quick Meat
Quick Mustard
Quick Sweet and
    Sour
Red Pepper and
    Tomato
Satay

Steaks

Béarnaise
Beurre Bercy
Citronaise
Cranberry
Creamy and
    Dreamy
    Horseradish
Curry Butter
Espagnole 1
Espagnole 2
Lemon Butter
Maître d'hôtel
    Butter
Au Poivre
Poivrade
Shallot Butter
Sparkling Cognac

Lamb

Barbecue 1
Barbecue 2
Beurre Bercy
Châteaubriand
Currant
Curry Butter
Dill
Espagnole 1
Espagnole 2
Garden
Leek and Pepper
Madeira 1
Madeira 2
Mint
Mint (Blender)
Aux Olives
Piquant Pepper
Portuguese (Cold)
Quick Sweet and
    Sour
Redcurrant 1
Reform
Soubise 1
Soubise 2
Tomato and Apple

Pork

Apple 1
Canada Ginger
Cherry 1
Chilli Tomato
Chinese Pork
Cider
Cranberry
Devil
Diable
Galliano
Garden
Ketchican
    Barbecue
Mild Sweet and
    Sour
Panache
Quick Sweet and
    Sour
Sweet and Sour 1
Tomato and Apple

Ham

Allspice Raisin
Cherry 1
Cider
Galliano Barbecue
Madeira 1
Madeira 2
Mild Sweet and
    Sour
Raisin and
    Almond
Raisin Cider
Redcurrant 1

Veal

Chutney Butter
Lemon and
    Beetroot
Mint
Miroton
Onion and
    Mushroom 1
Simple Tomato
Sorrel
Soubise 1
Soubise 2
Sparkling Cognac
Sweet and Sour 2

Offal

Breton
Maître d'hotel
    Butter (liver)
Olive and Bacon
    (kidneys)
Panache (kidneys)
Poivrade (liver and
    brains)
Soubise 1
    (sweetbreads)
Soubise 2
    (sweetbreads)

Sauces that appear in this section but are not mentioned here either have serving suggestions with the recipe or can be served with anything. See also the sauces under the following sections:

Poultry

Cumberland 1
Cumberland 2
Cumberland 3
Orange and
    Redcurrant
Paprika
Soured Cream
    Cranberry

Game

Anise
Cranberry with
    Pork
Financière
Game Fruit
Redcurrant 2
Spiced Apple
Textured
    Cumberland

Fish

Choron
Cucumber and
    Tomato Relish
Hollandaise 1
Hollandaise 2
Hungarian
Mustard Butter
Normande
Paprika Butter

Shellfish

Gribiche
Supreme

Vegetables

Poulette

Allemande Sauce

Requires care in cooking · Microwave (see notes page 12) · Do not freeze · Serve hot · Makes 1 pt/600 ml/2½ cups

1 oz/25 g/2 tbsp butter	Melt in a heavy-based saucepan over gentle heat.
1 oz/25 g/¼ cup plain or all-purpose flour	Stir into the melted butter and cook, stirring continuously, for 2 minutes. Remove from the heat.
1 pt/600 ml/2½ cups chicken stock	Gradually stir into the roux mixture in the pan and, when no longer lumpy, return the pan to the heat. Cook over medium heat, stirring continuously, until the sauce thickens to the consistency of single or light cream. Cook for a further 5 minutes, then remove the pan from the heat.
1 egg yolk 1 tbsp double or heavy cream	Beat together in a small bowl adding 2 tablespoons of the hot sauce. Pour into the sauce and place the pan over the lowest possible heat. Stir continuously with a wooden spoon until the sauce thickens slightly. Remove the pan from the heat.
Salt Pepper ¼ tsp nutmeg 1 tsp fresh lemon juice ½ oz/15 g/1 tbsp unsalted butter	Whisk into the sauce, seasoning to taste. Strain through a nylon sieve and serve at once.

Allspice Raisin Sauce

Easy to make · Do not microwave · No need to freeze or refrigerate · Store in a screw-top jar · Serve hot or cold · Makes ¾ pt/ 450 ml/2 cups

3 oz/75 g/6 tbsp dark soft brown sugar 4 tbsp red wine vinegar ½ pt/300 ml/1¼ cups water ¼ tsp ground cloves ¼ tsp mustard powder 2 tsp ground allspice 1 tbsp cornflour (cornstarch) 5 oz/150 g/⅞ cup seedless raisins	Combine in a large heavy-based saucepan. Bring to the boil, then simmer for 3 minutes, stirring constantly, until the sauce is thick and the raisins are plump.

Beurre Diable

Easy to prepare · No cooking required · Freeze · Refrigerate · Serve cold · Makes 4 oz/100 g/½ cup

4 oz/100 g/½ cup butter	Beat in a bowl until smooth.
½ tsp paprika ½ tsp curry powder 1 tbsp fresh lemon juice Pinch cayenne pepper Salt Pepper	Blend into the softened butter, adding seasoning to taste. Shape into a cylinder, roll up tightly in wax or greaseproof paper and cover with foil, folding in the ends securely. Chill. Slice as required.

Apple Sauce (1)

Easy to cook · Microwave · Freeze · Serve hot · Makes ½ pt/300 ml/ 1¼ cups

1½ lb/700 g cooking apples, peeled, cored and sliced 3 tbsp water 1 slice lemon	Combine in a large heavy-based pan and cook for 10 minutes or until the apple is soft and pulpy. Remove the lemon slice and purée the apple pulp. **Note:** If the purée is too thin, return to the saucepan and cook for a little longer.

Apple and Date Chutney

Easy to cook but essential to stir frequently · Microwave · No need to freeze as chutney stores well in a screw-top jar, provided the top is first covered with plastic cling film · Serve with cold meats or curries · Makes 2 lb/1 kg

12 oz/350 g cooking apples, peeled and cored 1 medium onion, peeled 4 oz/100 g/⅔ cup stoned dates	Cut up, then mince finely.
1 tsp mixed spice ½ tsp ground ginger ½ tsp ground cloves	Put into a heavy-based saucepan, add the minced mixture and stir thoroughly.
7 fl oz/200 ml/⅞ cup vinegar	Mix into the fruit mixture. Place the pan over moderate heat and bring to the boil, stirring frequently. Reduce the heat to minimum and cook, stirring, for 35-45 minutes until the mixture is thick. Leave to cool, then pot in the usual way.

Ambassadrice Sauce

Easy to cook if espagnole sauce is prepared in advance · Microwave · Freeze · Serve hot · Makes ¾ pt/450 ml/2 cups

2 oz/50 g/⅓ cup sultanas or golden raisins Juice of 1 orange	Soak for 2-3 hours.
½ pt/300 ml/1¼ cups espagnole sauce 1 tbsp redcurrant jelly 2 tsp lemon juice Salt Pepper	Combine in a saucepan with the soaked sultanas. Bring to the boil, then season to taste.

Barbecue Sauce (1)

Easy to prepare · Microwave – reduce the butter by half · Do not refrigerate · Store in a screw-top jar · Serve hot with lamb chops · Makes ½ pt/300 ml/1¼ cups

2 tbsp vegetable oil	Place in a heavy-based saucepan.
1 large onion, peeled and finely chopped	Fry in the oil until the onion is browned.
3 tbsp tomato purée 3 tbsp bottled sweet pickle ¼ tsp mustard powder ½ pt/300 ml/1¼ cups water	Stir into the onion, bring to the boil, then simmer for 15 minutes or until the mixture is reduced by one-third

Barbecue Sauce (2)

Easy to cook · Microwave · No need to freeze · Use to brush on meat before barbecuing · Makes ¾ pt/450 ml/2 cups

1 oz/25 g/2 tbsp butter or margarine	Melt in a heavy-based frying pan.
2 medium onions, peeled and finely chopped	Stir into the melted fat and fry for 8-10 minutes until golden brown.
2 tbsp soft dark brown sugar 2 tbsp malt vinegar 2 tbsp Worcestershire sauce ¼ pt/150 ml/⅔ cup tomato ketchup ¼ pt/150 ml/⅔ cup water 4 tbsp fresh lemon juice	Add to pan, cover and simmer for 15 minutes, stirring occasionally to prevent sticking.

Beef and Mushroom Sauce

Easy to cook using convenience foods · Microwave · Freeze · Serve hot with beefburgers · Makes ¾ pt/450 ml/2 cups

1 small onion, peeled and finely chopped ½ oz/15 g/1 tbsp butter	Cook gently until the onion is soft.
1 x 7½ oz/215 g can button mushrooms	Drain, reserving the juice. Add mushrooms to the pan.
1 x 10 oz/285 g/1¼ cup can condensed beef consommé 1 tbsp red wine vinegar	Stir into the mushroom mixture. Bring to the boil and cook for 2-3 minutes.
2 tbsp arrowroot	Blend with the reserved mushroom juices. Pour into the pan, bring back to the boil and simmer for 2-3 minutes, stirring continuously, until the sauce thickens.

Béarnaise Sauce

Difficult to make · Do not microwave · Do not freeze · Serve warm · Makes ½ pt/300 ml/1¼ cups

½ oz/15 g/1 tbsp unsalted butter 2 shallots, peeled and finely chopped	Place in a heavy-based saucepan and cook gently, stirring continuously, until the shallots are tender.
6 tbsp tarragon vinegar Pinch salt ½ tsp chopped chervil Pinch white pepper	Add to the shallots, raise the heat and simmer until only 1 tablespoon of free running liquid remains. Strain into the top part of a double saucepan, put 1 in/2.5 cm of hot water in the base. Set over low heat.
4 egg yolks	Whip lightly in a small bowl, strain into a jug, then pour spoonful by spoonful into the reduced liquid in the saucepan, beating continuously. Be careful as too much heat will spoil the sauce. Cook until the mixture is like a thick cream.
7 oz/200 g/⅞ cup unsalted butter, soft enough to spread easily	Beat into the egg mixture a teaspoonful at a time. Remove from the heat and continue beating until the mixture is smooth.
½ tsp chopped chervil	Fold into the sauce.

Beurre Bercy (1)

Complicated to prepare · Requires meat glaze and beef marrow, but once these ingredients are assembled the sauce is easy to cook · Microwave · Freeze · Serve warm with grilled or broiled meat or fish · Makes ¾ pt/450 ml/2 cups

1 oz/25 g shallots, finely chopped ¼ pt/150 ml/⅔ cup dry white wine	Combine in a saucepan and place over moderate heat. Without covering, cook until the wine is reduced by half.
2 tbsp meat glaze (see page 24) 1 tsp fresh chopped parsley 2 tsp fresh lemon juice	Stir into the wine mixture. Remove the pan from the heat.
8 oz/225 g/1 cup unsalted butter	Cut into cubes and stir into the hot liquid. Cover and keep warm.
1 oz/25 g beef marrow Salt Freshly ground black pepper	Cut into dice, place in a small saucepan with a pinch of salt, just cover with water and cook gently until the marrow softens. Drain away the cooking liquor and stir the softened marrow into the sauce until it melts. Do not replace on the heat. Add seasoning to taste.

Ketchican Barbecue Sauce

Easy to cook · Microwave · No need to freeze · Keeps well in a screw-top jar fitted with a non-metallic lid · Use cold prior to barbecuing · Makes ¹/₂ pt/300 ml/1¹/₄ cups

¹/₄ pt/150 ml/²/₃ cup water 1 oz/25 g/2 tbsp muscavado sugar	Put the water in a heavy-based saucepan, stir in the sugar until it is dissolved.
¹/₄ pt/150 ml/²/₃ cup tomato ketchup 6 fl oz/175 ml/³/₄ cup cider vinegar 2 tbsp Worcestershire sauce 2 tsp chilli powder ¹/₄ onion, finely chopped until the juices flow	Stir into the dissolved sugar and simmer the sauce over gentle heat until it is reduced by about one-third – it should be thick enough to brush onto meat as a coating. The sauce is very hot and peppery.

Sauce Robert

Easy to cook · Do not microwave · Freeze · Serve hot · Makes ¹/₂ pt/ 300 ml/1¹/₄ cups

1 small onion, peeled and finely chopped ¹/₂ oz/15 g/1 tbsp butter or margarine	Cook gently until the onion is soft but not brown.
6 tbsp dry white wine 2 tsp white vinegar	Add to onions and cook gently for about 5 minutes.
8 fl oz/250 ml/1 cup Demi-glace (page 150) 1 tsp French mustard	Stir into the sauce and cook until thoroughly reheated.

Above: Ketchican Barbecue Sauce

Chinese Pork Sauce

Easy to prepare · Microwave · Freeze · Serve hot · Makes 1 pt/600 ml/ 2¹/₂ cups

1 x 14 oz/400 g can pineapple chunks in syrup	Drain, reserving both the pineapple and the juice. Add sufficient water to the juice to make up to ¹/₂ pt/300 ml/1¹/₄ cups. Chop the pineapple finely.
2 tsp walnut oil 4 tsp vegetable oil 1 tbsp white wine vinegar 2 tbsp sweet sherry 1 tsp grated ginger root 2 medium green peppers, cored, seeded and cut into very thin strips 1 small red pepper, cored, seeded and cut into very thin strips Salt Pepper	Combine with the reserved diluted juice in a medium saucepan and bring to the boil, seasoning to taste. Simmer, uncovered, for 5 minutes to lightly cook the peppers.
2 tsp cornflour (cornstarch) 2 tbsp cold water	Blend together in a small bowl. Add 1 or 2 tablespoons of the hot juices and pour into the saucepan. Bring back to the boil, stirring continuously. Add the reserved pineapple and reheat for 2-3 minutes. **Note:** This sauce is thick, colourful and chunky.

Breton Sauce

Slightly complicated to prepare · Requires Chicken Velouté sauce · Microwave · Freeze – add butter and cream after reheating · Serve hot · Makes ³/₄ pt/450 ml/2 cups

1 medium onion, peeled	Slice vertically, then cut into thin strips.
1 medium leek, white part only	Cut into 1-in/2.5-cm lengths, slice vertically and cut into strips.
1 stick celery, scraped	Cut into 1-in/2.5-cm lengths, slice vertically and slice again into thin strips. Combine in a heavy-based saucepan and set over low heat.
Pinch salt Pinch sugar ¹/₂ oz/15 g/1 tbsp butter or margarine	Add to the vegetables, cover with the lid and cook until the vegetables are soft, shaking the pan occasionally.
2 oz/50 g mushrooms, finely sliced 4 tbsp dry white wine	Remove the lid from the pan, stir the mushrooms and wine into the other vegetables, then continue cooking until the liquid is almost completely absorbed.
¹/₄ pt/150 ml/²/₃ cup Chicken Velouté sauce (page 53)	Stir into the vegetables and cook briskly for about 1 minute or until the sauce comes to the boil. Remove the pan from the heat.
1¹/₂ oz/40 g/3 tbsp unsalted butter 2 tbsp whipped double or heavy cream	Stir into the hot sauce. **Note:** This is a textured sauce and should not be strained.

Opposite: Chinese Pork Sauce

Sauce Châteaubriand

Fairly easy to cook · The colour of the sauce is dependent upon the complete cooking of the roux · As cooking is slow use a heavy-based pan · Do not microwave · Freeze · Serve hot · Makes 1 pt/600 ml/ 2½ cups

2 oz/50 g/¼ cup butter or margarine 4 oz/100 g streaky bacon, diced	Combine in a heavy-based saucepan over moderate heat and fry gently, stirring occasionally, until the bacon sizzles.
1 small onion, peeled and finely chopped	Stir the onion into the bacon mixture and cook over minimum heat until the onion is a golden colour.
2 oz/50 g/½ cup flour	Stir into the mixture until every particle of flour has been incorporated and leave without stirring until the flour is nut brown.
1½ pt/900 ml/3¾ cups meat stock	Gradually add to the saucepan, stirring until the liquid is well mixed. Raise the heat and bring to the boil, stirring continuously. Reduce heat to minimum.
Bouquet garni	Add to the pan.
Salt Freshly ground black pepper	Season to taste.
2 tbsp fresh chopped tarragon leaves 6 tbsp fresh chopped parsley 3 tbsp fresh lemon juice	Stir into the sauce and cook gently for 10-15 minutes, stirring occasionally. Strain into another saucepan and reheat.
1 tsp butter	Draw the spoon of butter over the surface of the sauce, allowing the butter to melt gradually. Stir before serving.

Cherry Sauce (1)

Fairly easy to prepare · Microwave · Freeze · Serve hot or warm · Makes ½ pt/300 ml/1¼ cups

2 x 14 oz/400 g cans stoned black cherries	Put the cherries in a saucepan. Measure the juice and make up to 1 pt/600 ml/2½ cups with water. Pour over the cherries.
2 oz/50 g/¼ cup sugar 2 tbsp red wine vinegar	Add to the cherries and stir until the sugar is dissolved. Bring slowly to the boil, stirring frequently.
2 tbsp cornflour (cornstarch) 2 tbsp cold water	Blend together in a small bowl. Add 2-3 tablespoons of the hot cherry juice and stir thoroughly. Pour into the syrup in the pan. Reduce the heat to medium and bring to the boil, stirring continuously until the sauce thickens.
½ oz/15 g/1 tbsp butter	Stir into the hot sauce.

Carolina Relish

Fairly easy to prepare · No need to freeze as relish keeps well in a screw-top jar fitted with a non-metallic lid · Keep for 2 months before using · Makes 2 lb/1 kg

3 x 12 oz/350 g corn cobs	Using a sharp knife and a chopping board, scrape the corn kernels off the cob, making sure you scrape away from the body. It helps to do this if the cobs are still in the husk which can be peeled back and held securely in one hand.
1 large onion, peeled and finely chopped 1 red pepper, cored, seeded and finely chopped 1 green pepper, cored, seeded and finely chopped 2 oz/50 g white cabbage, shredded 1 tsp salt ¼ tsp freshly ground black pepper 1 tbsp mustard powder 5 oz/150 g/⅝ cup demerara sugar ½ pt/300 ml/1¼ cups cider vinegar	Mix with the corn, place the lid tightly on the pan and cook over the lowest possible heat for 1-1½ hours, stirring occasionally, or until the mixture is thick and the vegetables are soft. Coarsely chop in a liquidizer or blender, then pack into sterilized jars and seal. If too much moisture has evaporated during storage, stir in a little wine before using.

Chutney Butter

Easy to prepare · No cooking required · Freeze · Refrigerate · Serve cold · Makes 4 fl oz/120 ml/½ cup

1 oz/25 g/2 tbsp butter	Put into a small bowl and beat until soft.
1 tbsp sweet chutney ½ tsp French mustard	Gradually beat into the butter.
Salt Pepper	Season to taste.
2 tbsp double or heavy cream	Stir into the butter mixture. Spoon into a serving dish and serve soft.

Cider Sauce

Easy to cook provided espagnole sauce is prepared in advance · Microwave · Freeze · Serve hot · Makes ½ pt/300 ml/1¼ cups

¼ pt/150 ml/⅔ cup espagnole sauce 6 tbsp dry cider 1 green dessert apple, peeled, cored and finely chopped 1 clove ½ tsp bay leaf powder Salt Freshly ground pepper	Combine in a heavy-based saucepan and cook gently for 5-10 minutes until the apple is soft. Adjust seasoning. Strain, pressing the cooked apple through the sieve – make sure you scrape it from underneath.

Sauce Citronaise

Fairly easy to cook · Do not microwave · Freeze – take care when thawing: do not use microwave · Serve hot · Makes ½ pt/300 ml/ 1¼ cups

3 hard-boiled eggs	Mash, then press through a sieve into a small saucepan.
5 oz/150 g/½ cup plus 2 tbsp butter	Add half the butter in small pieces, place the pan over minimum heat and cook slowly, stirring continuously, until the butter has melted. Add the remaining butter and beat until the mixture is well blended. Remove the pan from the heat.
2 tsp fresh lemon juice 1 tsp French mustard 1 tsp tomato purée	Gradually work into the sauce.
1 tsp chopped chives ½ tsp dried chervil Salt Pepper	Stir in, seasoning to taste.

Cranberry Sauce

Easy to prepare in a food processor · No cooking required · Freeze – sauce will not solidify · Serve cold – good with hamburgers and meat balls · Makes ¾ pt/450 ml/2 cups

8 oz/225 g/2 cups cranberries	Place in the processor bowl and pulse until well chopped.
2 medium oranges	Squeeze the juice from 1 orange. Peel, coarsely chop and remove the pips from the remaining orange. Add to the food processor bowl.
8 oz/225 g/1 cup caster or superfine sugar	Add to the food processor bowl. Switch on the motor until all the ingredients are well mixed. Pot and refrigerate for 3-4 days before using, during which time the sugar will completely dissolve and the sauce will become cohesive.

Creamy and Dreamy Horseradish Sauce

Very easy to prepare · No cooking required · Do not freeze · Refrigerate · Serve cold · Makes 7 fl oz/200 ml/⅞ cup

4 oz/100 g/½ cup cream cheese 2 tbsp horseradish sauce 2 tbsp lemon mayonnaise	Blend together with a wooden spoon until smooth.
2 tbsp double or heavy cream	Mix in thoroughly. Chill until required.

Currant Sauce

Easy to cook · Do not microwave . Freeze · Serve hot or warm with lamb chops · Makes ½ pt/300 ml/1¼ cups

3 oz/75 g/½ cup currants ½ pt/300 ml/1¼ cups water	Combine in a saucepan, bring to the boil, then reduce the heat and simmer for 5 minutes until the currants swell.
1 oz/25 g/½ cup fresh soft breadcrumbs ½ tsp ground cloves 3 tbsp red wine 1 tsp butter	Stir into the mixture in the saucepan, reduce the heat to minimum and cook gently, stirring occasionally, until the sauce is evenly mixed.

Curry Butter

Easy to prepare but use a non-plastic bowl and a spoon or fork that will not be spoilt by the curry paste · No cooking required · Freeze · Refrigerate – wrap tightly to prevent the odours from transferring to other items in the refrigerator · Serve cold · Makes 4 oz/100 g/½ cup

4 oz/100 g/½ cup butter or firm margarine 1 tsp tomato purée 1 tsp curry paste (hot, medium or mild) Salt	Blend together until smooth and season to taste. Shape into a cylinder, roll up tightly in wax or greaseproof paper and cover with foil, folding in the ends securely. Chill until firm. Serve in slices.

Elderberry Sauce

Time-consuming to prepare the elderberries · Suitable for bottling · Microwave · Freeze · Serve as a chutney with cold meats · Makes 3 lb/1.5 kg

2 lb/1 kg elderberries	Pick over, discarding stalks. Rinse in cold water and drain thoroughly.
1 medium onion, peeled and chopped ½ oz/15 g salt ½ tsp mustard powder ½ pt/300 ml/1¼ cups spiced vinegar	Combine with the elderberries in a heavy-based saucepan, cover with the lid and cook over gentle heat until the elderberries are soft. Shake the pan frequently during cooking. Press through a sieve into another saucepan to remove the skins and onions.
1½ lb/750 g/3¾ cups granulated sugar	Stir into the hot elderberry mixture and cook gently without covering until the mixture is thick.

Note: The sauce will seem to thicken when the sugar is first stirred in but when dissolved will become liquid again. The sauce thickens again when the sugar is fully cooked.

Garden Sauce

Considerable chopping involved · No cooking required · Serve cold with cold meats, cooked potatoes or kebabs · Makes ¾ pt/450 ml/2 cups

4 tbsp salad oil 1 tbsp red wine vinegar 1 tsp salt ½ tsp freshly ground black pepper	Mix together thoroughly in a large non-metallic bowl.
2 oz/50 g gherkins, finely sliced 1 oz/25 g drained capers, chopped 6 chives, finely chopped 4 tbsp finely chopped parsley 1 small green pepper, cored, seeded and finely sliced 4 oz/100 g piece cucumber, peeled and diced 4 medium tomatoes, skinned and chopped 1 small onion, peeled and finely chopped 1 small courgette (zucchini), diced 1 small beetroot or beet, cooked, skinned and finely diced	Mix into the bowl and toss thoroughly. Cover tightly and leave at room temperature for 24 hours before serving.

Lemon Butter

Easy to prepare · Do not microwave · Do not freeze · Do not refrigerate · Serve hot · Makes 4 fl oz/120 ml/½ cup

4 oz/100 g/½ cup salted butter	Heat until bubbling. Strain through muslin and keep warm.
3 tbsp fresh lemon juice	Boil in a small saucepan until reduced by half. Remove the pan from the heat. Mix in the butter.
Salt White pepper	Season to taste and serve at once.

Devil Sauce

Very easy to cook · Microwave · Freeze · Serve hot with spare ribs · Makes ½ pt/300 ml/1¼ cups

2 oz/50 g/¼ cup butter 1 oz/25 g/¼ cup flour 1 tsp curry powder ½ pt/300 ml/1¼ cups milk Salt Pepper	Place all ingredients in a heavy-based saucepan and bring to the boil, whisking continuously until the sauce thickens. Continue cooking for 2-3 minutes.

Lemon and Beetroot Sauce (Liquidizer or blender)

Easy to prepare – heating only required · Microwave – for reheating · Freeze · Serve hot · Makes ¹/₂ pt/300 ml/1¹/₄ cups

1 small cooked beetroot or beet, peeled and diced
1-2 tbsp fresh lemon juice
1 small onion, peeled and diced
6 fl oz/175 ml/³/₄ cup thickened gravy
¹/₄-¹/₂ tsp salt
¹/₄ tsp freshly ground black pepper
2 tsp soft brown sugar

Purée in the liquidizer or blender.
Pour into a saucepan and heat just before serving.

Chilli Tomato Sauce

Easy to cook but take care the sauce does not burn · Do not microwave · Freeze · Serve hot with beefburgers or hamburgers · Makes ³/₄ pt/450 ml/2 cups

1 x 14 oz/400 g can tomatoes

Empty into a heavy-based saucepan.

¹/₄ pt/150 ml/²/₃ cup water

Stir into tomatoes.

1 large onion, peeled and finely chopped
A little garlic salt
Pinch mixed dried herbs
1 bay leaf
¹/₄ tsp chilli compound powder
1 tbsp tomato purée
¹/₄ tsp sugar
Salt
Pepper

Add to the tomatoes, bring to the boil, then reduce the heat and simmer gently for 20-25 minutes or until the sauce is thick. Remove the bay leaf. Crush with a potato masher or purée in a blender. Reheat the sauce and adjust the seasoning.

Opposite: Garden Sauce with cold meats

Above: Lemon and Beetroot Sauce with veal

Sauce Diable

Some care required · Microwave – stir frequently · Freeze · Serve hot with spare ribs · Makes 1 pt/600 ml/2½ cups

3 shallots, peeled and minced *1 clove garlic, peeled and crushed* *1 tsp mild curry paste* *1 tbsp tomato purée* *1 tsp Worcestershire sauce* *1 tsp hot chilli sauce* *2 tbsp salad oil*	Combine together in a heavy-based saucepan.
3 sprigs parsley *1 bay leaf* *6 black peppercorns* *1 sprig thyme*	Tie together in muslin to make a bouquet garni.
1 pt/600 ml/2½ cups hot beef stock	Stir into the shallot mixture, adding the bouquet garni. Place the pan over moderate heat and bring to the boil. Reduce to simmering, place the lid on the pan and cook for 10 minutes. Remove the bouquet garni.
2 tbsp potato flour *2 tbsp medium red wine*	Mix together in a small bowl, pour into the simmering sauce and stir for a few minutes until sauce thickens.

Hamburger Sauce

Easy to make using convenience foods · Do not microwave · Do not freeze · Serve hot with hamburgers or meat loaf · Makes ¾ pt/450 ml/ 2 cups

1 x 10 oz/285 g/1¼ cup can ready-to-serve tomato sauce *4 tbsp malt vinegar* *4 tbsp clear honey* *½ tsp chilli compound powder* *½ tsp salt* *1 tsp black pepper* *2 tbsp dried chopped chives*	Combine all ingredients in a heavy-based saucepan. Bring to the boil, then reduce the heat and simmer, covered, for 10 minutes.

Mustard Sauce

Easy to cook · Microwave · Freeze · Serve hot · Makes ¼ pt/150 ml/ ⅔ cup

1 oz/25 g/2 tbsp butter	Melt in a saucepan.
½ oz/15 g/2 tbsp plain or all-purpose flour	Stir into butter, cook for 1 minute.
¼ pt/150 ml/⅔ cup milk *1 tsp French mustard* *Salt* *Pepper*	Add to butter mixture and beat vigorously with a whisk. Gradually bring to the boil over medium heat until the sauce thickens.

Dill Sauce

Fairly easy to cook but take care when blending in eggs and cream · Do not microwave · Do not freeze · Serve hot · Makes 1 pt/600 ml/2½ cups

1 pt/600 ml/2½ cups lamb stock (substitute beef stock if sauce is to be served with beef)	Pour into a large saucepan and simmer until the liquid is reduced by one-quarter.
1½ oz/40 g/3 tbsp butter, softened *¾ oz/20 g/3 tbsp plain or all-purpose flour* *2 tsp dill weed*	Blend together to a paste in a small bowl. Making sure that the stock is at simmering point, whisk in the paste a teaspoonful at a time and continue beating until the sauce thickens slightly.
2 egg yolks, beaten *¼ pt/150 ml/⅔ cup single or light cream*	Beat together until well blended, then add 3 tablespoons of the hot stock. Reduce the heat under the pan to a minimum, pour in the cream mixture and beat continuously until the sauce thickens further.
1 tsp fresh lemon juice *Salt* *Freshly ground black pepper*	Add, seasoning to taste.

Espagnole Sauce (1)

Easy to cook · Do not microwave . Freeze · Serve hot · Makes ¾ pt/ 450 ml/2 cups

1 small carrot, peeled and finely chopped *1 small onion, peeled and finely chopped* *1 oz/25 g/2 tbsp dripping*	Combine in a heavy-based pan and fry gently until the vegetables are tender, approximately 5 minutes.
1 oz/25 g/¼ cup flour	Stir into the vegetables and cook, stirring constantly, until the mixture browns, approximately 5 minutes.
¾ pt/450 ml/2 cups beef stock	Gradually add to the saucepan, stirring occasionally, and bring to the boil.
3 tbsp tomato purée	Stir into the sauce, reduce the heat and simmer for 20 minutes for the flavour to develop.
Salt *Freshly ground black pepper*	Season to taste. Strain and reheat before serving. **Note:** The sauce thickens on standing. It may be necessary to add extra stock or water to thin down the consistency.

Italian Sauce

Easy to cook provided espagnole sauce is prepared in advance · Do not microwave · Freeze · Serve hot · Makes ½ pt/300 ml/1¼ cups

2 shallots, peeled and finely chopped *1 oz/25 g/½ cup chopped mushrooms* *1 oz/25 g/2 tbsp butter*	Place in a heavy-based saucepan and stir over medium heat until the butter is melted and the vegetables well coated. Continue cooking until the shallots and mushrooms are tender.
4 tbsp beef stock *5 tbsp medium sherry*	Stir into vegetables, bring to the boil and simmer for 4 minutes to partially reduce the liquid.
½ pt/300 ml/1¼ cups espagnole sauce *Bouquet garni*	Stir into the mixture in the saucepan and cook gently for 10-15 minutes. Skim and strain, then pour the mixture back into the saucepan.
Salt *Freshly ground black pepper*	Season to taste.

Leek and Pepper Sauce

Easy to cook · Microwave · Freeze · Serve hot · Makes 1 pt/600 ml/ 2½ cups

8 oz/225 g leeks, trimmed, finely sliced and washed *1½ oz/40 g/3 tbsp butter or margarine*	Place in a heavy-based pan. Cover with the lid and cook, shaking the pan occasionally, until the leeks are soft but not brown.
1 oz/25 g/¼ cup plain or all-purpose flour	Stir into leeks, set lid aside. Cook for 3 minutes, stirring continuously.
¾ pt/450 ml/2 cups milk	Add gradually to pan, stir thoroughly and simmer for 2 minutes.
2 canned red peppers, drained	Cut into strips and stir into sauce.
Salt *Pepper*	Season to taste. Reheat before serving.

Peanut Butter Barbecue Sauce

Easy to prepare using convenience foods · Microwave – stir frequently · Will keep in a screw-top jar in the refrigerator for 2 weeks · Makes ¾ pt/ 450 ml/2 cups

4 oz/100 g/½ cup smooth peanut butter *4 fl oz/120 ml/½ cup soy sauce* *4 fl oz/120 ml/½ cup water* *4 tbsp dry sherry* *3 tbsp fresh or bottled lemon juice* *2-3 tbsp honey*	Mix together in a pan and heat over moderate heat, stirring continuously until the sauce is smooth. Leave to cool before putting in a screw-top jar.

Fondue de Tomates

Fairly easy to cook · Prepare when tomatoes are at their cheapest; although cooking tomatoes will suffice, they are more difficult to skin · Microwave · Freeze · Use as a side sauce or chutney or to give flavour to other savoury sauces · Serve hot or cold · Makes 2 pt/1.2 litres/ 5 cups

3 lb/1.5 kg tomatoes	Place in a bowl of boiling water until the skins wrinkle. Remove the tomatoes from the water, discard the skins, then coarsely cut up and set aside.
3 tbsp vegetable oil	Place in a heavy-based saucepan.
2 lb/1 kg onions, peeled and very finely chopped	Place the pan of oil over a moderate heat and, when the oil is hot, stir in the onions and cook, stirring frequently, until they are golden. Stir in the chopped tomatoes.
½ tsp dried tarragon *1 clove garlic, peeled and crushed* *Salt* *Pepper*	Stir into the tomatoes, adding seasoning to taste. Place the lid on the pan and cook until the tomatoes are soft. Remove the lid and continue cooking until the mixture is thick.
1 large red pepper, cored, seeded and finely diced	Stir into the tomato pulp.
2 tbsp white wine	Stir into the vegetables, cover the pan with the lid and cook over a minimum heat until the pepper is soft. Purée in a liquidizer or food processor, then strain through a sieve.

Espagnole Sauce (2)

Easy to prepare, quick to mix, slow to cook · Do not microwave · Freeze · Serve hot · Makes 1 pt/600 ml/2½ cups

2 oz/50 /¼ cup butter or margarine	Melt in a large heavy-based saucepan.
2 oz/50 g/½ cup plain or all-purpose flour *2 oz/50 g bacon, rind removed and chopped* *1 medium onion; peeled and roughly chopped* *1 medium carrot, peeled and sliced* *4 oz/100 g mushrooms, sliced*	Stir into butter, making sure that the butter coats all the vegetables, and cook over low heat for 10 minutes or until the onion is soft.
1½ pt/900 ml/3¾ cups brown stock *2 tbsp tomato purée* *¼ tsp mixed dried herbs*	Stir into the vegetables, bring to the boil, then lower the heat and simmer for 1 hour, stirring occasionally to prevent sticking. Purée in a liquidizer or blender, then press through a sieve into a saucepan.
Salt *Freshly ground black pepper*	Season to taste.

Madeira Sauce (Sauce Madère)(1)

Easy to cook but espagnole sauce must be prepared in advance – takes 30-40 minutes · Do not microwave · Freeze · Serve hot · Makes ½ pt/ 300 ml/1¼ cups

2 shallots, finely chopped 1 sprig thyme 1 bay leaf ¼ pt/150 ml/²⁄₃ cup medium white wine	Combine in a saucepan and simmer until reduced by half.
½ pt/300 ml/1¼ cups espagnole sauce	Stir into the reduced wine. Bring back to the boil, then reduce the heat and cook gently for 10 minutes, stirring occasionally. Strain into another saucepan.
Salt Freshly ground black pepper Pinch cayenne pepper	Season to taste.
2 oz/50 g flat mushrooms, finely sliced ¼ pt/150 ml/²⁄₃ cup gravy 4 tbsp Madeira	Stir into the sauce, bring to the boil, then reduce the heat and cook gently for 10 minutes or until the mushrooms are soft. Purée in a liquidizer or blender.

Madeira Sauce (2)

Easy to cook but espagnole sauce must be prepared in advance · Reserve gravy after cooking the roast · Do not microwave · Freeze · Serve hot · Makes ½ pt/300 ml/1¼ cups

½ pt/300 ml/1¼ cups espagnole sauce ¼ pt/150 ml/²⁄₃ cup well-flavoured gravy, skimmed	Combine in a saucepan, bring to the boil, then simmer for 10 minutes or until of coating consistency.
4 tbsp Madeira	Stir into sauce and immediately remove pan from the heat.

Sauce Miroton

Easy to cook · Use a heavy-based saucepan and cook the flour mixture until it is brown · Microwave – more successful when using the browning dish · Freeze · Serve hot · Makes ½ pt/300 ml/1½ cups

2 oz/50 g/¼ cup butter or margarine	Place in a heavy-based saucepan over strong heat until the butter sizzles.
2 large onions, peeled and finely chopped	Stir into the sizzling butter and cook until the onions are just coloured.
1½ oz/40 g/6 tbsp flour	Stir into the onion mixture. Reduce the heat to minimum and cook until the flour is brown. Remove the pan from the heat.
12 fl oz/350 ml/1½ cups chicken stock 1 tbsp tomato purée 1 tsp vinegar	Stir into the flour mixture and bring to the boil over moderate heat, beating continuously.
Salt Pepper	Season to taste. Cook over minimum heat for a further 10 minutes.

Roquefort and Chive Butter

Easy to prepare · No cooking required · Freeze · Refrigerate · Serve cold with hamburgers or meat loaf · Makes 6 oz/175 g/¾ cup

2 oz/50 g/½ cup crumbled Roquefort cheese 4 oz/100 g/½ cup butter, at room temperature 4 tbsp finely chopped chives	Beat together until smooth.
1 tbsp fresh lemon juice ¼ tsp ground white pepper Pinch bay leaf powder	Beat into the butter mixture. Place between two sheets of wax or greaseproof paper and flatten to a ¼-in/5-mm depth. Chill without blending until firm, then place on a board and cut into 1-in/2.5-cm squares with a very sharp knife, cutting through both sheets of paper. Stack neatly in a covered plastic box and serve as required, removing the paper wrappings at the time of serving.

Above: Madeira Sauce with lamb cutlets

Maître d'Hôtel Butter

Fairly easy to prepare · No cooking required · Freeze · Refrigerate · Serve cold · Makes 4 oz/100 g/¹/₂ cup

4 oz/100 g/¹/₂ cup butter *1-2 tbsp fresh lemon* *juice* *6 tbsp fresh chopped* *parsley* *Pinch cayenne pepper*	Combine in a bowl and beat until the butter is well blended. Shape into a 1-in/2.5-cm cylinder, roll in wax or greaseproof paper and cover with foil, folding in the ends securely. Store in the refrigerator or freezer until required and serve cut into slices or as butter curls.

Shallot Butter

Easy to prepare · Microwave · Freeze · Refrigerate · Serve cold · Makes 4 oz/100 g/¹/₂ cup

4 oz/100 g shallots, *peeled and finely* *chopped*	Place in a saucepan and cover with cold water. Bring to the boil, then drain through a strainer and refresh under cold water. Drain.
4 oz/100 g/¹/₂ cup butter *2 tbsp fresh lemon juice* *Salt* *Pepper*	Combine in a bowl and beat until smooth. Add the shallots and mix thoroughly. Shape into a cylinder, roll up in wax or greaseproof paper and cover with foil, folding in the ends securely. Chill until firm. Slice and use as required.

Above: (left) Paprika and Orange Butter (see page 56), (centre) Piccalilli Butter and (right) Maître d'hôtel Butter

Piccalilli Butter

Easy to prepare · No cooking required · Freeze · Serve cold on hot food · Makes 4 oz/100 g/¹/₂ cup

2 tbsp chunky mustard *pickle* *Few drops fresh lemon* *juice*	Chop very finely but do not purée.
2 oz/50 g/¹/₄ cup butter	Cut into five or six pieces and place in a warmed basin. Beat until smooth.
2 tbsp double or heavy *cream, whipped*	Beat gradually into the butter to form a smooth paste. Gradually beat in the mustard pickle until the butter is an even yellow colour. Shape into a cylinder, roll in wax or greaseproof paper and cover with foil, folding in the ends securely. Chill. Slice and use as required.

Sorrel Sauce

Easy to cook · Do not substitute dried herbs · Do not microwave · Do not freeze · Serve warm · Makes ¹/₄ pt/150 ml/²/₃ cup

¹/₂ oz/15 g/1 tbsp butter *3-4 oz/75-100 g fresh* *sorrel leaves, rinsed and* *dried*	Cook over low heat until the sorrel leaves are tender.
4 fl oz/120 ml/¹/₂ cup *evaporated milk* *4 tbsp chicken stock*	Stir into the sorrel mixture. Purée in a liquidizer or blender. Return to the saucepan, place over minimum heat and warm through.
Salt *Pepper*	Season to taste

Mint Béarnaise Sauce

Fairly easy to cook · Requires double saucepan · Do not microwave · Do not freeze · Serve warm · Makes 8 fl oz/250 ml/1 cup

2 shallots, peeled and finely chopped 3 tbsp white wine vinegar	Combine in a heavy-based saucepan and cook gently for 10 minutes until the shallots have softened and the mixture thickens. Transfer to the top part of a double saucepan, put 1 in/ 2.5 cm of hot water in the base and replace over gentle heat.
4 tbsp fresh chopped mint 1 tbsp water 1 tbsp lemon juice 2 egg yolks, beaten Salt	Stir into the shallot mixture and beat vigorously until the sauce thickens.
4 oz/100 g/½ cup butter, cut into small pieces	Add a little at a time to the sauce, beating continuously until the sauce thickens.

Mint Sauce

Easy to prepare · Requires little cooking · Microwave · Stores well in a corked bottle · Makes ¼ pt/150 ml/⅔ cup

3 tbsp water	Bring to the boil.
1 tsp caster or superfine sugar	Stir into the boiling water. Remove the pan from the heat.
2 tbsp white vinegar	Stir into the sugar mixture. Leave until cool.
4 tbsp finely chopped fresh mint	Stir into the liquid.

Mint Sauce (Blender)

Easy to make · No cooking required · No need to freeze · Store in a screw-top jar · Serve cold · Makes ¼ pt/150 ml/⅔ cup

Generous handful fresh mint	Remove the stems and put the leaves in the blender.
1 tbsp demerara sugar 1 tbsp boiling water 4 tbsp malt vinegar	Switch on the blender and pour through the feed tube. Blend for 20 seconds. Leave to stand for 30 minutes before serving.

Quick Mustard Sauce

Easy to prepare · No cooking required · Do not freeze · Serve cold · Makes 4 fl oz/120 ml/½ cup

2 tbsp mustard powder	Place in a small bowl.
4 fl oz/120 ml/½ cup single or light cream	Gradually stir into the mustard powder. Cover and leave to stand for 15 minutes before using.

Lyonnaise Sauce

Easy to make but Demi-glace must be prepared ahead · Do not microwave · Freeze · Serve hot · Makes 1 pt/600 ml/2½ cups

3 oz/75 g/⅜ cup butter	Melt in a heavy-based saucepan.
4 oz/100 g onions, peeled and thinly sliced	Fry gently in the butter until the onion is soft.
¼ pt/150 ml/⅔ cup white wine ¼ pt/150 ml ⅔ cup wine vinegar	Add to the onion mixture and cook until reduced by half.
1½ pt/900 ml/3¾ cups Demi-glace (page 150)	Stir into wine mixture and simmer until reduced to 1 pt/600 ml/2½ cups.
Salt Pepper	Skim the sauce and season to taste.
Few tbsp stock	If necessary, add to thin the sauce.
½ oz/15 g/1 tbsp butter	Stir into the hot sauce.

Mild Sweet and Sour Sauce

Easy to cook but sauce is inclined to spatter during simmering · Do not microwave · Freeze · Serve hot or cold · Makes 1 pt/600 ml/2½ cups

1 medium carrot, peeled and finely diced 1 large onion, peeled and finely chopped	Drop into a pan of boiling water, then bring back to the boil and simmer for 3 minutes. Drain thoroughly.
1 x 14 oz/400 g can tomatoes 1 x 8 oz/227 g can pineapple chunks in syrup, finely diced 8 cocktail gherkins, sliced ½ oz/15 g/1 tbsp demerara sugar 1 tbsp malt vinegar 1 tbsp soy sauce 1 tsp salt Black pepper	Combine in a large heavy-based saucepan with the blanched carrots and onions. Bring to the boil, then reduce the heat and simmer for 10 minutes to blend the flavours and thicken this textured sauce. **Note:** The sauce is for those who like just a hint of sweet and sour and it is a chunky sauce. If you prefer, it can be puréed in a blender and served smooth.

Galliano Barbecue Sauce

Easy-to-make using convenience foods · Microwave · Store in a screw-top jar · Serve hot with hamburgers or use as a marinade · Makes ¾ pt/450 ml/2 cups

8 fl oz/250 ml/1 cup tomato ketchup 4 fl oz/120 ml/½ cup bottled chilli sauce 4 tbsp Galliano 2 tbsp Worcestershire sauce 4 tbsp fresh lemon juice 5-6 tbsp dark soft brown sugar	Combine all the ingredients in a saucepan, bring just to boiling point and use as required.

Piquant Pepper Sauce

Easy to cook · Do not microwave · Freeze · Serve hot or cold · Makes
¼ pt/150 ml/⅔ cup

1 tbsp oil 2 medium red peppers, cored, seeded and diced	Combine in a heavy-based saucepan and cook gently until the peppers are tender.
3 large tomatoes, skinned and roughly chopped ¼ tsp sweet paprika Pinch dried mace	Stir into the softened peppers and cook over minimum heat until the mixture is reduced to a thick pulp. Stir frequently during cooking.
2 cocktail gherkins, finely chopped 1 tbsp red wine vinegar Salt Freshly ground black pepper	Add to the saucepan, seasoning to taste. Raise the heat, then remove the pan as soon as the mixture bubbles.

Sauce Piquante

Easy to prepare · Add only sufficient vinegar to taste · Microwave ·
Freeze · Serve hot · Makes ¾ pt/450 ml/2 cups

1½ oz/40 g/3 tbsp butter or margarine 3 shallots, peeled and finely chopped	Combine in a heavy-based saucepan and cook over moderate heat, until the onions are just beginning to brown.
½ pt/300 ml/1¼ cups red wine ¼ pt/150 ml/⅔ cup canned condensed beef consommé ¼ pt/150 ml/⅔ cup boiling water Bouquet garni	Stir into the onion mixture. Bring to the boil, then reduce the heat to minimum and cook gently until the liquid is reduced by a quarter. Remove the bouquet garni.
3-5 tbsp red wine vinegar Salt Pepper	Add vinegar and seasoning to taste. Strain the mixture and reheat to boiling point.
3 oz/75 g cocktail gherkins, finely sliced	Add to the sauce.
¾ oz/20 g/1½ tbsp butter 1½ tbsp flour	Blend together in a small bowl. Add to the boiling liquid in small quantities, beating in between each addition, and cook until the sauce thickens.

Poivrade Sauce

Easy to cook but espagnole sauce should be prepared ahead ·
Microwave (see notes page 12) · Freeze · Serve hot · Makes ½ pt/300
ml/
1¼ cups

¼ pt/150 ml/⅔ cup wine vinegar 14 white peppercorns, crushed	Combine in a saucepan, bring to the boil and simmer until reduced by half.
½ pt/300 ml/1¼ cups espagnole sauce	Stir into vinegar mixture and simmer over a low heat for 10 minutes.
Few tbsp beef stock Salt Freshly ground black pepper	Add stock to adjust consistency and season. Strain through a fine nylon sieve and reheat before serving.

Olive and Bacon Sauce

Fairly easy to cook · Do not microwave · Freeze – add olives after
thawing · Serve hot · Makes ½ pt/300 ml/1¼ cups

1 small onion, peeled and chopped 1½ oz/40 g/3 tbsp butter	Combine in a heavy-based saucepan and cook for 5 minutes or until the onion is soft.
1 medium carrot, peeled and finely sliced 2 bacon rashers, rinds removed and chopped	Stir into the onion mixture and cook for a further 5 minutes or until the bacon is brown.
1 oz/25 g/¼ cup plain or all-purpose flour	Stir into vegetables and cook over the lowest possible heat for 15 minutes. Stir frequently and take care that the flour does not scorch.
¾ pt/450 ml/2 cups water 1 beef stock cube, crumbled	Gradually stir into the mixture in the pan, bring to the boil, then simmer for 3 minutes, stirring continuously.
3 large tomatoes, skinned and quartered 1 tbsp tomato purée 1 bay leaf 1 tbsp sherry Salt Freshly ground black pepper	Add to the pan and simmer for 15 minutes until a rich sauce is formed. Stir to prevent sticking. Press the mixture through a nylon sieve and discard the pulp. Return the sauce to the pan.
10 stuffed olives	Slice thinly, add to the sauce and reheat.

Onion and Mushroom Sauce (1)

Easy to cook · Microwave – (see notes page 12) · Freeze – add soured cream after thawing and reheating · Serve hot · Makes ¹/₂ pt/300 ml/1¹/₄ cups

2 tbsp vegetable oil	Heat in a heavy-based pan.
3 oz/75 g onions, peeled and chopped	Stir into the oil and cook until soft.
3 oz/75 g mushrooms, finely sliced	Add to the onion mixture and cook for 1 minute.
¹/₄ pt/150 ml/²/₃ cup dry white wine ¹/₄ pt/150 ml/²/₃ cup veal bone stock 1 tsp fresh lemon juice Salt Pepper	Stir into the vegetable mixture and simmer for 10 minutes or until the liquid is reduced by half. Season to taste.
¹/₄ pt/150 ml/²/₃ cup soured cream	Stir into the pan and immediately remove from the heat.

Note: This is a textured sauce containing chopped onions and sliced mushrooms.

Sauce Savigny

Fairly easy to cook · Do not microwave · Freeze – add cream and port after thawing and reheating · Serve hot · Makes 12 fl oz/350 ml/1¹/₂ cups

12 fl oz/350 ml/1¹/₂ cups good quality red Burgundy wine Pinch nutmeg Pinch ground cloves Pinch ground cinnamon Pinch ground ginger ¹/₄ tsp ground black pepper 1 medium onion, peeled and roughly chopped 1 clove garlic, peeled and sliced 1 bay leaf 1 sprig parsley 1 sprig thyme ¹/₄ tsp celery salt	Combine in a medium saucepan, bring to the boil, then lower the heat and simmer until the liquid is reduced by half. Remove the pan from the heat.
1 oz/25 g/2 tbsp butter or margarine	Melt in a heavy-based saucepan.
³/₄ oz/20 g/3 tbsp plain or all-purpose flour	Stir into the melted fat, cook over low heat for 5-6 minutes, stirring continuously, until the mixture browns. Off the heat, strain in the reduced wine liquid. Return to the heat and whisk continuously until the sauce boils and thickens.
Salt Freshly ground black pepper	Season to taste.
¹/₄ pt/150 ml/²/₃ cup beef stock 1 tsp sugar	Stir into the sauce and bring back to the boil. Remove the pan from the heat.
2 tbsp double or heavy cream 2 tbsp port	Stir into the sauce just before serving.

Roquefort and Meaux Butter

Easy to prepare · No cooking required · Make fresh as needed · Serve cold on hot meat so that the sauce melts on the plate · Makes 4 oz/100 g/¹/₂ cup

1 oz/25 g/¹/₄ cup crumbled Roquefort cheese 2 oz/50 g/¹/₄ cup butter, at room temperature 1 tbsp Moutarde de Meaux 1 tsp bottled savoury fruit sauce	Beat together until creamy and soft.
Salt Freshly ground black pepper	Season to taste if necessary. Spread on hot meat.

Galliano Sauce

Easy to make if you can get Galliano – miniature bottles are sometimes available · No cooking required · Do not freeze · Refrigerate · Serve chilled with pork chops · Makes ¹/₂ pt/300 ml/1¹/₄ cups

¹/₂ pt/300 ml/1¹/₄ cups soured cream 2 small shallots, peeled and finely chopped 1 tsp mustard powder 1 tsp salt 2 tbsp Galliano	Beat thoroughly together. Cover and chill for 6-8 hours before serving.

Canada Ginger Sauce

Easy to cook · Do not microwave · Freeze · Serve hot · Makes ³⁄₄ pt/450 ml/2 cups

1 small green pepper, cored, seeded and finely sliced *1 small onion, peeled and finely sliced* *1 tbsp vegetable oil*	Combine in a heavy-based saucepan and cook until the onion and pepper slices are soft.
7 fl oz/200 ml/⁷⁄₈ cup ginger ale *1 tsp cornflour (cornstarch)* *1 tbsp tomato ketchup* *1 tsp Worcestershire sauce*	Mix together thoroughly, then pour onto the vegetables. Bring to the boil and simmer for 10 minutes.
1 x 8 oz/225 g can tomatoes *2 tbsp soft brown sugar*	Empty into the saucepan and simmer for a further 10 minutes. Purée in a blender.
Salt *Freshly ground black pepper*	Reheat the sauce and season to taste.

Sauce Bordelaise Blanche

Fairly easy to cook · Microwave (see notes page 12) · Freeze · Serve hot · Makes 1 pt/600 ml/2¹⁄₂ cups

3 tbsp vegetable oil *1 medium onion, peeled and finely chopped* *1 small clove garlic, peeled and finely chopped* *2 oz/50 g mushrooms, finely chopped*	Cook together in a heavy-based saucepan for 15 minutes or until the onion is soft and the mushrooms begin to brown. Remove the pan from the heat.
1¹⁄₂ oz/40 g/3 tbsp butter	Melt in a clean saucepan.
1¹⁄₂ oz/40 g/6 tbsp plain or all-purpose flour	Stir into the butter and cook for 2 minutes, stirring all the time.
8 fl oz/250 ml/1 cup water *8 fl oz/250 ml/1 cup medium white wine*	Gradually stir the water then the wine into the flour mixture. Bring to the boil, stirring continuously until the sauce thickens.
Salt *Pepper*	Season to taste. Add the reserved onion mixture, stir thoroughly and cook for 5 minutes over gentle heat until the sauce is very thick. Purée in a blender, adding extra hot stock if necessary.

Opposite: Roquefort and Meaux Butter on grilled or broiled steak

Above: (left) Canada Ginger Sauce and *(right)* Sauce Bordelaise Blanche

Tomato and Apple Sauce

Easy to cook but must be stirred frequently during boiling to prevent spattering · Do not microwave · Freeze · Serve hot or cold with chops or sausages · Can also be used for flavouring soups or stews · Makes 1¹/₄ pt/ 750 ml/3 cups

1¹/₂ lb/700 g ripe tomatoes, skinned and quartered 1 small onion, peeled and sliced 1 medium cooking apple, peeled, quartered and cored 4 fl oz/120 ml/¹/₂ cup wine vinegar 1 tsp salt ¹/₄ tsp freshly ground black pepper Pinch celery salt ¹/₄ tsp ground allspice ¹/₄ tsp ground juniper berries 2 bay leaves	Combine in a large heavy-based saucepan, cover with a lid and cook over gentle heat until the onion is soft. Remove the lid, bring to the boil and simmer until the mixture thickens. Remove the pan from the heat.
1¹/₂ oz/40 g/3 tbsp granulated sugar	Stir into the sauce until dissolved, then put the pan back on the heat and boil for 3-4 minutes. Remove the bay leaves. Purée in two or three batches in the liquidizer.

Sparkling Cognac Sauce

Easy to prepare · To save expense serve a sparkling white wine with the meal and use a small amount for the sauce · Do not microwave · Do not freeze · Makes ¹/₂ pt/300 ml/1¹/₄ cups

¹/₂ pt/300 ml/1¹/₄ cups red wine 1 clove garlic, peeled and halved 1 shallot, peeled and quartered Bouquet garni	Combine in a medium saucepan over moderate heat and bring to steaming point. Reduce the heat to minimum and cook without the lid until the liquid is reduced by one-third. Remove the pan from the heat.
1¹/₂ oz/40 g/3 tbsp butter	Place in a medium heavy-based saucepan and cook over gentle heat until melted.
1¹/₂ oz/40 g/6 tbsp flour	Stir into the melted butter and cook, stirring continuously, until the mixture turns nut brown. Strain the reduced liquid into the butter paste and bring to the boil, stirring continuously until the sauce thickens.
Salt Pepper	Season to taste
4 tbsp Cognac	Stir into the sauce and remove the pan from the heat.
6 tbsp sparkling white wine ¹/₂ oz/15g/1 tbsp butter	Stir into the sauce and serve at once.

Sauce Panache

Easy to cook · Use dried onion flakes · Microwave · Freeze · Serve hot with pork sausages or kidneys · Makes ¹/₂ pt/300 ml/1¹/₄ cups

1 x 8 oz/225 g can tomatoes	Empty into a saucepan.
1 tsp dried onion flakes ¹/₂ beef stock cube, crumbled ¹/₄ pt/150 ml/²/₃ cup water ¹/₄ tsp sugar 3 tbsp Worcestershire sauce	Stir into the tomatoes, bring to the boil, crushing the tomatoes with a potato masher or fork.
¹/₂ oz/15 g/2 tbsp flour 2 tbsp oil	Blend together to form a paste and whisk in small amounts into the boiling sauce. Reduce the heat and simmer, uncovered, for 10 minutes to combine the flavours.
Salt Pepper	Season to taste.

Sauce au Poivre

Fairly easy to cook · Microwave – the colour will not be as deep · Do not freeze unless the sauce is prepared in two stages, adding the cream, brandy and thickening after reheating · Serve hot · Makes ¹/₂ pt/300 ml/ 1¹/₄ cups

2 oz/50 g/¹/₄ cup butter	Melt in a heavy-based saucepan over moderate heat.
1 rasher bacon, diced 1 small onion, peeled and minced or very finely chopped ¹/₄ small carrot, finely sliced 1 oz/25 g mushroom stems, sliced	Stir into the melted butter and sauté until the vegetables are brown.
1 tbsp drained green peppercorns	Add to the mixture and cook for about 1 more minute.
1 oz/25 g/¹/₄ cup flour	Stir into the sautéed vegetables and cook over moderate heat, stirring continuously, until the flour is brown.
¹/₄ pt/150 ml/²/₃ cup dry white wine 6 tbsp meat stock 1 bay leaf 1 tbsp tomato purée	Blend thoroughly into the vegetables, cover with a lid and cook over minimum heat for 30 minutes, shaking the pan occasionally.
Salt Pepper	Season to taste. Strain into another saucepan.
1 tsp potato flour 1 tbsp water	Stir together, pour into the sauce and reheat, stirring continuously, until the sauce thickens.
¹/₄ pt/150 ml/²/₃ cup double or heavy cream ¹/₂ tsp Dijon mustard	Stir into the sauce, bring back to the boil, stirring continuously. Remove the pan from the heat.
2 tbsp brandy	Stir into the sauce.
1 tsp butter	Draw the spoon of butter across the top of the sauce to leave a thin melted layer and stir in just before serving.

Redcurrant Sauce (1)

Very easy to prepare · Microwave – frequent beating required · Store in a screw-top jar · Serve warm · Makes ½ pt/300 ml/1¼ cups

8 fl oz/250 ml/1 cup redcurrant jelly	Melt in a saucepan over low heat.
4 tbsp red wine vinegar	Stir into the redcurrant jelly until all the lumps are removed. Bring to the boil, then simmer for 3-4 minutes or until the sauce is reduced by about one-third.

Reform Sauce

Easy to cook provided espagnole sauce is prepared in advance · Microwave · Freeze · Serve hot · Makes 14 fl oz/400 ml/1¾ cups

¼ pt/150 ml/⅔ cup red wine vinegar *12 peppercorns, crushed*	Combine in a saucepan and boil until the liquid is reduced by half. Strain and return liquid to saucepan.
½ pt/300 ml/1¼ cups espagnole sauce	Stir into the reduced vinegar.
Few tbsp beef stock *Salt* *Pepper*	Add to obtain the correct consistency and seasoning.
2 tbsp port *2 tsp redcurrant jelly*	Stir into the sauce, reheat but do not boil and serve at once.

Sweet and Sour Sauce (1)

Easy to cook · Can be made in two stages if preferred · Microwave · Freeze · Makes 2½pt/1.5 litres/6¼ cups

2 tbsp salad oil *1 large onion, peeled and finely diced*	Cook together in a large heavy-based pan until the onion is soft.
1½ pt/900 ml/3¾ cups meat stock *¼ pt/150 ml/⅔ cup dry sherry* *¼ pt/150 ml/⅔ cup orange juice* *6 tbsp soy sauce* *2 tbsp tomato purée* *½ tsp ground ginger* *1 x 8¾ oz/240 g can crushed pineapple* *4 oz/100 g/¾ cup sultanas or golden raisins*	Combine in a large heavy-based saucepan, add the drained onion and bring to the boil over moderate heat. Reduce to simmering point and cook without covering for 10 minutes.
3 tbsp arrowroot *6 tbsp water*	Blend together in a small bowl. Pour into the sauce, then bring back to the boil, stirring continuously until the sauce thickens.
Salt *Freshly ground black pepper*	Season to taste.

Sauce Soubise (1)

Easy to cook but take care the milk does not boil over · Do not microwave · Do not freeze · Serve hot or cold · Makes 1 pt/600 ml/2½ cups

1 lb/450 g shallots, peeled and finely sliced *1 pt/600 ml/2½ cups milk*	Combine in a heavy-based saucepan. Bring to the boil, then reduce the heat and cook gently until the shallots are tender and the milk is reduced by half. Purée in a liquidizer or blender. Return to the saucepan and reheat to steaming but not boiling point.
4 fl oz/120 ml/½ cup double or heavy cream, half whipped *Salt* *Pepper*	Stir into the saucepan, remove from the heat and season to taste. **Note:** This sauce can be prepared ahead and reheated in the top section of a double saucepan.

Sauce Soubise (2)

Fairly easy to cook but béchamel sauce should be prepared in advance · Do not microwave · Do not freeze · Serve hot · Makes ¾ pt/450 ml/2 cups

8 oz/225 g Spanish onions, peeled and finely chopped *Salt*	Cook in boiling salted water until the onions are soft. Drain thoroughly. **Note:** This can be done in the microwave.
1 oz/25 g/2 tbsp butter	Combine with the onions in a saucepan over minimum heat and cook for 15 minutes, stirring continuously. Do not allow to colour.
¾ pt/450 ml/2 cups béchamel sauce (made using ¾ oz/20 g/1½ tbsp butter, ¾ oz/20 g/3 tbsp flour and ¾ pt/450 ml/2 cups milk)	Stir into the onion mixture and cook over minimum heat for 10 minutes. Pour the sauce through a nylon sieve, rinse the saucepan and reheat the sauce to steaming point. Remove the pan from the heat.
3 tbsp double or heavy cream *1 oz/25 g/2 tbsp butter, at room temperature* *Salt* *Pepper*	Stir into the sauce, seasoning to taste, and serve immediately.

Takeaway Sauce

Easy to prepare · No cooking required · Store in a screw-top jar · Serve cold with Indian foods · Makes 12 fl oz/350 ml/1½ cups

1 tbsp golden syrup *8 fl oz/250 ml/1 cup peach jam* *4 tbsp mango chutney* *1 tbsp malt vinegar* *2 tbsp boiling water* *Salt* *Pepper*	Combine together in a liquidizer or food processor and purée until the peel is finely chopped.

Walnut Sauce

Easy to prepare · Use a liquidizer or food processor · No cooking required · Do not freeze · Refrigerate · Serve cold with smoked tongue · Makes ½ pt/300 ml/1¼ cups

1 thick slice wholemeal bread, crusts removed Few tbsp cold milk	Put in a dish with sufficient milk to cover. Squeeze to remove all the liquid.
3 oz/75 g/¾ cup shelled walnuts Water	Combine in a small saucepan, using sufficient water to cover. Bring to the boil, then discard the water and repeat the process twice more. Cool in ice cold water. Drain the walnuts.
1 clove garlic peeled 1½ tbsp fresh lemon juice ½ tsp salt ¼ tsp pepper	Place in the liquidizer with the walnuts and bread and purée until smooth.
¼ pt/150 ml/⅔ cup olive oil	With the motor running, add a teaspoonful at a time to the liquidizer and continue puréeing until the mixture is thick and creamy.

Red Pepper and Tomato Sauce

Very easy to cook · Do not microwave · Freeze · Serve hot or cold with meat loaf · Makes ½ pt/300 ml/1¼ cups

1 large red pepper, cored, seeded and finely chopped 1 lb/450 g firm tomatoes, skinned, seeded and finely chopped 1 small onion, peeled and finely chopped 1 clove garlic, peeled and finely chopped ¼ pt/150 ml/⅔ cup dry white wine ¼ tsp dried rosemary Pinch sugar	Combine in a heavy-based pan, bring to the boil, then simmer without a lid until the sauce thickens. Purée in a liquidizer or blender, return to the saucepan.
Salt Freshly ground black pepper	Season to taste and reheat the sauce.

Opposite: Walnut Sauce

Below: (left) Sauce au Poivre *(see page 44) and (right)* Red Pepper and Tomato Sauce

Portuguese Sauce (Cold)

Fairly easy to prepare · Microwave – reduce oil to 1 tablespoon ·
Freeze · Serve cold · Makes 1 pt/600 ml/2½ cups

1 large onion 2 shallots	Peel and finely chop.
3 tbsp olive oil	Place in a heavy-based pan and sauté the onion and shallots until translucent.
½ pt/300 ml/1¼ cups dry white wine	Stir into the onion mixture. Bring to the boil over moderate heat, then simmer without a lid until the wine is reduced to 2 tablespoons.
12 oz/350 g tomatoes, peeled, seeded and chopped	Stir into the onion mixture and cook over a gentle heat until the tomato pulp is really soft. Remove the pan from the heat.
4 tbsp olive oil	Beat into the tomato sauce.
2 tbsp fresh lemon juice	Stir into the sauce.
Salt Freshly ground black pepper	Add seasoning to taste. Leave until cold and stir before use.

Portuguese Sauce (Hot)

Easy to cook · Do not microwave · Freeze · Serve hot · Makes 12 fl oz/
350 ml/1½ cups

½ pt/300 ml/1¼ cups port	Place in a small saucepan and simmer until reduced by half.
8 fl oz/250 ml/1 cup beef stock 2 tsp fresh lemon juice 1 tbsp fresh orange juice 1 tsp grated lemon rind 1 tsp grated orange rind	Stir into the port and bring back to the boil.
2 tbsp cornflour (cornstarch) 4 tbsp cold water	Blend together in a small bowl, pour into the boiling sauce and beat vigorously. Reduce the heat to minimum.
1 tbsp seedless raisins 1 tbsp chopped blanched almonds 1 small red pepper, cored, seeded and finely chopped	Stir into the thickened sauce and simmer for 5 minutes until the red pepper is tender but firm.
Salt Pepper	Add seasoning to taste.
Pinch sugar	Stir in.

Quick Sweet and Sour Sauce

Very easy to make using convenience foods · Do not microwave · Do not
freeze · Refrigerate · Serve hot · Makes ½ pt/300 ml/1¼ cups

¼ pt/150 ml/⅔ cup clear honey ¼ pt/150 ml/⅔ cup white wine vinegar 3 tbsp soy sauce 3 tbsp Worcestershire sauce	Combine in a saucepan, bring to the boil, then reduce the heat and simmer, uncovered, for 5 minutes until the sauce is reduced by about one-third. Serve straightaway or reheat before serving.

Sauce aux Olives

Easy to cook · Microwave · Freeze – but the olives tend to soften · Serve
hot · Makes 1 pt/600 ml/2½ cups

2 oz/50 g/¼ cup butter or margarine	Melt in a heavy-based saucepan over minimum heat.
4 oz/100 g onions, peeled and finely sliced	Add to the melted butter and fry gently until the onions are golden.
1½ oz/40 g/6 tbsp flour	Stir into the onion mixture and cook, stirring continuously, until the flour browns.
½ pt/300 ml/1¼ cups dry white wine 8 fl oz/250 ml/1 cup cold water	Add the liquid to the browned flour and bring to the boil, stirring continuously.
Bouquet garni	Add to the sauce.
Salt Pepper	Add seasoning to taste and cook in the pan without a lid for 15-20 minutes. Strain the sauce, reheat.
6 tbsp Madeira 6 oz/175 g/1 cup stoned green olives	Stir into the sauce and serve hot.

Sweet and Sour Sauce (2)

Easy to cook · Microwave · Freeze · Serve hot · Makes ½ pt/300 ml/
1¼ cups

6 fl oz/175 ml/¾ cup water 4 oz/100 g/½ cup soft dark brown sugar 3 fl oz/90 ml/⅜ cup red wine vinegar	Bring to the boil over gentle heat, stirring continuously until the sugar is dissolved. Cook for another minute.
2 tbsp arrowroot 2 tbsp soy sauce 4 tbsp cold water	Blend together in a small bowl and stir into the syrup. Bring back to the boil, stirring continuously until the sauce thickens.
2 drops red food colouring	Stir into sauce.

Quick Meat Sauce

Easy to cook · Microwave · Freeze · Serve hot · Makes 1 pt/600 ml/
2½ cups

1 tbsp vegetable oil 1 oz/25 g/¼ cup flour	Combine in a heavy-based saucepan and stir over minimum heat for 5 minutes or until the mixture is nut brown in colour.
¾ pt/450 ml/2 cups hot brown stock	Gradually stir into the flour mixture and bring to the boil, stirring continuously. Skim if necessary.
2 tbsp tomato purée 2 oz/50 g ham, finely chopped 2 oz/50 g/½ cup raw minced or ground beef Bouquet garni	Stir into the thickened sauce, reduce the heat to moderate and cook in the uncovered pan for 15 minutes. Remove the bouquet garni.
Salt Freshly ground black pepper	Season to taste.

Satay Sauce

Very easy to prepare using a food processor but more difficult if preparing by hand · Do not microwave · Freeze · Serve hot · Makes 1 pt/ 600 ml/2½ cups

6 oz/175 g/1¼ cups shelled roasted unsalted peanuts	Pulverise in the food processor.
1 onion, peeled and coarsely cut	Add to the processor and blend until the onion is finely chopped.
1 tsp chilli powder 2 tsp soft brown sugar	Blend into the peanut mixture.
1 tbsp peanut oil	Heat in a frying pan, then stir in the paste and cook for 3-4 minutes, stirring continuously.
Juice of 1 lime ½ pt/300 ml/1¼ cups Coconut Milk (page 150) 2 tbsp water	Stir into the fried mixture and cook over moderate heat, stirring continuously, until the sauce thickens to the consistency of cream.
Salt	Add to taste.

Raisin Cider Sauce

Easy to prepare · Do not microwave · Freeze · Serve very hot · Makes ½ pt/300 ml/1¼ cups

½ pt/300 ml/1¼ cups dry cider	Put into a saucepan.
2 oz/50 g/¼ cup soft brown sugar Pinch salt 1 tbsp cornflour (cornstarch) 1 oz/25 g/3 tbsp raisins, chopped	Stir into the cider, making sure that the cornflour is thoroughly blended.
6 cloves 2-in/5-cm piece cinnamon stick	Tie together in muslin and add to the pan. Bring to the boil over moderate heat, stirring continuously until the sauce thickens. Reduce the heat and cook for a further 4-5 minutes, then remove the pan from the heat. Take out the bag of spices.
½ oz/15 g/1 tbsp butter	Stir into the sauce until melted. Serve at once.

Simple Tomato Sauce

Easy to cook · Microwave · Do not freeze · Serve hot or cold · Makes ½ pt/300 ml/1¼ cups

1 lb/450 g tomatoes, quartered	Place in a heavy-based saucepan, cover tightly with a lid and cook over low heat, shaking the pan occasionally, until the tomatoes pulp. Press through a sieve. Discard pips and skin. Reheat.
Salt Pepper	Season to taste.
4 tbsp double or heavy cream, unwhipped	Stir into sauce just before serving.

Quick Brown Sauce

Easy to cook · Do not microwave · Freeze – add cream after thawing and reheating · Serve hot · Makes ¾ pt/450 ml/2 cups

2 tbsp salad oil 1 oz/25 g/¼ cup flour	Blend together in a medium pan over minimum heat, then cook, stirring continuously, until a brown paste forms.
½ pt/300 ml/1¼ cups meat or vegetable stock	Pour into the pan and stir vigorously until the mixture is well blended. Bring to the boil, stirring continuously until the sauce thickens.
2 tbsp tomato purée 1 tsp Worcestershire sauce 1 tsp meat extract ¼ tsp bay leaf powder ¼ tsp dried basil 4 oz/100 g button mushrooms, finely chopped	Stir into the thickened sauce and cook, stirring frequently, until the mushrooms are cooked.
Salt Pepper	Season to taste.
2 tbsp fresh or canned cream	Stir in and serve immediately.

Raisin and Almond Sauce

Fairly easy to cook · Do not microwave · Freeze · Serve hot or cold with braised ham or tongue · Makes ¾ pt/450 ml/2 cups

1 pt/600 ml/2½ cups medium red wine 4 oz/100 g/¾ cup seedless raisins 2 oz/50 g/½ cup shredded blanched almonds ½ tsp ground cinnamon Thin strip lemon peel	Combine in a heavy-based saucepan and simmer over a moderate heat for 20 minutes. Take out the lemon peel. Remove the pan from the heat.
1½ oz/40 g/3 tbsp butter ½ oz/15 g/1 tbsp dark brown sugar	Put into a large saucepan and stir over moderate heat until the butter is melted. Continue cooking, stirring continuously, until the sugar has dissolved and turned brown. Remove the pan from the heat.
½ oz/15 g/2 tbsp flour	Blend into the butter and sugar mixture. Replace on the heat and cook, stirring continuously, until the mixture browns further. Stir in the wine mixture, then bring to the boil. Reduce the heat to minimum and cook for 15 minutes, stirring occasionally.

Yogurt and Mint Sauce

Easy to prepare · No cooking required · Do not freeze · Refrigerate · Serve cold with curries · Makes ¼ pt/150 ml/⅔ cup

2 tsp bottled mint sauce 1 x 5 fl oz/142 ml/⅔ cup carton natural yogurt	Mix thoroughly together.
Salt Freshly ground pepper	Add seasoning to taste.

POULTRY

Chicken	Turkey	Duck	Goose	Poussin
Aurore	Chestnut	Bigarade 1	Orange and	Cucumber and
Avgolemono	Cumberland 1	Bigarade 2	Curaçao	Marjoram
Chaud-froid	Cumberland 2	Cherry 2		
Chestnut	Cumberland 3	Cherry 3		
Cold Curry	Sherry	Orange, Lemon		
Honey and Lemon	Soured Cream	and Redcurrant		
Mango Butter	Cranberry	Orange and		
	Xerex	Redcurrant		
		Raspberry		

Sauces that appear in this section but are not mentioned here either have serving suggestions with the recipe or can be served with anything. See also sauces under the following sections:

Meat	Game	Fish	Shellfish	Pasta	Vegetables
Breton	Game Fruit	Béchamel	Gribiche	Five Spice Cream	Mushroom 3
Cider	Textured	Choron			Poulette
Onion and	Cumberland	Hungarian			
Mushroom 1		Mornay			
		Normande			
		Velouté			

Sauce Bigarade (1)

Easy to cook provided espagnole sauce is prepared in advance · Do not microwave · Freeze · Serve hot · Makes ¾ pt/450 ml/2 cups

½ pt/300 ml/1¼ cups espagnole sauce 1 strip lemon peel Rind of ½ Seville orange	Bring to the boil, switch off the heat and leave to infuse for 10 minutes. Strain into another saucepan.
Juice of ½ Seville orange 1 tsp fresh lemon juice ¼ pt/150 ml/⅔ cup claret Pinch cayenne pepper Pinch salt 1 tsp sugar	Stir into sauce and reheat but do not boil.

Sauce Bigarade (2)

Fairly easy to cook · Do not microwave · Freeze · Serve hot · Makes ¼ pt/150 ml/⅔ cup

¾ pt/450 ml/2 cups chicken or duck stock, skimmed 2 tbsp Demi-glace (page 150) Grated rind of 2 Seville oranges 1 tbsp sugar	Combine in a large heavy-based saucepan, bring to the boil, then simmer for about 10 minutes until reduced by one-third.
½ oz/15 g/1 tbsp butter ¼ oz/7 g/1 tbsp plain or all-purpose flour	Blend together in a small bowl. Add to the sauce in small dabs beating each in thoroughly before the next is added.
1 tsp fresh lemon juice 2 tsp Seville orange juice	Stir into the sauce.
Salt Pepper	Season to taste.

Opposite: Sauce Bigarade (1) with roast duck

Sauce Aurore

Easy to cook but time-consuming · Do not microwave · Do not freeze · Serve hot with boiled poultry or eggs · Makes 2 pt/1.2 litres/ 5 cups

1 oz/25 g fatty pork, diced 1/4 oz/7 g/2 tsp butter	Place in a heavy-based pan and fry gently until the meat browns.
1 onion, peeled and diced 1 small carrot, peeled and diced	Stir into the meat. Put a lid on the pan, reduce the heat and cook gently, shaking the pan every 2 or 3 minutes, until the vegetables are tender.
1 oz/25 g/1/4 cup flour	Stir into the vegetables. Do not replace the lid on the pan.
1 lb/450 g tomatoes, skinned	Chop finely and add to pan.
3/4 pt/450 ml/2 cups white bone stock	Blend into the sauce. Bring to the boil and skim.
Pinch sugar Sprig thyme 1 clove garlic 1 bay leaf Salt Freshly ground black pepper	Stir into the sauce. Replace the lid and cook over moderate heat for 3/4 hour or until 1 pt/ 600 ml/2 1/2 cups remain. Pass through a fine nylon sieve, pressing the pulp firmly. About 1/2 pt/300 ml/1 1/4 cups will remain.
1 pt/600 ml/2 1/2 cups Chicken Velouté sauce (page 53)	Add to the tomato sauce, heat, stirring constantly, but do not allow to boil. Remove the pan from the heat.
6 tbsp fresh double or heavy cream	Stir into the sauce.
Salt Freshly ground black pepper	Add salt and pepper to taste. Pass through the fine nylon sieve once more.
3 oz/75 g/6 tbsp butter	Add to the sauce in small pieces, whisking each piece in separately. **Note:** If the sauce is too cool for the butter to melt, reheat gently over the lowest possible heat.

Avgolemono Sauce

Easy to cook · Microwave – only partially · Do not freeze · Serve hot · Makes 1 pt/600 ml/2 1/2 cups

1 oz/25 g/2 tbsp butter	Melt in a heavy-based saucepan.
1/2 oz/15 g/2 tbsp flour	Stir into melted butter. Cook for a few minutes, stirring continuously.
1/2 pt/300 ml/1 1/4 cups chicken stock	Slowly add to the butter mixture, stirring in thoroughly. Cook, stirring continuously, until the sauce thickens. Switch off the heat.
2 eggs 2 tbsp fresh lemon juice 2 tbsp cold water	Beat vigorously together until the mixture is frothy. Put the thick sauce into the top section of a double saucepan or in a bowl over a saucepan of hot water. Slowly pour in the egg mixture beating all the time. Heat but do not boil. The frothy white sauce has a slightly sour lemony taste.

Beurre Noisette

Fairly easy to cook but take care not to burn the butter · Microwave – only suitable if you use browning dish · Freeze · Serve hot · Makes 2 1/2 fl oz/75 ml/5 tablespoons

4 oz/100 g/1/2 cup butter	Place in a frying pan and melt over moderate heat.
1/4 tsp salt	Sprinkle over the surface of the melted butter, raise the heat and cook briskly until the butter browns.
1 tbsp fresh lemon juice	Stir into the browned butter, taking care as the mixture will spatter. Immediately remove the pan from the heat.

Mushroom Sauce (1)

Easy to cook · Do not microwave · Freeze · Serve hot · Makes 1/2 pt/ 300 ml/1 1/4 cups

2 oz/50 g/1/4 cup unsalted butter	Put into a saucepan and melt gently.
1 small shallot, finely chopped	Add to the pan and fry gently until soft.
1 tbsp fresh chopped parsley 4 oz/100 g button mushrooms, finely chopped	Add to pan, stir thoroughly and cook over medium heat until the liquid has evaporated.
1/4 pt/150 ml/2/3 cup dry white wine 1/2 pt/300 ml/1 1/4 cups beef stock 4 tbsp tomato purée	Blend into the mixture in the saucepan. Cook over moderate heat, stirring occasionally, until the volume is reduced to one-third.
2 oz/50 g/1/4 cup unsalted butter	Whisk into pan in small portions using a fork.
Salt Pepper	Season the sauce to taste with salt and pepper. Strain and reheat the sauce before serving.

Sauce Xerez

Easy to cook but espagnole sauce should be prepared in advance · Microwave · Freeze · Serve hot · Makes 1 pt/600 ml/2 1/2 cups

1 pt/600 ml/2 1/2 cups espagnole sauce 2 chicken stock cubes, crumbled	Combine in a large saucepan and bring to the boil over moderate heat. Reduce the heat to minimum and leave to cook, without covering, while continuing with the recipe.
1 small onion, peeled and finely chopped 1 tbsp vegetable oil	Combine in a small saucepan and cook until the onion is soft and golden in colour. Drain the onion and add to the sauce.
8 fl oz/250 ml/1 cup medium sherry 1 oz/25 g lean ham, diced	Add to the sauce and cook over moderate heat for 15 minutes. Purée in the liquidizer and return to the saucepan.
Salt Freshly ground black pepper	Add to taste if necesary and reheat the sauce.

Chaud-froid Sauce

Fairly easy to prepare but success depends upon using well-flavoured béchamel and chicken stock, which must be clear · Microwave · Freeze · Use cold · Makes 3/4 pt/450 ml/2 cups

2 tsp powdered gelatine 2 tbsp hot water	Sprinkle gelatine into the water and stir until completely dissolved.
1/4 pt/150 ml/2/3 cup jellied chicken stock	Heat in a saucepan and stir in the dissolved gelatine.
1/2 pt/300 ml/11/4 cups béchamel sauce, coating consistency	Blend with the chicken stock, stirring thoroughly. Strain through a fine nylon sieve into a clean bowl.
Ice cubes	Half-fill a large bowl with ice and stand bowl of sauce on top. Stir occasionally, but keep covered.
	To use, place chicken on a wire tray, spoon over one coat of the sauce and leave to set before applying second coat. Keep the sauce warm in between the coatings and cool on ice to regain the consistency.

Chicken Velouté Sauce

Easy to make · Do not microwave · Freeze · Serve hot · Makes 1 pt/ 600 ml/21/2 cups

11/2 oz/40 g/3 tbsp butter or margarine	Place in a heavy-based pan over minimum heat until melted.
11/2 oz/40 g/6 tbsp flour	Stir into the butter and cook, stirring continuously, for 3-4 minutes until the mixture just colours. Remove the pan from the heat.
1 pt/600 ml/21/2 cups chicken stock	Gradually stir into the flour mixture, return the pan to the heat and raise the heat to moderate. Bring the sauce to the boil, stirring continuously. Reduce the heat to minimum and continue cooking for 10 minutes, stirring continuously.
Salt Freshly ground pepper	Season to taste.

Mango Butter

Easy to prepare · No cooking required · Freeze · Refrigerate · Serve cold · Makes 6 oz/175 g/3/4 cup

2 oz/50 g/1/3 cup chopped mango chutney peel	Remove three or four large pieces of mango peel from the bottle of chutney and finely chop. Weigh the chopped peel and return the surplus to the jar. Place the chopped peel in a medium bowl.
4 oz/100 g/1/2 cup salted butter 1 tbsp fresh lemon juice Pinch ground ginger Pinch cayenne pepper Pinch ground cloves Pinch salt	Add to the bowl and beat until the mixture is well blended. Shape into a cylinder about 1in/ 2.5 cm in diameter, roll in wax or greaseproof paper and cover with foil, folding in the ends securely. Refrigerate or freeze until required. Cut into slices before serving.

Cumberland Sauce (1)

Very easy to cook · Microwave – ideal. Allow about 30 seconds on Full Power for melting. Reheat by microwave if desired · Freeze – this does not set · Serve hot or cold · Makes 1/4 pt/150 ml/2/3 cup

4 fl oz/120 ml/1/2 cup redcurrant jelly	Half-melt in a saucepan over a gentle heat.
1/2 tsp Dijon mustard 2 tbsp port 2 tbsp fresh orange juice 1 tbsp fresh lemon juice	Stir into the jelly, and cook until steaming but not boiling point is reached. Serve hot or leave to cool.

Cumberland Sauce (2)

Very easy to prepare · No cooking required · Freeze · Serve cold · Makes 6 fl oz/175 ml/3/4 cup

5 tbsp redcurrant jelly 1 tbsp Madeira 1 tsp mustard powder	Stir thoroughly until well blended and no lumps of jelly remain.
2 medium oranges, washed and dried	Finely grate the rind. Squeeze the orange juice. Stir into the jelly mixture until all the ingredients are well blended.
	If you have difficulty in blending the jelly, warm the mixture gently in a bowl over warm water or in the microwave oven on Defrost 35%. Chill until required.

Sauce Chasseur

Easy to cook but espagnole sauce should be prepared in advance · Do not microwave · Freeze · Serve hot · Makes 1 pt/600 ml/21/2 cups

8 oz/225 g mushrooms 2 shallots, peeled and quartered	Chop very finely by hand or chop in a food processor.
2 oz/50 g/1/4 cup butter	Melt in a heavy-based saucepan. Add the mushrooms and shallots and sauté until all the butter is absorbed.
7 fl oz/200 ml/7/8 cup medium white wine	Stir into mushroom mixture, bring to the boil, then simmer until reduced by one-third
1/2 pt/300 ml/11/4 cups espagnole sauce	Add and bring to the boil.
1 tbsp fresh chopped parsley Salt Pepper	Stir into the sauce, seasoning to taste. Reheat and serve immediately.

Cherry Sauce (2)

Easy to prepare · A cherry stoner is useful · Microwave · Freeze – thaw carefully · Serve hot · Makes 8 fl oz/250 ml/1 cup

8 oz/225 g black cherries	Wash and remove the stalks and stones.
1 tbsp vegetable oil *1 onion, peeled and finely chopped*	Cook gently until the onion is soft but not coloured. Remove the pan from the heat. Stir in the cherries.
4 tbsp water *1 rasher bacon, all fat removed*	Add to the pan, cover with a lid and cook over low heat for 10 minutes, shaking the pan occasionally, until the cherries are soft. Remove and discard the bacon.
1 tsp white wine vinegar *¹/₄ tsp sugar* *¹/₄ tsp pepper* *¹/₄ tsp brandy*	Stir into the sauce. Reheat but do not boil.

Cherry Sauce (3)

Easy to cook · Microwave · Do not freeze · Serve hot or cold · Makes ¹/₂ pt/300 ml/1¹/₄ cups

8 oz/225 g black cherries, stoned *¹/₄ pt/150 ml/²/₃ cup water*	Combine in a saucepan and cook over gentle heat until the cherries are tender. Strain into a measuring jug and set the cherries aside. Make up the liquid to ¹/₄ pt/150 ml/²/₃ cup, return to the saucepan.
2 oz/50 g/¹/₄ cup caster or superfine sugar	Stir into the cherry liquid and bring to the boil, stirring constantly until the sugar is dissolved.
2 tsp arrowroot *Few drops almond essence* *1 tbsp cold water*	Blend together, stir into the sugar liquid, raise the heat and bring to the boil, stirring constantly until the sauce clears. Chop the reserved cherries, stir into the sauce, then remove the pan from the heat.
1 tbsp cherry brandy	Stir into the cherry sauce.

Above: (left) Cherry Sauce (2) *and (right)* Chestnut Sauce

Chestnut Sauce

*Easier to prepare if canned chestnuts are substituted for fresh ·
Microwave – use to remove shells and cook chestnuts · Freeze · Serve
hot or warm · Makes ³/₄ pt/450 ml/2 cups*

1 lb/450 g chestnuts	Slit the shells, put into a saucepan, cover with cold water, bring to the boil and cook for 2 minutes. Drain, peel and skin while hot.
³/₄ pt/450 ml/2 cups chicken stock *1 tsp grated lemon rind*	Combine with the chestnuts in a saucepan and cook gently until the chestnuts are tender. Purée in a blender in one or two batches. Return the mixture to the pan.
¹/₂ oz/15 g/1 tbsp butter *4 tbsp double or heavy cream* *Salt* *Pepper*	Add to the sauce, seasoning to taste. Remove the pan from the heat at once.
1 tsp butter	Draw over the surface of the hot sauce. Mix in just before serving.

Mushroom and Coffee Cream Sauce

*Easy to prepare · Microwave · Do not freeze · Serve hot – do not boil
when reheating · Makes ¹/₂ pt/300 ml/1¹/₄ cups*

2 oz/50 g/¹/₄ cup butter or margarine *6 spring onions or scallions, trimmed and finely chopped*	Cook in a heavy-based saucepan until the onion is translucent.
1 tbsp flour	Stir into the onion. Cook for 30 seconds.
1 tbsp tomato purée *¹/₄ pt/150 ml/²/₃ cup well-flavoured chicken stock* *Pinch sugar* *Pinch ground nutmeg*	Add to the onion mixture and bring to the boil over minimum heat. Simmer for 2-3 minutes until the sauce thickens.
4 oz/100 g button mushrooms, finely sliced	Stir into the sauce. Cook for 3 minutes.
1 tsp instant coffee granules *6 tbsp evaporated milk*	Stir in, remove pan from heat.
Salt *Pepper*	Season to taste.

Above: Mushroom and Coffee Cream Sauce

Curry Sauce

Easy to cook · Choose a good curry powder · Microwave – reduce to Medium Low 35% after the sauce has boiled and cook uncovered · Freeze – add soured cream after thawing and reheating · Serve hot · Makes 1 pt/600 ml/2½ cups

1½ oz/40 g/3 tbsp butter or margarine	Melt in a medium saucepan over minimum heat.
1½ oz/40 g/6 tbsp flour	Add to the melted butter and stir in until well blended.
1 pt/600 ml/2½ cups water	Add all at once to the saucepan and whisk over minimum heat until there are no lumps.
Pinch salt 1 tbsp curry powder	Stir into the sauce. Raise the heat and bring to the boil, stirring continuously. Reduce the heat to minimum and continue simmering for 10 minutes for the curry flavour to blend in completely.
Salt Pepper	Add seasoning to taste.
1 tbsp soured cream	Stir in just before serving.

Cold Curry Sauce

Very easy to prepare using convenience foods · Vary flavours by adding a pinch ground cardamom, pinch ground cumin or pinch turmeric · No cooking required · Do not freeze · Refrigerate – leave sauce at room temperature for ½ hour before using · Serve cold · Makes 3 fl oz/90 ml/ ⅓ cup

5 tbsp good quality mayonnaise 1 tsp curry paste 1 tbsp mango chutney	Combine in a bowl, cutting up the larger pieces of mango peel with scissors.

Crème de Volaille Sauce

Fairly easy to cook but requires care when adding eggs and cream · Microwave (see notes page 12) · Do not freeze · Serve hot · Makes ½ pt/300 ml/1¼ cups

¾ oz/20 g/1½ tbsp butter	Melt in a saucepan over low heat.
½ oz/15 g/2 tbsp flour	Stir into the butter and remove the pan from the heat.
8 fl oz/250 ml/1 cup home-made chicken stock 7 tbsp top of the milk Salt Pepper	Gradually add to the butter mixture and blend thoroughly with a wooden spoon. Replace over medium heat and cook for 4-5 minutes, stirring constantly until the sauce thickens. Add seasoning sparingly.
1 egg yolk 2 tbsp double or heavy cream	Mix together in a small bowl, stir into the sauce and immediately remove from the heat. The sauce should be thick enough to coat the back of a spoon and is shiny and creamy in texture. Strain into a sauce boat.

Cumberland Sauce (3)

Easy to cook · Microwave · Do not freeze · Refrigerate · Serve cold · Makes ½ pt/300 ml/1¼ cups

1 lemon 1 orange	Finely grate the rind. Squeeze the juice from the whole orange and half the lemon. Strain the juice and set aside.
4 fl oz/120 ml/½ cup port	Place in a small saucepan, add the orange and lemon strips and bring to the boil. Remove the pan from the heat.
4 tbsp redcurrant jelly 1 tsp mustard powder	Stir into the hot port mixture and add the reserved juices. Leave to cool before serving.

Paprika and Orange Butter

Easy to prepare · No cooking required · Freeze · Serve cold · Makes 4 oz/100 g/½ cup

1 tbsp freshly grated orange rind 1 tsp sweet paprika 4 oz/100 g/½ cup salted butter	Place in a warmed basin, cut the butter into five or six pieces, then beat until smooth.
1 tbsp fresh orange juice	Beat into the butter mixture drop by drop. Do not add more than the butter will incorporate. Shape into a cylinder, roll up in wax or greaseproof paper and cover with foil, folding in the ends securely. Refrigerate or freeze until required. Serve sliced.

Orange and Redcurrant Sauce

Easy to make · Microwave · Freeze · Serve hot or cold · Makes ½ pt/ 300 ml/1¼ cups

1 oz/25 g/2 tbsp butter or margarine	Heat in a heavy-based saucepan until melted.
1 medium onion, peeled and finely chopped	Stir into butter and cook until onion is tender.
¾ oz/20 g/3 tbsp flour	Stir into softened onion and cook for 1 minute, stirring continuously. Remove the pan from the heat.
½ pt/300 ml/1¼ cups fresh orange juice	Gradually stir into onion mixture. Return to heat and bring to the boil stirring continuously.
2 tbsp redcurrant jelly	Add to sauce, reduce the heat and cook gently for 5 minutes to blend the flavours.
Salt Freshly ground black pepper	Season to taste.

Note: The sauce is a yellow/orange colour and the smooth texture of the sauce is laced with small pieces of onion. |

Paprika Sauce

Easy to cook · Microwave · Freeze · Serve hot · Makes ¹⁄₂ pt/300 ml/ 1¹⁄₄ cups

¹⁄₄ pt/150 ml/²⁄₃ cup milk ¹⁄₄ pt/150 ml/²⁄₃ cup chicken stock ³⁄₄ oz/20 g/1¹⁄₂ tbsp butter ¹⁄₂ oz/15 g/2 tbsp plain or all-purpose flour	Beat thoroughly together in a saucepan over low heat. Cook, stirring continuously, until the sauce thickens to a pouring consistency. Remove pan from the heat and keep covered.
1 small onion, peeled and finely chopped ¹⁄₂ oz/15 g/1 tbsp butter	Combine in a small saucepan and fry gently until the onion is cooked. Drain thoroughly and stir the onion into the sauce.
1 tbsp sweet paprika Salt	Add to the sauce and cook over gentle heat, stirring continuously, for 5 minutes.
1 egg yolk, beaten 1 tbsp single or light cream	Beat together, then mix in 2 tablespoons of the hot sauce. Pour into the sauce, beat thoroughly and immediately remove from the heat.
¹⁄₂ oz/15 g/1 tbsp butter	Stir in and serve immediately

Rich Bread Sauce

Easy to cook · Requires 1 hour to infuse · Do not microwave · Do not freeze · Serve hot · Makes 12 fl oz/350 ml/1¹⁄₂ cups

4 cloves 1 medium onion, peeled	Press cloves into onion and place in a medium saucepan.
4 black peppercorns 2 bay leaves, roughly torn ¹⁄₂ pt/300 ml/1¹⁄₄ cups milk	Pour over the onions in the pan. Bring to the boil slowly over a gentle heat. Remove the pan from the heat, cover with a lid and set aside for 1 hour. Strain to remove the peppercorns and bay leaves.
2 oz/50 g/1 cup fresh soft breadcrumbs 1 oz/25 g/2 tbsp butter	Stir into the infused milk. Place the pan over medium heat and bring to the boil, stirring constantly. Remove the pan from the heat.
3 tbsp double or heavy cream Salt Freshly ground white pepper	Stir into the sauce, adding seasoning to taste. Do not reheat.

Honey and Lemon Sauce

Very easy to cook · Prepared in 10 minutes · Microwave · Freeze · Serve hot or cool but not cold · Makes 7 fl oz/200 ml/⁷⁄₈ cup

5 tbsp clear honey 1 oz/25 g/2 tbsp butter ¹⁄₄ pt/150 ml/²⁄₃ cup water ¹⁄₄ chicken stock cube, crumbled Juice of 1 lemon (3 tbsp) 4 sprigs fresh or ¹⁄₄ tsp dried rosemary	Place in a heavy-based saucepan and heat gently until the butter is melted. Bring to the boil, then simmer until the sauce is the consistency of thin syrup.
Pepper Salt	Season, adding salt sparingly.

Orange, Lemon and Redcurrant Sauce

Easy to cook · Microwave · Freeze – flavour becomes less fresh · Serve hot · Makes 7 fl oz/200 ml/⁷⁄₈ cup

1 small onion, peeled and finely chopped Salt	Cook in salted water for 5 minutes or until tender. Drain and set aside.
Juice and grated rind of 1 small orange Juice and grated rind of 1 small lemon 5 tbsp redcurrant jelly	Combine in a medium saucepan, bring to the boil and simmer for 2 minutes.
2 tsp arrowroot 2 tbsp cold water	Blend thoroughly, stir into the saucepan, add the reserved onion. Bring the sauce to the boil and cook for 1 minute, stirring continuously. **Note:** The sauce will not be entirely smooth as it contains the fine particles of onion and grated orange and lemon rinds.

Cucumber and Marjoram Sauce

Fairly easy to cook · Microwave · Do not freeze · Serve warm · Makes 1 pt/600 ml/2¹⁄₂ cups

1 large cucumber, peeled, seeded and chopped 1 tsp dried marjoram Salted water	Place in a saucepan with only just enough salted water to cover. Cover with a lid and cook for 10 minutes over low heat, shaking the pan from time to time. Strain, reserving the liquid. Make up the liquid to ¹⁄₂ pt/300 ml/1¹⁄₄ cups with water. Purée the cucumber in a liquidizer or blender and combine in the saucepan with the liquid. Bring to simmering point.
1 oz/25 g/2 tbsp butter ¹⁄₄ oz/7 g/1 tbsp plain or all-purpose flour	Mix together to a paste. Add to the simmering liquid a little at a time, beating vigorously in between each addition.
1 egg yolk 4 tbsp double or heavy cream 1 tsp grated lemon rind	Beat together in a small bowl. Add 2-3 tablespoons of the hot sauce. Reduce the heat under the saucepan to minimum, pour the egg mixture into the pan and beat vigorously. Do not allow to boil.
Salt Pepper	Season to taste.

Soured Cream Cranberry Sauce

Easy to prepare · Take care not to boil after soured cream has been added · Do not microwave · Do not freeze · Serve warm · Makes ¾ pt/ 450 ml/2 cups

¼ pt/150 ml/⅔ cup water 2 oz/50 g/¼ cup sugar	Bring to the boil over medium heat, stirring constantly until the sugar is dissolved. Raise the heat and boil for 1 minute.
8 oz/225 g cranberries	Stir into the syrup and cook until the mixture thickens. Remove the pan from the heat.
1 tbsp vegetable oil 1 medium onion, peeled and finely chopped	Combine in a saucepan and cook, stirring frequently, for about 10 minutes or until the onion is golden. Stir into the cranberry mixture. Purée in a liquidizer or blender. Reheat.
¼ pt/150 ml/⅔ cup soured cream Few drops Worcestershire sauce	Add to the cranberry mixture and reheat gently but do not boil.

Chaud-froid Sauce Verte

Easy to make but time is saved if white sauce and aspic jelly are made in advance · No cooking required · Freeze · Warm slightly before applying · Can be used as a coating for cold cooked fish, chicken or eggs · Makes 1 pt/600 ml/2½ cups

2 oz/50 g cooked peas 1 drop green food colouring ½ pt/300 ml/1¼ cups white sauce, coating consistency	Purée in a liquidizer or blender, then press through a nylon sieve to remove the pea skins.
¼ pt/150 ml /⅔ cup Aspic Jelly (page 18)	Melt in a small saucepan.
2 tbsp boiling water	Stir into the aspic.
1 tsp powdered gelatine	Sprinkle into the hot aspic and stir thoroughly. Leave to cool but not set. Stir into the green sauce.
2 tbsp single or light cream	Stir into the sauce.
Salt White pepper	Season to taste. Strain through muslin and use as required.

Above left: (top) Soured Cream Cranberry Sauce and *(bottom)* Rich Bread Sauce *(see page 57)*

Opposite: Cucumber and Marjoram Sauce

Above right: Chaud-froid Sauce Verte on chicken breasts

Bread Sauce

Easy to prepare · Microwave · Do not freeze · Serve hot · Makes ½ pt/ 300 ml/1¼ cups

1 medium onion, peeled 2 cloves	Press cloves into the onion.
¾ pt/450 ml/2 cups milk 8 peppercorns	Place in large saucepan and add the prepared onion. Bring almost to the boil, reduce the heat to the lowest possible, then cover and cook for 20 minutes. Switch off the heat and remove the peppercorns but not the onion.
¾ oz/20 g/1½ tbsp unsalted butter 3 oz/75 g/1½ cups fresh soft breadcrumbs	Add to the milk, mixing thoroughly so that the butter is melted and the breadcrumbs well incorporated. Cover and, without cooking further, leave for 15 minutes, then remove onion.

Roquefort Sauce

Fairly easy to cook · Do not overheat once the cream and cheese have been added · Do not microwave · Do not freeze · Serve hot or warm · Makes 12 fl oz/350 ml/1½ cups

1 oz/25 g/2 tbsp butter 3 spring onions or scallions, white part only, finely chopped	Cook over gentle heat until the onions are tender.
4 fl oz/120 ml/½ cup dry white wine 4 tbsp cider ¼ pt/150 ml/⅔ cup strained vegetable stock	Add to the saucepan, bring to the boil, then reduce the heat and simmer until reduced by about half. Strain through a fine nylon sieve. Return the sauce to the pan and reheat.
4 fl oz/120 ml/½ cup double or heavy cream 3 oz/75 g/¾ cup crumbled Roquefort cheese 1 tbsp fresh chopped chives	Stir into the sauce, remove from the heat and continue stirring until the cheese has melted.
Pepper	Add to taste.

Sherry Sauce

Fairly easy to prepare · Do not overboil the cream · Do not microwave · Do not freeze · Serve hot · Makes ½ pt/300 ml/1¼ cups

½ pt/300 ml/1¼ cups double or heavy cream 1 tbsp mustard powder	Stir together in a saucepan and bring to the boil over a gentle heat, stirring frequently. Remove the pan from the heat.
1 tbsp wine vinegar Few drops Tabasco sauce Few drops Worcestershire sauce	Add to the pan, place over the lowest possible heat and cook, stirring continuously, until the sauce is thick enough to coat the back of a wooden spoon.
2 tbsp sweet sherry	Stir in just before serving.

Onion and Mushroom Sauce (2)

Easy to cook · Microwave · Freeze · Serve hot · Makes ½ pt/300 ml/ 1¼ cups

¼ pt/150 ml/⅔ cup meat stock ¼ pt/150 ml/⅔ cup dry white wine 1 tsp lemon juice	Combine in a saucepan and bring to the boil. Reduce the heat and simmer without a lid until the liquid is reduced by half. Remove the pan from the heat.
3 oz/75 g mushrooms, sliced 1 medium onion, peeled and finely chopped 1 tbsp salad oil	Combine in a heavy-based saucepan and cook, stirring frequently, until the onion is soft. Stir in the reduced wine liquid.
Salt Pepper	Add seasoning to taste.
2 tbsp double or heavy cream	Stir into the sauce, reheat to steaming point, stirring continuously.

Mushroom Sauce (2)

Very easy to prepare · Microwave · No need to freeze as recipe uses a can of soup · Serve hot · Makes ½ pt/300 ml/1¼ cups

1 x 10 oz/285 g/1¼ cup can condensed mushroom soup	Empty into a heavy-based saucepan.
4 tbsp sherry 2 tbsp fresh chopped parsley	Stir into the soup, place the pan over moderate heat, then bring to the boil.
4-6 tbsp water	Stir in until the required consistency, then bring back to the boil.

Raspberry Sauce

Easy to cook · Microwave · Freeze · Serve hot · Makes ½ pt/300 ml/ 1¼ cups

1 tbsp oil	Heat in a heavy-based saucepan.
3 shallots or 1 onion, finely chopped	Add to pan and cook gently until soft.
2 tbsp raspberry vinegar 2 tbsp wine vinegar 1 tbsp redcurrant jelly	Add to pan and bring to the boil. Lower the heat and simmer until slightly reduced (about 5 minutes).
8 fl oz/250 ml/1 cup good white stock or white wine	Add to the pan, bring to the boil, reduce heat and simmer for 5 minutes.
Salt	Taste and add salt if necessary.
1½ oz/40 g/3 tbsp unsalted butter, cut into cubes	Beat into the sauce a cube at a time, beating well between each addition, until all the butter is added.
5 oz/150 g/1 cup raspberries, fresh or frozen	Add to the sauce and heat gently until warmed through. Serve immediately.

GAME

Hare	Rabbit	Venison	Guinea Fowl
Alsatian Bourguignonne	Cucumber, Caper and Fennel Thin Onion	Alsatian Anise Cranberry with Port Grand Veneur Oxford Redcurrant 2	Financière

Sauces that appear in this section but are not mentioned here either have serving suggestions with the recipe or can be served with anything.
See also sauces under the following sections:

Meat	Poultry
Cherry 1	Bread Cumberland 1 Cumberland 2 Cumberland 3 Orange and Redcurrant Rich Bread

Cucumber, Caper and Fennel Sauce

Easy to cook · Microwave · Do not freeze · Serve cold · Makes ½ pt/ 300 ml/1¼ cups

2 oz/50 g piece cucumber, peeled and finely diced 2 tsp chopped capers 1 tsp fennel seed	Mix together in a small bowl. Set aside.
1 oz/25 g/2 tbsp butter	Melt in a heavy-based saucepan over gentle heat.
½ oz/15 g/2 tbsp flour	Stir into melted butter and cook for 30 seconds, stirring all the time. Remove the pan from the heat.
½ pt/300 ml/1¼ cups milk	Gradually stir into flour mixture until smooth, then cook over medium heat, stirring continuously, until the sauce thickens. Add the cucumber mixture and cook for 1 minute. Remove from the heat.
Salt Pepper	Season to taste.

Grand Veneur Sauce

Easy to cook · Do not microwave · Freeze · Serve hot · Makes 8 fl oz/250 ml/1 cup

½ oz/15 g/1 tbsp butter 1 small carrot, peeled and finely sliced 4 shallots, peeled and finely sliced 1 bay leaf 1 sprig thyme 1 clove 1 sprig parsley	Cook together gently until the carrot and shallots are golden in colour.
¾ oz/20 g/3 tbsp plain or all-purpose flour ½ pt/300 ml/1¼ cups medium red wine 1 tbsp red wine vinegar	Stir into the vegetables. Bring to the boil, then simmer for 15-20 minutes or until the sauce is reduced by one-third.
1 tbsp Demi-glace (page 150) 3 tbsp redcurrant jelly 1 tsp freshly ground black pepper	Add to the sauce, stirring until the jelly is melted. Strain through a nylon sieve. Reheat.
Salt	Add to taste.

Port Wine Sauce

Easy to cook · Do not microwave · Freeze · Serve hot with any game birds · Makes 8 fl oz/250 ml/1 cup

1 bay leaf *1 small shallot, peeled and finely chopped* *1 sprig thyme* *6 tbsp port*	Combine in a saucepan, bring to the boil, then simmer until reduced to about 3 tablespoons. Remove the pan from the heat.
Juice of 1 large orange *1 tbsp fresh lemon juice* *Pinch grated orange rind* *7 fl oz/200 ml/⁷⁄₈ cup well-flavoured brown stock* *2 tsp tomato purée*	Stir into the reduced liquid. Place the pan on the heat and simmer until boiling point is reached. Strain into another saucepan.
2 tsp flour *2 tsp butter*	Blend together to make *beurre manié*. Reheat the sauce to simmering and add in small quantities, whisking between each addition.
Salt *Pepper*	Adjust seasoning.

Opposite: (left) Cucumber, Caper and Fennel Sauce *(see page 61)* and *(right)* Port Wine Sauce

Above: Grand Veneur Sauce with roast pheasant *(see page 61)*

Sauce Anise

Difficult to cook · Requires gravy left over from roast · Do not microwave · Freeze · Serve hot · Makes ½ pt/300 ml/1¼ cups

3 tbsp wine vinegar 1 tbsp sugar	Combine in a small heavy-based saucepan. Cook over medium heat, stirring constantly, until the sugar has dissolved. Bring to the boil and simmer until the syrup caramelizes and turns light brown. Immediately remove the pan from the heat and dip the base in a bowl of hot water to prevent the caramel from becoming dark. Wipe the base of the pan dry and set aside on a heatproof surface.
4 fl oz/120 ml/½ cup medium white wine ½ tsp aniseed	Stir into the caramel until the mixture is blended. Replace on the heat and bring to the boil. Reduce the heat to medium and simmer until the mixture is reduced by one-third.
½ pt/300 ml/1¼ cups gravy 1 tsp cornflour (cornstarch)	Blend together, then gradually add to the wine. Bring back to the boil and cook for 1 minute, stirring continuously.
Salt Pepper	Season to taste. Strain through a fine nylon sieve or piece of muslin. Serve immediately.

Thin Onion Sauce

Easy to cook · Do not microwave · Do not freeze · Serve hot · Makes 1 pt/600 ml/2½ cups

1 lb/450 g onions, thinly sliced 1 pt/600 ml/2½ cups creamy milk 2 sage leaves	Combine in a large saucepan, bring to the boil, then reduce the heat and simmer until the onions are tender. Stir occasionally during cooking to prevent the milk from boiling over. Strain the milk into another large pan, leaving 3 tablespoons with the onions, and simmer until only ½ pt/300 ml/1¼ cups remain. Purée the onions and sage leaves in a blender. Stir into the milk.
2 tbsp double or heavy cream Salt Pepper	Stir cream into the sauce, immediately remove the pan from the heat and season to taste.

Oxford Sauce

Easy to cook · Microwave · Freeze · Serve cold · Makes ¾ pt/450 ml/2 cups

8 fl oz/250 ml/1 cup redcurrant jelly 1 shallot, peeled and finely chopped Juice and grated rind of 1 orange Juice and grated rind of 1 lemon 1½ tsp made English mustard ¼ tsp ground ginger ¼ pt/150 ml/⅔ cup sweet red wine	Combine all the ingredients in a heavy-based saucepan, set over minimum heat and bring to the boil, stirring frequently. Pour into jars or a jug and leave until cool.

Cranberry Sauce with Port

Easy to cook · Microwave · Freeze · Serve hot or cold · Makes ¾ pt/450 ml/2 cups

6 oz/175 g/¾ cup caster or superfine sugar ¼ pt/150 ml/⅔ cup water	Stir together in a saucepan placed on minimum heat until the sugar has dissolved.
8 oz/225 g/2 cups cranberries	Stir into the sugar syrup, bring to the boil then reduce to simmering point. Cook in the pan without a lid, stirring frequently, until the cranberries are soft and the mixture is thick.
2 tbsp port	Remove the pan from the heat and stir in the port.

Sauce Financière

Easy to cook · An expensive sauce to make properly · Requires truffles which are obtainable in small cans from exclusive grocers · Microwave · Freeze · Serve hot · Makes 1 pt/600 ml/2½ cups

1½ oz/40 g/3 tbsp butter	Melt over gentle heat in a heavy-based saucepan.
1½ oz/40 g/6 tbsp flour	Stir into the melted butter and cook for 4-5 minutes, stirring continuously, until the mixture is a biscuit colour.
1 pt/600 ml/2½ cups chicken stock	Gradually blend into the butter mixture, bring to the boil over moderate heat, stirring continuously
8 oz/225 g button mushrooms, quartered	Stir into the sauce and cook over minimum heat for 15-20 minutes until the mushrooms are soft, stirring occasionally.
6 tbsp Madeira	Stir into the sauce.
1 truffle, thinly sliced	Add to the sauce and cook for a further 5 minutes.
Salt Pepper	Season to taste.

Sauce Bourguignonne

Fairly easy to cook · Use a good quality wine, as cheap acid wine will produce a sour flavour · Do not microwave · Freeze · Serve hot · Makes ³/₄ pt/450 ml/2 cups

1 bottle red Burgundy wine ¹/₂ tsp quatre-épices Pinch grated nutmeg 1 small onion, peeled and stuck with 4 cloves 1 clove garlic, peeled and chopped 1 sprig parsley 1 sprig thyme 2 bay leaves 6 black peppercorns	Combine in a large saucepan and bring to the boil over moderate heat. Reduce to simmering and cook without a lid until the liquid is reduced by half. Remove the pan from the heat.
2 oz/50 g/¹/₄ cup butter	Melt in a large heavy-based saucepan over minimum heat.
1 oz/25 g/¹/₄ cup flour	Stir into the butter and cook over minimum heat for about 6-7 minutes, stirring frequently until the flour is nut brown. Strain the wine mixture into the browned flour and bring to the boil, stirring continuously until the sauce thickens slightly.
Salt Pepper	Season to taste
1 tsp butter	Draw over the surface of the sauce, allowing the butter to form a melted layer. Stir before serving.

Game Fruit Sauce

Easy to cook but the orange peel must be pared thinly and finely shredded · Do not microwave · Serve hot or cold · Makes ¹/₂ pt/300 ml/ 1¹/₄ cups

1 Seville orange 1 lemon	Wash and dry the fruit and pare away the peel thinly so that no pith is attached. Shred the peel finely, put into a small saucepan, cover with water and simmer until the peel is tender. Drain. Halve the fruit and extract the juice. Reserve the strips of peel and the juice.
¹/₄ pt/150 ml/²/₃ cup redcurrant jelly 3 tbsp water	Combine in a saucepan and heat until the jelly is melted. Add the reserved fruit juices and the peel.
5 tbsp Madeira	Stir into the pan and simmer the sauce for 5 minutes until it is slightly reduced.
1 tsp Dijon mustard Salt Freshly ground black pepper	Add mustard and season to taste.

Orange Curaçao Sauce

Easy to prepare · Microwave · Freeze · Serve hot or cold · Makes 12 fl oz/ 350 ml/1¹/₂ cups

1 tbsp arrowroot	Place in a saucepan away from the heat.
¹/₂ pt/300 ml/1¹/₄ cups fresh orange juice	Stir into the arrowroot until well blended.
Grated rind of 1 orange	Stir into the orange mixture and bring to the boil over moderate heat, stirring continuously until the sauce thickens. Remove the pan from the heat.
Chopped flesh of 1 orange 1 tbsp Orange Curaçao	Stir into the orange sauce.

Redcurrant Sauce (2)

Easy to cook · Microwave · Freeze · Serve hot or cold · Makes 8 fl oz/ 250 ml/1 cup

4 fl oz/120 ml/¹/₂ cup redcurrant jelly	Melt in a saucepan over moderate heat.
6 tbsp water 1 tbsp fresh lemon juice Pinch ground cloves	Stir into the jelly until the liquid is hot and the jelly melted.
1 tsp arrowroot 3 tbsp red wine	Blend together, stir into the sauce, then bring to the boil, stirring continuously until the sauce is clear.
1 tsp butter	Draw the spoon of butter across the surface, allowing it to form a melted layer. Stir in just before serving.

Spiced Apple Sauce

Easy to cook but stir frequently as bubbles tend to spatter · Microwave – use only 1 tablespoon water · Freeze · Serve hot · Makes ½ pt/300 ml/ 1¼ cups

8 oz/225 g cooking apples	Peel, core and finely slice.
5 tbsp water ¼ tsp mixed spice ¼ tsp ground ginger 3 tbsp sugar	Combine with the apples in a heavy-based saucepan. Cook, stirring occasionally, over moderate heat until the apple is pulpy.
¼ pt/150 ml/⅔ cup dry ginger ale	Pour into the apple mixture, stirring vigorously to prevent foaming up. Reheat, then remove the pan from the heat.
½ oz/15 g/1 tbsp butter	Stir into the sauce until melted. Strain through a nylon sieve.

Textured Cumberland Sauce

Fairly easy to cook · Microwave · Freeze · Serve hot or cold · Makes ¾ pt/450 ml/2 cups

1 shallot, peeled and finely chopped	Put into small saucepan.
2 oranges 1 lemon	Pare thinly and add peel to the pan. Cover the shallot and peel with cold water, bring to the boil, then reduce the heat and simmer for 5 minutes. Drain. Squeeze the juice from the fruit and reserve.
12 fl oz/350 ml/1½ cups redcurrant jelly	Put in a bowl over a pan of boiling water and stir until melted. Mix in the onion and orange peel. Purée in a liquidizer or blender
2 tsp Dijon mustard ¼ pt/150 ml/⅔ cup port Reserved fruit juice	Mix together in the saucepan. Pour in the puréed mixture and reheat until steaming but not boiling.

Alsatian Sauce

Easy to make · Do not microwave · Freeze – remains liquid · Serve hot · Makes ¼ pt/150 ml/⅔ cup

3 fl oz/90 ml/⅜ cup port Pinch nutmeg Salt Pepper	Combine in a saucepan and cook over medium heat until the volume is reduced to two-thirds.
3 fl oz/90 ml/⅜ cup redcurrant jelly	Stir into the port until melted.
1 tbsp grated horseradish 1 tbsp double or heavy cream	Stir into the mixture in the saucepan. Cook for 1 minute until the sauce is hot. Stir before serving.

Above: Spiced Apple Sauce

FISH

Sauces that appear in this section but are not mentioned here either have serving suggestions with the recipe or can be served with anything. See also the sauces under the following sections:

Black Grape Sauce

Requires care in cooking · Microwave – cook on Defrost setting (see notes page 12) · Do not freeze · Serve hot or warm · Makes ¾ pt/450 ml/ 2 cups

5 oz/150 g/½ cup plus 2 tbsp unsalted butter	Place in a saucepan over minimum heat until melted. Set aside.
¼ pt/150 ml/⅔ cup double or heavy cream	Put into a bowl over a saucepan containing 1 in/2.5 cm of hot water. Place over minimum heat.
2 egg yolks, beaten	Beat into the cream.
Salt Pepper	Season to taste. Cook, beating continuously, until the sauce thickens slightly. Gradually pour in the melted butter a few drops at a time and continue beating until the sauce is pale and creamy.
6 oz/175 g black grapes, skinned, pipped and quartered	Stir into the sauce, then reheat gently just enough to warm the grapes.

Right: Black Grape Sauce with sole

Aïoli (Traditional)

Requires practice for success · Microwave – it helps if the oil is heated for 30 seconds before using · Do not freeze · Serve cold · Makes ¼ pt/ 150 ml/²/₃ cup

5 cloves garlic, peeled	Place in a glass or glazed bowl that will not absorb the odour. Using the end of a rolling pin or pestel, pound to a pulp.
2 egg yolks	Beat into the pulped garlic.
4 fl oz/120 ml/½ cup first grade olive oil	Beat in drop by drop until the mixture begins to thicken.
1 tsp fresh lemon juice 1 tsp water	Mix together, then beat into the sauce a few drops at a time, alternating with the remainder of the oil.
Salt Freshly ground pepper	Season to taste.

Anchovy Butter

Very easy to prepare · No cooking required · Do not freeze · Refrigerate – use earthenware pot · Serve cold · Makes 1½ oz/40 g/3 tablespoons

1 oz/25 g/2 tbsp butter ½ oz/15 g/1 tbsp anchovy paste ¼ tsp fresh lemon juice Pinch cayenne pepper	Beat together until well blended. Serve in dabs.

Anchovy and Egg Sauce

Easy to make · Microwave · Do not freeze · Serve hot · Makes 8 fl oz/ 250 ml/1 cup

¾ oz/20 g/1½ tbsp butter	Melt in a saucepan.
½ oz/15 g/2 tbsp plain or all-purpose flour	Stir into the melted butter and cook for 1 minute, stirring continuously.
6 fl oz/175 ml/¾ cup milk	Gradually add to the mixture in the saucepan off the heat. Return the saucepan to the heat and bring to the boil, stirring continuously until the sauce thickens. Remove the pan from the heat.
4 anchovies	Remove any bones and chop until puréed. Stir into the sauce.
¼ tsp freshly ground black pepper	Add to sauce. Reheat sauce to steaming point, stirring continuously. Remove the pan from the heat.
1 hard-boiled egg, finely chopped 1 tbsp fresh chopped parsley	Stir into the sauce.

Beurre Blanc (1)

Fairly easy to prepare · Do not microwave · Do not freeze · Do not refrigerate · Serve hot · Makes 12 fl oz/350 ml/1½ cups

4 shallots, peeled and finely chopped ¼ pt/150 ml/²/₃ cup dry white wine	Place in an enamel or non-metallic saucepan, bring to the boil, then reduce the heat and simmer until only 1 tablespoon of the wine runs freely. Pour the mixture into a bowl set over a pan of hot water.
7 oz/200 g/⁷/₈ cup butter, at room temperature, diced	Whisk into the onion mixture a few pieces at a time until well blended and the sauce thickens.
1 tsp white wine vinegar	Whisk into the sauce.
Salt Freshly ground black pepper	Season to taste. Strain through a fine nylon sieve and serve immediately.

Beurre Blanc (2)

Requires care · Do not microwave · Do not freeze · Serve warm · Makes ¼ pt/150 ml/²/₃ cup

2 tbsp white wine vinegar 4 fl oz/120 ml/½ cup dry white wine 1 shallot, peeled and finely minced or chopped ½ tsp roughly crushed black peppercorns	Combine in an enamel, glass or non-stick saucepan and cook over medium heat until only 1 tablespoon of liquid remains. Remove the pan from the heat.
1 tbsp single or light cream	Stir into liquid remaining in pan. Bring to the boil and immediately remove from heat.
4½ oz/125 g/½ cup plus 1 tbsp unsalted butter, diced	Add quickly to the liquid in the hot pan and swirl the pan round to hasten melting.
Salt	Season to taste. Strain through a fine nylon sieve. Keep warm in a bain-marie or over a bowl of hot water.

Sauce Bercy

Fairly easy to cook · Microwave – results are not quite as good as when cooked in a saucepan · Freeze · Serve hot with baked or boiled fish · Makes ¹/₂ pt/300 ml/1¹/₄ cups

1-2 shallots, peeled and finely chopped ¹/₂ oz/15 g/1 tbsp butter	Cook together until the shallots are tender but not coloured.
4 fl oz/120 ml/¹/₂ cup white wine	Stir into the shallots and cook over moderate heat until the liquid is reduced by half.
8 fl oz/250 ml/1 cup fish stock Salt Pepper 1 tbsp fresh lemon juice 1 tbsp fresh chopped parsley	Add to the reduced wine liquor, then bring back to the boil. Remove the pan from the heat.
¹/₂ oz/15 g/1 tbsp butter ¹/₄ oz/7 g/1 tbsp flour	Mix together to a smooth paste. Add to the pan in pieces, then stir until well blended and bring back to the boil, beating continuously.
Salt Pepper	Season to taste.

Béchamel Sauce

Easy to cook · Microwave · Freeze · Use ¹/₄ pt/150 ml/²/₃ cup additional milk for a pouring sauce · Serve hot · Makes ¹/₂ pt/300 ml/1¹/₄ cups

¹/₂ pt/300 ml/1¹/₄ cups milk 1 slice onion 1 bay leaf 1 blade mace 1 slice carrot 3 sprigs parsley 6 peppercorns 1 sprig thyme	Combine in a saucepan and bring to simmering point over moderate heat. Place the lid on the pan, switch off the heat and leave the saucepan on the hob. Leave to stand for 15-30 minutes.
³/₄ oz/20 g/1¹/₂ tbsp butter or margarine	When the sauce infusion time is completed, place the butter in a heavy-based saucepan and melt over moderate heat.
³/₄ oz/20 g/3 tbsp flour	Stir into the melted butter and cook, stirring, for 1-2 minutes. Remove the pan from the heat. Strain the infused milk into the butter mixture and blend thoroughly with a wooden spoon. Replace the pan over moderate heat and bring to the boil, whisking continuously until the sauce boils and thickens. Reduce the heat to minimum and cook for a further 2 minutes.
Salt Pepper	Season to taste

Asparagus Sauce

Very easy to cook using convenience foods · Microwave · Freeze · Serve hot · Makes ³/₄ pt/450 ml/2 cups

1 oz/25 g/2 tbsp butter or margarine 1 oz/25 g/¹/₄ cup flour 1 x 14 oz/400 g can asparagus soup 4-6 tbsp milk	Place all the ingredients in a heavy-based saucepan and stir until as smooth as possible. Put the saucepan on the heat and gradually bring to the boil, stirring continuously until the sauce thickens. Reduce the heat and cook for a further 3-4 minutes, still stirring.
Salt Pepper	Season to taste.

Fennel Sauce

Easy to cook · Microwave · Do not freeze · Serve hot · Makes ¹/₄ pt/150 ml/²/₃ cup

1 tbsp fresh chopped fennel Salt	Cook in boiling salted water for 5 minutes. Drain thoroughly.
2 tsp butter 1 tbsp flour ¹/₄ pt/150 ml/²/₃ cup milk	Combine in a saucepan, blend until smooth, then place over low heat. Whisk continuously until the sauce boils and thickens. Stir in the chopped fennel.
Few drops fresh lemon juice Salt Pepper	Add to sauce, seasoning to taste.

Sauce Maigre

Easy to cook · Microwave · Freeze · Serve hot · Makes ¹/₂ pt/300 ml/1¹/₄ cups

¹/₂ oz/15 g/1 tbsp low calorie margarine 1 small onion, peeled and finely chopped 2 oz/50 g button mushrooms, finely sliced	Cook gently for 5 minutes or until the mushrooms and onion are soft.
¹/₂ oz/15 g/2 tbsp flour	Stir into the vegetable mixture.
¹/₂ pt/300 ml/1¹/₄ cups beef stock 1 tbsp tomato purée	Add to the saucepan, stir thoroughly and simmer for 10 minutes.
2 drops liquid sweetener	Stir in to taste.

Beurre Montpellier

Easy to prepare but fresh herbs are essential · Can be made in a food processor · Microwave · Freeze · Refrigerate · Serve cold · Makes 5 oz/ 150 g/¹⁄₂ cup plus 1 tablespoon

2 oz/50 g fresh spinach leaves	Wash, then drop into a saucepan of boiling water. Bring back to the boil, drain in a colander and place under cold running water until the spinach is cold. Drain thoroughly. Finely chop and set aside.
2 anchovies 4 tbsp cold milk	Soak for 15 minutes. Drain thoroughly, discarding the milk, and finely chop the anchovies.
8 oz/225 g/1 cup butter, at room temperature 4 hard-boiled eggs, peeled and chopped 2 cocktail gherkins, chopped 1 tsp capers, rinsed and finely chopped	Add to the anchovies and pound to a smooth paste. Stir in the spinach, then rub the mixture through a fine strainer or sieve.
1 tbsp fresh chopped chives 1 tbsp fresh chopped chervil 1 tbsp fresh chopped tarragon 2 tbsp fresh chopped parsley	Chop as finely as possible, mix into the butter paste. Smooth to a 6 in/15 cm square on wax or greaseproof paper and refrigerate or freeze until required. Serve in slices or dabs.

Butter Nut Sauce

Fairly easy to cook · Microwave – care required when browning nuts · Freeze · Serve hot · Makes 8 fl oz/250 ml/1 cup

1 stick celery, finely sliced Salted water	Boil celery in salted water for 2 minutes, then drain thoroughly.
4 oz/100 g/¹⁄₂ cup salted butter	Melt in a frying pan.
1 oz/25 g/¹⁄₄ cup cashew nuts, slivered	Stir into the butter and fry gently, stirring continuously, until light brown. Stir in the celery and cook for 2 more minutes. Serve immediately.

Above: (left) Butter Nut Sauce *and (right)* Beurre Montpellier

Fish Curry Sauce

Easy to cook · Microwave · Freeze – liquidize before serving · Serve hot ·
Makes just under ³/₄ pt/450 ml/2 cups

1 oz/25 g/2 tbsp butter or margarine	Melt in a heavy-based saucepan.
1 onion, peeled and finely diced	Stir into the melted butter and cook until the onion is soft but not brown.
¹/₄ tsp dried thyme 1 bay leaf 2 blades mace Pinch ground cardamom 2 tbsp mild curry paste	Add to the onions, stir thoroughly and cook gently for 10 minutes. Strain into a clean pan. Discard the pulp.
1 pt/600 ml/2¹/₂ cups fish stock	Add to the strained liquor and cook until reduced by one-third.
4 tbsp Coconut Milk (page 150) 1 tsp cornflour (cornstarch)	Blend together in a small bowl. Pour into the simmering sauce and stir briskly until well blended and the sauce thickens.
1 tsp salt 1 tsp fresh lemon juice	Stir in, adding more salt if preferred.

Sauce Vin Blanc

Easy to cook · Requires velouté sauce · Microwave · Do not freeze ·
Serve hot · Makes 1 pt/600 ml/2¹/₂ cups

¹/₂ pt/300 ml/1¹/₄ cups fish stock 4 fl oz/120 ml/¹/₂ cup dry white wine	Combine in a saucepan, bring to the boil, then reduce to simmering point and cook until only 1 tablespoon of liquid remains. Remove the pan from the heat.
³/₄ pt/450 ml/2 cups velouté sauce 1 clove garlic, peeled	Add to the saucepan, place the pan over minimum heat and bring to the boil, stirring continously. Take out the garlic and remove the pan from the heat.
2 egg yolks 4 tbsp double or heavy cream	Beat together in a small bowl. Stir in 2 tablespoons of the hot sauce, return the mixture to the pan and whisk thoroughly.
¹/₂ oz/15 g/1 tbsp butter	Stir into the sauce until the butter is melted.
Salt Pepper	Adjust seasoning if necessary.

Above: Fish Curry Sauce

Black Butter

Easy to cook but take care not to burn the butter · Microwave – only if browning dish is available · Do not freeze · Serve hot with baked or steamed white fish · Makes 5 tablespoons

2 oz/50 g/¼ cup unsalted butter	Heat in a small saucepan until a nut brown colour. Remove from the heat.
1 tbsp white wine vinegar	Stir into butter.
Salt Freshly ground black pepper	Add seasoning to taste.

Beurre Meunière

Fairly easy to cook but take care when browning the butter as it burns easily · Microwave – use browning dish · Freeze · Serve hot with fish fillets · Makes ¼ pt/150 ml/⅔ cup

4 oz/100 g/½ cup butter	Place in a frying pan and melt over moderate heat.
¼ tsp salt	Sprinkle over the surface of the butter, raise the heat and cook briskly until the butter browns.
2 tsp fresh lemon juice 1 tbsp fresh chopped parsley	Stir into the browned butter, remove the pan from the heat and serve at once.

Microwave Hollandaise Sauce (1)

Easy to cook · Microwave · Freeze · Serve warm · Makes ¼ pt/150 ml/⅔ cup

3 oz/75 g/¼ cup plus 2 tbsp unsalted butter	Place in a suitable bowl and microwave on Full Power for 30 seconds to 1 minute or until the butter is melted.
2 egg yolks Juice of 1 small lemon (2 tbsp) Pinch mustard powder Pinch salt Pinch white pepper	Whisk together with a fork until well mixed. Remove the bowl from the microwave and strain the egg mixture into the hot butter, beating thoroughly. Replace the bowl in the microwave oven, set the timer for 45 seconds and switch on. Open the door and whisk the sauce every 15 seconds until it thickens slightly and leaves a trail when the whisk is drawn across the surface. Remove the bowl and whisk while the sauce cools. **Note:** Take care not to overcook or the sauce will curdle.

Fish Satin Sauce

Easy to prepare · Do not microwave · Do not freeze · Serve hot · Makes ½ pt/300 ml/1¼ cups

½ oz/15 g/1 tbsp butter	Place in a small bowl and beat until soft.
1 tbsp flour	Stir into butter and beat to a smooth paste.
¾ pt/450 ml/2 cups liquid in which fish was poached	Place in a saucepan and cook until reduced by one-quarter. Keep the liquid at simmering but not boiling point and add the butter mixture in teaspoonfuls, beating in between each addition. Switch off the heat as soon as the sauce thickens. do not allow to boil.

Fresh Green Herb and Egg Sauce

Easy to cook · Microwave · Do not freeze · Serve hot or cold · Makes 1 pt/600 ml/2½ cups

1½ oz/40 g/3 tbsp butter	Melt in a heavy-based saucepan.
1½ oz/40 g/¼ cup plus 1 tbsp plain or all-purpose flour	Stir into melted butter and cook over gentle heat for 1 minute, stirring continuously. Remove pan from heat.
6 fl oz/175 ml/¾ cup evaporated milk 14 fl oz/400 ml/1¾ cups well-flavoured chicken stock	Gradually blend into butter mixture and, when well mixed, return pan to heat and cook until the sauce thickens. Cook for a minute more, stirring continuously.
3 tbsp fresh chopped parsley 3 tbsp fresh chopped chives 1 hard-boiled egg, finely chopped	Fold into the sauce and immediately remove from the heat.
Salt Pepper	Season if required.

Sauce Mornay

Easy to cook · Microwave · Freeze · Serve hot or warm · Makes 1 pt/600 ml/2½ cups

1¼ oz/35 g/2½ tbsp butter or margarine	Heat in a medium saucepan over low heat until melted.
1 oz/25 g/¼ cup flour	Add to the melted butter. Cook, stirring continuously, for 1 minute.
¾ pt/450 ml/2 cups cold milk	Add all at once to the butter mixture and bring to the boil, stirring continuously until the sauce thickens.
4 oz/100 g/1 cup grated Gruyère cheese	Mix into the sauce and stir until the cheese is melted. Remove the pan from the heat.
Salt Pepper	Season to taste.

Cardinal Sauce

Easy to prepare · Microwave – this is particularly good for making small quantities of fish stock · Freeze – thaw at room temperature or in a microwave oven set on low · Serve hot with poached fish · Makes 12 fl oz/350 ml/1½ cups

1 oz/25 g/2 tbsp butter	Melt over moderate heat in a medium saucepan.
1 oz/25 g/¼ cup flour	Stir into the butter and cook, stirring continuously, for 1 minute. Remove the pan from the heat.
½ pt/300 ml/1¼ cups fish stock 5 tbsp double or heavy cream ¼ tsp cayenne ¼ tsp salt	Stir into the butter mixture and, when completely blended, bring to the boil over gentle heat, whisking continuously.
1 tsp fresh lemon juice.	Stir in.
2 tbsp Lobster Butter (page 86)	Whisk into the sauce in small pieces. Strain through muslin or a fine nylon sieve and reheat but do not boil.

Choron Sauce

Fairly easy to cook · Do not microwave · Do not freeze · Serve hot · Makes ¾ pt/450 ml/2 cups

8 fl oz/250 ml/1 cup dry white wine 1 tbsp tarragon vinegar 1 tbsp finely chopped spring onions or scallions 3-4 sprigs parsley 2 sprigs chervil 4 white peppercorns, crushed	Combine in a saucepan, bring to the boil, then simmer until the liquid is reduced by one-third. Pour the liquid into the top section of a double saucepan and put 1 in/2.5 cm hot water in the lower section.
1 tbsp water 3 egg yolks	Beat together, pour into the reduced liquid and cook over minimum heat, beating continuously, until the sauce begins to thicken.
8 oz/225 g/1 cup butter	Melt in a small pan. Pour slowly into the thickened sauce, beating continuously, until the consistency of double or heavy cream. Strain through a nylon sieve or muslin.
6 tbsp tomato purée	Warm gently in a small saucepan. Stir thoroughly into the sauce.
Salt Pepper	Season to taste.

Beurre Noir (1)

Fairly easy to prepare but needs care when browning · Do not let the butter become darker than hazelnut brown · Microwave – use browning dish but prepare half quantity only · Freeze – thaw and reheat gently · Serve hot · Makes 6 fl oz/175 ml/¾ cup

4 oz/100 g/½ cup salted butter	Melt gently in a frying pan, then cook for about 5 minutes until the butter browns. Remove the pan from the heat.
1 tbsp white wine vinegar 1½ tbsp fresh lemon juice ½ oz/15 g/⅜ cup fresh chopped parsley	Stir into the browned butter and serve immediately.

Beurre Noir (2)

Fairly easy to cook but take care not to burn the butter · Microwave – use browning dish but prepare half quantity only · Freeze · Serve very hot · Makes 6 fl oz/175 ml/¾ cup

4 oz/100 g/½ cup salted butter	Heat in a heavy-based pan until the butter is golden brown. Remove pan from heat.
2 tbsp malt vinegar 3 tbsp chopped capers Salt Freshly ground black pepper	Stir into the melted butter and reheat until the sauce boils. Season to taste. Serve at once.

Aillarde

Fairly easy to prepare · Best to use electric beater · No cooking required · Do not freeze · Serve cold · Makes ¼ pt/150 ml/⅔ cup

3 cloves garlic ¼ tsp salt	Crush the garlic with a flat-bladed knife on a chopping board, adding salt during crushing. Mix together well. Place in a 1 pt/600 ml/2½ cup pudding basin.
1 egg yolk	Add to garlic and beat thoroughly.
4 fl oz/120 ml/½ cup vegetable oil	Put into jug, then add to the garlic mixture drop by drop, whisking continuously, until the mixture thickens.
2 tsp cold water	Whisk into the sauce.
1 oz/25 g/¼ cup blanched grated walnuts	Beat into the sauce.
½ tsp lemon juice	Stir into the sauce. Taste and add more salt if preferred. The sauce is a light greyish colour textured with the grated walnut and garlic.

Watercress Sauce

Easy to cook · Microwave · Freeze · Serve hot · Makes 7 fl oz/200 ml/ ⁷/₈ cup

1 bunch watercress	Wash, dry and remove all the hard stalks.
1 shallot, peeled and roughly cut ¼ pt/150 ml/²/₃ cup milk	Place in the liquidizer and add the watercress leaves. Blend until smooth. Put in a saucepan and simmer over moderate heat for 2 minutes.
1 tsp arrowroot 2 tbsp cold milk	Blend together in a small bowl and pour into the bubbling sauce. Stir continuously until the sauce thickens.
½ oz/15 g/⅛ cup grated Cheddar cheese Salt Pepper	Stir into the sauce, seasoning to taste, and remove from the heat immediately.

Egg and Lemon Sauce

Easy to prepare but remember to move the pan away from the heat when adding the egg yolks · Microwave · Do not freeze · Serve hot · Makes 12 fl oz/350 ml/1½ cups

½ oz/15 g/1 tbsp butter ½ oz/15 g/2 tbsp flour ½ pt/300 ml/1¼ cups cold milk	Combine together in a saucepan and place over gentle heat. Bring to the boil, beating continuously, then cook for 1 more minute and switch off the heat.
2 egg yolks 3 tbsp fresh lemon juice	Beat together, then strain into the hot sauce, and beat thoroughly. The sauce should thicken further without requiring additional heat.
Salt Pepper	Add seasoning to taste.

White Wine Butter

Easy to prepare but the wine must be beaten in only a few drops at a time · No cooking required · Freeze · Refrigerate · Use cold · Makes 4 oz/ 100 g/½ cup

4 oz/100 g/½ cup butter, softened	Beat until light and fluffy.
5 tbsp dry white wine	Add a few drops at a time, beating vigorously after each addition.
3 tbsp fresh chopped parsley	Beat into the softened mixture.
Salt Freshly ground black pepper	Mix in, seasoning to taste. Pot and chill.

Sauce Cresson

Easy to prepare · excellent in a liquidizer or blender · No cooking required · Do not freeze · Refrigerate · Serve cold with trout – also good with eggs · Makes ¼ pt/150 ml/²/₃ cup

1 box cress	Wash thoroughly and drain. Place the cut cress in a sieve and pour boiling water through. Drain again, then purée in a liquidizer.
1 egg yolk 1 tsp mustard powder 2 tbsp fresh lemon juice ½ tsp salt Pinch cayenne pepper	Add to the liquidizer and purée with the cress.
2 tbsp salad oil	Switch on the liquidizer and pour the oil in in a thin stream.
2 tbsp single or light cream	Fold into the cress purée. Leave until cold, but do not chill.

Velouté Sauce

Easy to make · Do not microwave · Freeze · Serve hot · Makes ½ pt/ 300 ml/1¼ cups

¾ oz/20 g/1½ tbsp butter or margarine	Place in a heavy-based pan over minimum heat until melted.
¾ oz/20 g/3 tbsp flour	Stir into the butter and cook, stirring continuously, for 2-3 minutes until the mixture just colours. Remove the pan from the heat.
½ pt/300 ml/1¼ cups fish stock	Gradually stir into the flour mixture, return the pan to the heat and raise the heat to moderate. Bring the sauce to the boil, stirring continuously. Reduce the heat to minimum and continue cooking for 10 minutes, stirring continuously.
Salt Freshly ground black pepper	Season to taste.

Opposite: Watercress Sauce

Lobster Sauce Substitute

Easy to cook · Do not microwave · Freeze – add the brandy and cream after thawing and reheating · Serve hot · Makes 1 pt/600 ml/2½ cups

2 oz/50 g/¼ cup butter	Melt in a heavy-based saucepan.
1 small onion, peeled and finely chopped 1 small clove garlic, peeled and crushed	Fry gently in the butter until the onion is golden brown.
2 oz/50 g/½ cup plain or all purpose flour	Stir into the onion mixture and cook for 3 minutes, stirring continuously.
1 pt/600 ml/2½ cups jellied fish stock 4 tbsp tomato purée 1 bay leaf 2 sprigs thyme	Stir into the onion mixture, bring to the boil, stirring continuously. Reduce the heat and simmer for 30 minutes until the liquid is reduced by one-third. Remove bay leaf and thyme. Purée in a liquidizer or blender. Return the sauce to the pan and reheat but do not boil.
Salt Pepper	Season to taste. Remove the pan from the heat.
1 tbsp brandy 2 tbsp double or heavy cream	Stir into the sauce and serve immediately.

Thick Mushroom Sauce

Fairly easy to cook · Microwave · Do not freeze · Serve hot as a filling for vol-au-vents, pancakes, etc. · Makes ¾ pt/450 ml/2 cups

8 oz/225 g button mushrooms, sliced 2 oz/50 g/¼ cup butter Salt Pepper ¼ tsp grated nutmeg	Combine in a heavy-based saucepan and stir until the butter has melted. Do not overseason. Cook over low heat, stirring frequently, until the mushrooms have softened.
½ pt/300 ml/1¼ cups single or light cream	Stir into the sauce and cook over low heat, stirring continuously, until the sauce is thick.

Tartare Sauce (Quick)

Easy to prepare using good quality commercial or home-made mayonnaise · No cooking required · Do not freeze · Refrigerate – must be left at room temperature for 15 minutes and stirred before serving · Serve cold · Makes ¼ pt/150 ml/⅔ cup

2 tbsp chopped gherkins 2 tbsp chopped drained capers 2 tbsp fresh chopped parsley ¼ pt/150 ml/⅔ cup good quality mayonnaise	Mix all the ingredients thoroughly together.

Leveller Sauce

Easy to cook · Microwave · Freeze · Serve hot · Makes ½ pt/300 ml/ 1¼ cups

8 oz/225 g leveller gooseberries, topped and tailed 5 tbsp water	Place in a heavy-based saucepan and cook over minimum heat, stirring occasionally, until the gooseberries are soft. Purée in a liquidizer or blender, return to the saucepan and reheat gently.
2 tsp unsalted butter Sugar to taste	Stir into the hot sauce until the butter and sugar have dissolved.

Mariner's Sauce

Easy to prepare using convenience foods · Microwave · Freeze · Serve hot with fish steaks · Makes ½ pt/300 ml/1¼ cups

½ pt/300 ml/1¼ cups white sauce, home-made, canned or packaged 2 tbsp pickled relish 1 tsp dried onion flakes 2 tsp mustard powder ¼ tsp garlic powder	Combine in a saucepan and bring to the boil. Cook for 5 minutes, stirring constantly.
Salt Pepper	Season to taste.

Sea Shell Sauce

Quick to make using convenience foods, provided white sauce is already prepared · No extra cooking required · Freeze · Serve cold · Makes ½ pt/ 300 ml/1¼ cups

½ pt/300 ml/1¼ cups basic white sauce, either home-made, canned or packaged, coating consistency 3 tbsp tomato ketchup 2 tbsp sweet pickle relish, finely chopped 2 tsp anchovy paste	Beat together until thoroughly mixed.

Lemon Caper Sauce

Easy to prepare · No cooking required · Recipe can be reduced easily · Do not freeze · Refrigerate – keeps a few days · Makes ½ pt/ 300 ml/1¼ cups

½ pt/300 ml/1¼ cups soured cream	Pour into a cold bowl and mix until smooth.
2 tbsp capers	Chop and stir into the sauce.
2 tsp grated lemon rind	Stir into the sauce.
Salt Pepper	Season to taste.

Lemon Sauce

Easy to make · Microwave · Do not freeze · Serve hot · Makes ³/₄ pt/ 450 ml/2 cups

1 oz/25 g/2 tbsp butter	Melt in a saucepan over medium heat.
1 oz/25 g/¹/₄ cup flour	Stir into melted butter.
³/₄ pt/450 ml/2 cups milk	Gradually stir into butter mixture and beat until sauce thickens.
Juice and grated rind of ¹/₂ lemon	Remove sauce from heat and stir in.
Salt *Pepper*	Season to taste. Return the pan to the heat and cook very gently for 2 minutes.

Jaffa Sauce

Easy to cook · Microwave · Freeze · Serve hot or cold · Makes ¹/₄ pt/ 150 ml/²/₃ cup

3 oranges	Thinly pare the peel from 1 orange, shred finely and place in a small saucepan. Just cover with cold water, then bring to the boil over moderate heat and cook for 3 minutes. Drain and set aside. Grate the rind from the remaining 2 oranges and place in a medium saucepan. Add the juice from the 3 oranges.
3 tbsp dry white wine *2 spring onions or scallions, trimmed and sliced* *8 peppercorns, lightly crushed*	Add to the juice in the saucepan, bring to the boil, then reduce the heat and, without covering, simmer for 10-15 minutes until only 5 tablespoons of liquid remains. Strain into another pan to remove the grated rind, peppercorns and onions.
1 tbsp double or heavy cream *1¹/₂ oz/40 g/3 tbsp butter*	Stir into the strained juices.
Salt	Season to taste. Stir in the blanched shredded peel. Reheat to steaming but not boiling point. Serve hot or leave until cool and serve cold.

Quick Aurore Sauce

Very easy to cook · Microwave · Freeze · Serve hot · Makes ¹/₂ pt/300 ml/ 1¹/₄ cups

1 oz/25 g/2 tbsp butter *1 oz/25 g/¹/₄ cup flour* *¹/₂ pt/300 ml/1¹/₄ cups milk*	Place in a saucepan over moderate heat, bring to the boil, beating continuously. Cook for 2 minutes, beating all the time, until the sauce has thickened and is smooth and glossy.
2 tbsp tomato purée *¹/₄ bay leaf powder* *Pinch ground nutmeg*	Stir into sauce.
Salt *Pepper*	Season to taste. Remove pan from heat.
¹/₂ oz/15 g/1 tbsp butter	Stir into sauce.

Sauce Verte

Easy to prepare using a liquidizer or food processor · Prepare mayonnaise in advance · Microwave · Do not freeze · Refrigerate – only for a few hours · Serve cold with cold or fried fish · Makes 1¹/₄ pt/750 ml/ 3 cups

2 oz/50 g fresh spinach leaves *1 oz/25 g watercress leaves* *1 oz/25 g tarragon leaves* *1¹/₂ oz/40 g chervil leaves* *1¹/₂ oz/40 g chives, chopped*	Place in a large saucepan, just cover with cold water, bring to the boil and drain thoroughly. Purée in the liquidizer and leave in the liquidizer until the mixture is cool.
1 pt/600 ml/2¹/₂ cups mayonnaise	Add a few spoonfuls of the mayonnaise to the liquidizer and switch on until blended. Pour into the remaining mayonnaise and stir thoroughly.

Soured Cream and Horseradish Sauce

Easy to prepare using mainly convenience ingredients · No cooking required · Do not freeze · Serve cold · Makes 6 fl oz/175 ml/³/₄ cup

2 tbsp good quality mayonnaise *2 tbsp creamed horseradish sauce* *¹/₄ pt/150 ml/²/₃ cup soured cream* *¹/₄ tsp bay leaf powder* *1 tsp dried parsley (good colour)* *Salt* *Pepper*	Beat all the ingredients together, seasoning to taste, and leave for 1 hour before using. Stir before serving. **Note:** This is to allow the parsley to reconstitute.

Cucumber and Tomato Relish

Easy to cook but take care not to brown the onion · Microwave – stir frequently · Do not freeze · Serve cold · Makes 1/2 pt/300 ml/1 1/4 cups

1 small onion, peeled and finely chopped 1/2 oz/15 g/1 tbsp butter or margarine	Cook over moderate heat, stirring frequently, until the onion is soft but not brown.
1 x 8 oz/225 g can tomatoes	Empty into the onions, cover with a lid and cook over moderate heat for 10 minutes, stirring occasionally.
1 tbsp cornflour (cornstarch) 2 tbsp cold water	Blend together in a small bowl and add to the saucepan, removing the lid. Cook for 2 minutes, stirring constantly, until the sauce clears and thickens. Reduce the heat to minimum.
1/4 cucumber, unpeeled and finely diced 1/2 tsp dried dill weed Salt Pepper	Stir into the sauce and cook for 2 minutes. Remove from the heat, cover and leave until cold. Stir before serving.

Below: Cucumber and Tomato Relish with fried scampi

Cold Parsley Sauce

Easy to prepare · No cooking required · Do not freeze · Makes 1/2 pt/ 300 ml/1 1/4 cups

4 fl oz/120 ml/1/2 cup good quality mayonnaise 4 fl oz/120 ml/1/2 cup French dressing 3 tbsp boiling water	Beat together until the mixture is smooth.
1 oz/25 g/3/4 cup fresh chopped parsley	Stir into the sauce. Leave to cool before serving.

Walnut and Horseradish Sauce

Very easy to prepare · No cooking required · Do not freeze · Refrigerate · Serve cold · Makes 1/2 pt/300 ml/1 1/4 cups

2 oz/50 g/1/2 cup chopped shelled walnuts 2 tsp grated horseradish 1/4 pt/150 ml/2/3 cup whipping cream, lightly whipped	Gently mix together.
1 tbsp fresh lemon juice 2 tsp fresh orange juice 1 tsp sugar 1/2 tsp salt	Fold into the cream mixture.

Sauce Florentine

Easy to prepare · All ingredients should be prepared first making this time-consuming if you have to start from scratch · Microwave – can be used for preparing the white sauce and cooking the spinach · Freeze – liquidize before serving · Serve cold with cold fish balls · Makes 12 fl oz/ 350 ml/1 1/2 cups

5 tbsp basic white sauce, coating consistency 5 tbsp single or light cream 1/4 pt/150 ml/2/3 cup mayonnaise 2 hard-boiled egg yolks 4 oz/100 g spinach leaves, cooked 4 sprigs parsley, stalks removed 2 anchovy fillets	Place all the ingredients in a liquidizer or blender and purée until well blended.
Pepper	Taste the sauce, then season with pepper to taste and purée again to incorporate the pepper.

Opposite: (from top to bottom) Walnut and Horseradish Sauce, Sauce Florentine, Cold Parsley Sauce and Sauce Tartare *(see page 80)*

Hot Tartare Sauce

Easy to cook · Microwave · Do not freeze · Serve hot · Makes 12 fl oz/350 ml/1½ cups

½ oz/15 g/1 tbsp butter or margarine ½ oz/15 g/2 tbsp flour ½ pt/300 ml/1¼ cups milk	Combine in a saucepan and whisk continuously over minimum heat until the butter is melted. Bring to the boil over moderate heat, then cook for a further 2 minutes, whisking continuously. Remove the pan from the heat.
1 tbsp fresh chopped parsley 1 tsp chopped gherkins 1 tsp chopped capers ½ tsp fresh lemon juice Pinch cayenne pepper	Stir into the sauce.
2 tbsp double or heavy cream 1 egg yolk	Blend together, add 2 tablespoons of the hot sauce, stir thoroughly, then strain into the sauce. Replace the pan over minimum heat and whisk continuously until the sauce is hot.

Hungarian Sauce

Easy to cook · Microwave · Freeze · Serve hot · Makes ½ pt/300ml/1¼ cups

½ pt/300 ml/1¼ cups white sauce (made with ¾ oz/20 g/1½ tbsp butter, ¾ oz/20 g/3 tbsp flour, ½ pt/300 ml/1¼ cups milk)	Pour into a saucepan and heat gently.
1 small onion, peeled and finely chopped 1 oz/25 g/2 tbsp butter or margarine	Stir together in a small saucepan, cook over moderate heat until the onions are soft. Drain thoroughly and stir the onions into the hot sauce.
1 tbsp sweek paprika	Stir into the sauce, cook gently for 5 minutes. Strain through a nylon sieve and reheat.

Hollandaise Sauce (1)

Requires care in cooking · Microwave (see special recipe) · Do not freeze – unless a microwave is available for thawing · Serve warm · Makes ¼ pt/150 ml/⅔ cup

1 tbsp tarragon vinegar 2 tbsp cold water 2 egg yolks, beaten	Combine in the top section of a double saucepan, placing 1 in/2.5 cm hot water in the base. Cook over minimum heat, whisking continuously, until the sauce thickens. Remove the pan from the heat.
2 oz/50 g/¼ cup butter	Beat into the sauce in tiny pieces.
1 tbsp fresh lemon juice	Stir in.
Salt White pepper	Season to taste. Reheat gently in the top half of a double saucepan beating continuously. Do not overheat.

Beurre Raifort

Easy to prepare · Preferably use fresh horseradish; peel before grating · No cooking required · Freeze · Serve cold · Makes 4 oz/100 g/½ cup

4 oz/100 g/½ cup butter ½ oz/15 g grated horseradish 1½ tbsp fresh lemon juice ¼ tsp salt Pinch cayenne pepper	Beat together using two forks until the mixture is smooth. Shape the flavoured butter into an oblong and roll up tightly in wax or greaseproof paper. Chill until firm, then open the wrappings. Slice the butter, separating each with a small disc of wax or greaseproof paper and rewrap. Cover in foil and freeze until required.

Hollandaise Sauce (2)

Requires care in cooking · Do not microwave · Do not freeze – unless a microwave is available for thawing · Serve warm · Makes 8 fl oz/250 ml/1cup

1 tbsp water 2 tbsp wine vinegar	Boil in a small saucepan until only 1 tablespoon of liquid remains. Remove from heat and leave to cool.
3 egg yolks, beaten	Place in a heatproof bowl and beat in reduced liquid. Place bowl over a pan of hot water over minimum heat, but do not allow water to touch base of saucepan. Cook, stirring constantly, until the mixture thickens.
6 oz/175 g/¾ cup butter, cubed	Add to the egg mixture, beating after each addition. Continue cooking until the sauce thickens.
Salt Freshly ground pepper	Season to taste. Remove bowl from the pan and continue whisking as the sauce cools.

Sauce Tartare

Very easy to prepare · No cooking required · Do not freeze · Keeps in a screw-top jar in the refrigerator for 1 week · Serve with fish or steaks · Makes ½ pt/300 ml 1¼ cups

½ pt/300 ml/1¼ cups thick mayonnaise	Place in a mixing bowl.
6 cocktail gherkins 1 tbsp capers 12 chives 6 sprigs parsley 1 shallot	Chop finely and fold into the mayonnaise.
Salt Freshly ground black pepper	Season to taste if necessary.

Parsley Sauce

Easy to cook · A good first sauce to practise on · Microwave · Freeze · Serve hot · Makes ½ pt/300 ml/1¼ cups

1 oz/25 g/2 tbsp butter	Melt in a medium saucepan over gentle heat.
1 tbsp cornflour (cornstarch)	Blend into the melted butter, remove the pan from the heat.
½ pt/300 ml/1¼ cups milk	Stir into the butter mixture, return the pan to the heat and bring to the boil, stirring continuously. Simmer for 3 minutes, stirring all the time.
Salt Pepper	Add seasoning to taste.
1 tbsp fresh chopped parsley	Stir into the sauce just before serving.

Paprika Butter

Easy to prepare · No cooking required · Freeze · Serve cold · Makes 4 oz/ 100 g/½ cup

4 oz/100 g/½ cup unsalted butter 2 tsp hot paprika 1 tbsp Worcestershire sauce	Combine in a warmed bowl and cut the butter into four or five pieces. Beat until smooth.
Salt	Add to taste. Shape into a rectangle and chill in the refrigerator. Cut into thin cylinders with a butter curler, placing each in a chilled box in the freezer as it is prepared. Cover with the lid and freeze until required.

Shrimp Sauce (1)

Easy to cook · Microwave · Freeze · Serve hot · Makes 1¼ pt/750 ml/ 3 cups

1 x 7oz/200 g can shrimps	Drain the liquor into a measuring jug. Reserve and chop the shrimps.
About ¾ pt/450 ml/ 2 cups cold milk	Add to the shrimp juice to make up to 1 pt/ 600 ml/2½ cups
1½ oz/40 g/3 tbsp butter or margarine	Melt in a medium saucepan.
1½ oz/40 g/6 tbsp flour	Stir into the melted butter. Cook for 1 minute, stirring continuously, then remove the pan from the heat. Slowly add the milk and shrimp liquid until the mixture is well blended. Bring to the boil over moderate heat and continue cooking for 2-3 minutes until the sauce thickens. Remove the pan from the heat. Stir the chopped shrimps into the sauce.
Salt Pepper	Add to the shrimp mixture. Reheat briefly.

Sauce Noilly Prat

Fairly easy to cook · Do not microwave · Do not freeze · Serve hot · Makes ¼ pt/150 ml/⅔ cup

¼ pt/150 ml/⅔ cup fish stock 4 fl oz/120 ml/½ cup Noilly Prat 1 shallot, peeled and finely chopped	Combine in a heavy-based saucepan and cook over medium heat, stirring frequently, until the mixture is thick.
4 tbsp double or heavy cream, half whipped	Pour gradually into stock mixture and beat continuously until well incorporated. Remove the pan from the heat.
2 oz/50 g/¼ cup unsalted butter, diced	Beat in a piece at a time until melted, but do not return the pan to the heat.
Salt Pepper	Season to taste.

Sauce Normande

Fairly easy to prepare but take care not to boil after egg and cream have been added · Microwave – extreme care required when the egg and cream are added · Use minimum setting · Do not freeze · Serve hot · Makes ¾ pt/450 ml/2 cups

1 oz/25 g/2 tbsp butter or margarine	Place in a medium saucepan and melt over minimum heat.
1 oz/25 g/¼ cup flour	Stir into the melted butter.
8 fl oz/250 ml/1 cup cold water 4 fl oz/120 ml/½ cup milk	Pour together into the butter mixture and bring to the boil over moderate heat, stirring continuously until the sauce thickens slightly.
4 tbsp Crème Fraîche (page 150) 1 egg yolk	Stir together in a small bowl. Mix in 2 tablespoons of the hot sauce, then pour back into the sauce and immediately remove the pan from the heat. Beat vigorously.
Salt Pepper	Season to taste.

Shrimp Butter

Very easy to prepare · No cooking required · Freeze · Refrigerate · Serve cold · Makes 8 oz/225 g/1 cup

4 oz/100 g/½ cup unsalted butter	Beat together with a pestle and mortar or blend in a food processor until smooth.
4 oz/100 g/½ cup cooked shrimps	Rub the mixture through a nylon sieve. Shape into a block and wrap in wax or greaseproof paper. Chill until very hard. Coarsely grate, first chilling the grater. Carefully and loosely pack in a freezer box until required. Sprinkle over the food just before serving.

Sauce Tapenade

Easy to prepare in a liquidizer or food processor · No cooking required · Store in a tightly-closed jar in the refrigerator and leave at room temperature for 30 minutes or until the liquid in the sauce is clear before using, as olive oil tends to cloud when cold · A thick coating sauce for hard-boiled eggs · Makes ½ pt/300 ml/1¼ cups

24 stoned black olives 8 anchovy fillets 1½ oz/40 g canned tuna fish 4 tbsp capers	Place in the liquidizer and blend briefly.
7 tbsp olive oil	Pour slowly into the liquidizer while the motor is running.
1½ tbsp fresh lemon juice ½ tsp French mustard 2 tsp brandy ¼ tsp freshly ground black pepper	Add to the liquidizer and blend until smooth.

Above left: Grated Shrimp Butter

Above right: Sauce Tapenade on hard-boiled eggs

Opposite: Pernod and Fennel Sauce *(see page 84)*

Pernod and Fennel Sauce

Fairly easy to cook but take care after butter is added or sauce may curdle · Do not microwave · Do not freeze · Serve hot · Makes ¼ pt/ 150 ml/²⁄₃ cup

2 shallots, peeled and finely chopped 1 tbsp fresh chopped fennel 1 tsp white wine vinegar 4 fl oz/120 ml/½ cup dry white wine	Cook together over medium heat until 1 tablespoon of free running liquid remains. Reduce heat to minimum.
4 oz/100 g/½ cup butter, diced	Beat into the liquid a little at a time, stirring continuously. Remove the pan from the heat.
1 tsp Pernod Salt Pepper	Stir in and season to taste. **Note:** Keep warm in top section of double saucepan until required. The sauce solidifies when cold.

Blender White Sauce

Very easy to prepare and cook · Microwave · Freeze – make sauce thinner · Serve hot · Makes ¾ pt/450 ml/2 cups

¾ pt/450 ml/2 cups cold milk 1 oz/25 g/¼ cup self-raising flour ¼ tsp salt ¼ tsp pepper	Place in a food processor bowl or liquidizer and blend until smooth.
1 oz/25 g/2 tbsp butter or margarine	Place in a heavy-based saucepan and melt over gentle heat. Pour in blended sauce mixture and bring to the boil, stirring continuously. Cook for 2-3 minutes, still stirring.

Variations

Cheese sauce	Add 2 oz/50 g/½ cup grated cheese and ¼ teaspoon made mustard.
Parsley sauce	Add 1 tablespoon parsley when blending.
Hard-boiled egg sauce	Add 2 chopped hard-boiled eggs at end.

Garlic Butter (1)

Easy to prepare · No cooking required · Freeze · Refrigerate · Serve cold · Makes 4 oz/100 g/½ cup

4 oz/100 g/½ cup salted butter	Beat until soft in a bowl.
2 cloves garlic, finely chopped 2 tbsp fresh chopped parsley	Work into the butter until the mixture is smooth.
½ tsp fresh lemon juice	Work into the butter until all the lemon juice is incorporated.
Salt Freshly ground black pepper	Add seasoning to taste. Shape the garlic butter into an oblong, wrap tightly in foil and refrigerate until firm. Slice and freeze the slices flat in a sealed container until required.

Garlic Butter (2)

Easy to cook · Use an old saucepan to cook the garlic · Microwave – a better way to cook the garlic · Freeze – wrap carefully and completely to prevent odours from escaping · Serve cold · Makes 4 oz/100 g/½ cup

4 large cloves garlic	Peel and place in a small saucepan. Just cover with cold water, then bring to the boil over moderate heat. Place the lid on the pan and cook for 4-5 minutes. Drain, dry on kitchen paper towel, then chop and mash finely.
4 oz/100 g/½ cup salted butter	Place in a warmed bowl and beat until soft. Gradually beat in the mashed garlic.
¼-½ tsp salt	Mix into the butter to taste. Shape the butter into an oblong and roll up in wax or greaseproof paper. Cover in plastic cling film and foil, then chill until firm. Open out the wrappings, slice the garlic butter, then rewrap and freeze. Use as required.

Shrimp Sauce (2)

Easy to cook but requires Sauce Vin Blanc · Microwave · Do not freeze · Serve hot · Makes 1 pt/600ml/2½ cups

2 oz/50 g/¼ cup unsalted butter 2 oz/50 g/¼ cup shelled cooked shrimps	Place in a wooden bowl or mortar and pound with a pestle or the head of a rolling pin until the mixture is smooth. Rub through a sieve.
1 pt/600 ml/2½ cups Sauce Vin Blanc (page 71)	Place in a medium saucepan and heat until steaming but do not boil. Beat in the butter mixture.
About 2 drops red food colouring About 2 drops orange food colouring	Gradually beat into the sauce to achieve a shrimp colour.

Rhubarb Sauce

Very easy to cook · Microwave · Freeze · Serve hot · Makes ³/₄ pt/450 ml/ 2 cups

8 oz/225 g trimmed fresh or frozen rhubarb, coarsely sliced 1 tsp fresh lemon juice 4 tbsp sweet cider 3 tbsp demerara sugar Pinch grated nutmeg	Combine in a heavy-based saucepan and cook over minimum heat in a pan with a lid, shaking the pan occasionally, until the rhubarb is pulpy. Blend in a liquidizer or food processor and reheat.

Mustard Butter

Very easy to prepare · No cooking required · Freeze · Refrigerate · Serve cold · Makes 4 oz/100 g/¹/₂ cup

4 oz/100 g/¹/₂ cup butter	Place in a bowl and beat until soft and smooth.
1 tsp mustard powder 1 tbsp fresh lemon juice Pinch cayenne pepper Salt White pepper	Beat into the butter, adding seasoning to taste. Shape into a cylinder, roll up in wax or greaseproof paper and cover with foil, folding in ends securely. Refrigerate or freeze until required. Serve in slices.

Sauce Nantua

Fairly easy to prepare but needs care · Prepare Lobster Butter first · Requires double saucepan · Do not microwave · Serve hot with quenelles · Makes 1¹/₂ pt/900 ml/3³/₄ cups

1³/₄ pt/1 litre/4¹/₂ cups milk	Bring to the boil, then cover and leave until cold.
2 oz/50 g/¹/₄ cup butter	Melt in a heavy-based saucepan.
2¹/₂ oz/60 g/¹/₂ cup plus 1 tbsp plain or all-purpose flour	Add to the butter and cook for 1 minute, stirring continuously. Gradually blend in the milk.
Salt Pepper ¹/₄ tsp grated nutmeg	Season the sauce to taste and add the nutmeg. Bring to the boil over medium heat and cook for 2 minutes until the sauce thickens.
1 small onion, peeled 2 cloves Bouquet garni	Add to the sauce, reduce the heat and cook gently for 20 minutes, stirring frequently. Strain into the top half of a double saucepan and put 1 in/2.5 cm of hot water in the base.
¹/₄ pt/150 ml/²/₃ cup Crème Fraîche (page 150) 4 oz/100 g/¹/₂ cup Lobster Butter (page 86)	Add gradually to the sauce, stirring until well blended. Reheat in the double pan, stirring all the time.

Mock Hollandaise Sauce

Easy to cook · Microwave · Freeze · Serve warm · Makes ¹/₂ pt/300 ml/ 1¹/₄ cups

1 oz/25 g/2 tbsp butter 1 oz/25 g/¹/₄ cup plain or all-purpose flour ¹/₄ pt/150 ml/²/₃ cup milk ¹/₄ pt/150 ml/²/₃ cup fish stock	Place in a heavy-based saucepan and stir thoroughly before switching on the heat. Cook over medium heat, stirring continuously, until the sauce thickens. Cook for 2 minutes over gentle heat.
2 tsp tarragon vinegar	Stir into the sauce.
1 egg yolk, beaten	Remove the pan from the heat and whisk in the egg yolk.
¹/₂ oz/15 g/1 tbsp butter Salt Pepper	Stir briskly into sauce, seasoning to taste.
1 tbsp double or heavy cream	Fold into sauce.

SHELLFISH

Lobster

Diplomate
Oyster

Seafood

Cocktail 1
Cocktail 2
Gribiche

Oysters

Red Cabbage

Sauces that appear in this section but are not mentioned here either have serving suggestions with the recipe or can be served with anything.
See also the sauces under the following sections:

Fish

Aillarde
Garlic Butter 1
Garlic Butter 2

Vegetables

Hot Cucumber

Sauce Diplomate

Slightly complicated to prepare · Make sure that you have all ingredients ready before you begin · Microwave – thicken on the Defrost setting · Do not freeze · Serve hot · Makes 1 pt/600 ml/2½ cups

2½ oz/65 g/¼ cup plus 1 tbsp butter	Melt in a heavy-based saucepan over gentle heat.
2 oz/50 g/½ cup plain or all-purpose flour	Stir into the melted butter and cook for 1 minute, stirring continuously.
1 pt/600 ml/2½ cups shellfish stock	Gradually stir into the butter mixture until the sauce is lump-free.
1 tsp mushroom essence	Stir into the sauce. Bring the sauce to the boil, stirring continuously until thickened.
Salt Pepper	Season to taste. Remove the pan from the heat.
3 egg yolks 3 tbsp double or heavy cream	Blend together in a bowl. Stir in 2 tablespoons of the hot sauce, then pour the mixture back into the sauce and cook over a gentle heat, beating continuously, until the sauce thickens. Immediately remove the pan from the heat.
1 tbsp fresh lemon juice 1 oz/25 g/2 tbsp Coral Butter (page 150) Pinch cayenne pepper	Stir into the sauce and serve hot.

Lobster Butter

Easy to prepare in a blender · No cooking required · Freeze or use cooked lobster in another recipe · Refrigerate – keep 24 hours only · Serve cold · Makes 6 fl oz/175 ml/¾ cup

1 cooked lobster shell Coral from 1 cooked female lobster	Grind finely, either with a pestle and mortar or in a liquidizer or blender.
6 oz/175 g/¾ cup unsalted butter, at room temperature	Cut into pieces and beat thoroughly into the lobster shell and coral until the mixture is well blended. Heat in a bowl over a pan of boiling water until the butter comes to the top. Strain through a fine nylon sieve.
Salt	Season to taste. Pour into a shallow dish. Cool and chill until required. Cut out rounds to form pats.

Opposite: Lobster Butter

Cocktail Sauce (1)

Easy to prepare provided home-made tomato sauce is available · No cooking required · Store in a screw-top jar in the refrigerator · Serve cold · Makes ¼ pt/150 ml/⅔ cup

4 fl oz/120 ml/½ cup home-made tomato sauce	Blend all the ingredients together thoroughly. Chill.
1 tsp Worcestershire sauce	Stir thoroughly before serving.
1 tbsp very finely chopped onion	
1 tsp hot paprika	
1 tsp salt	
½ tsp white pepper	
Juice of ½ lime	

Supreme Sauce (1)

Fairly easy to cook but take care when adding the eggs and cream · Microwave – care required · Do not freeze · Serve hot · Makes 1 pt/600 ml/2½ cups

4 oz/100 g button mushrooms, finely chopped	Mix together and leave to stand while preparing the next stage.
1 tbsp lemon juice	
1½ oz/40 g/3 tbsp butter or chicken dripping	Place together in a heavy-based saucepan, and stir thoroughly over minimum heat until the butter is melted.
1½ oz/40 g/6 tbsp flour	Add the mushrooms and bring to the boil, stirring continuously. Reduce the heat and cook gently for 25-30 minutes until the mushrooms are soft.
1 pt/600 ml/2½ cups cold fish stock	
Salt Pepper	Add seasoning to taste.
4 tbsp double or heavy cream	Beat together in a small bowl, stir in 2 tablespoons of the hot sauce, then pour the mixture into the sauce. Remove the pan from the heat immediately and whisk the sauce vigorously.
2 egg yolks	

Sauce Gribiche

Fairly easy to prepare · Method is similar to making mayonnaise – add 1-2 tablespoons fast boiling water if the sauce starts to curdle · No cooking required · Do not freeze · Makes 12 fl oz/350 ml/1½ cups

2 hard-boiled eggs	Separate the yolks from the whites, sieve the yolks and chop the whites finely. Set the egg whites aside.
1 raw egg yolk	Stir into the cooked egg yolks, blending thoroughly.
¼ tsp salt	
1 tsp French mustard	
¼ tsp freshly ground black pepper	
6 fl oz/175 ml/¾ cup salad oil	Beat into the egg yolk mixture a few drops at a time until the mixture thickens, then pour in the oil in a thin stream, beating continuously.
4 tbsp white wine vinegar	Stir into the thickened egg mixture.
1 tsp fresh chopped parsley	Stir into the sauce.
1 tsp fresh chopped tarragon	
1 tsp fresh chopped chervil	
1 tsp fresh chopped chives	
1 oz/25 g piece sweet and sour gherkin	Press out all moisture, then chop finely. Stir into the thick sauce. Mix in the chopped egg white.
Salt Pepper	Add seasoning if necessary.

Beurre Bercy (2)

Fairly easy to prepare · Do not microwave · Freeze · Refrigerate · Serve cold with snails · Makes 4 oz/100 g/½ cup

4 shallots, peeled and finely chopped	Place in a small saucepan, just cover with cold water, then bring to the boil. Drain and cool under running water. Drain again thoroughly.
¼ pt/150 ml/⅔ cup beef stock	Place in a small saucepan and boil until only 1 teaspoon of liquid remains. Leave to cool.
1 small clove garlic, crushed	Beat together until creamy. Add the teaspoon of reduced stock and the shallots. Shape into a cylinder, roll up in wax or greaseproof paper and cover with foil, folding in the ends securely. Store in the refrigerator until required. Serve in slices.
Pinch cayenne pepper	
3 tbsp fresh chopped parsley	
1 tbsp lemon juice	
4 oz/100 g/½ cup butter	

Red Cabbage Sauce

Easy to prepare · Use food processor to finely chop the cabbage · No cooking required · Do not freeze · Serve cold · Makes ³/₄ pt/450 ml/ 2 cups

4 oz/100 g/1¹/₂ cups finely chopped raw red cabbage	Mix all the ingredients thoroughly together and keep cool but do not chill. Stir once before serving.
¹/₄ pt/150 ml/²/₃ cup good quality mayonnaise	**Note:** If preferred, purée the finished sauce in a liquidizer or blender.
4 tbsp single or light cream	
1 tsp salt	
¹/₄ tsp ground black pepper	
¹/₄ tsp ground juniper berries	
¹/₂ red dessert apple, peeled, cored and finely chopped	
Pinch cayenne pepper	
Pinch paprika	
2 tsp sweet pickle	

Cocktail Sauce (2)

Very easy to make · This recipe can be doubled or tripled · No cooking required · Do not freeze · Refrigerate – stir and leave at room temperature for ¹/₂ hour before using · Serve cold · Makes ¹/₄ pt/150 ml/ ²/₃ cup

4 tbsp good quality mayonnaise	Beat together until well blended and smooth.
1 tsp tomato purée	
3 drops Tabasco	
3 drops Worcestershire sauce	
1 tsp dry sherry	

Oyster Sauce

Easy to prepare · Do not microwave · Do not freeze · Serve hot · Makes ¹/₂ pt/300 ml/1¹/₄ cups

1 x 4 oz/100 g can smoked oysters, drained	Finely slice.
¹/₂ pt/300 ml/1¹/₄ cups béchamel sauce (made with 1 oz/25 g/2 tbsp butter, 1 oz/25 g/¹/₄ cup plain or all-purpose flour and ¹/₂ pt/300 ml/1¹/₄ cups milk)	Stir in the oysters.
¹/₄ pt/150 ml/²/₃ cup Rich Fish Stock (page 23)	Stir into the sauce. Pour into a heavy-based saucepan and bring to boiling point but do not boil.
Few drops fresh lemon juice Salt Pepper	Add to taste.

Salsa al Mare

Easy to cook · Allow about 5 minutes for the roux to cook before adding the liquid · Microwave – use a deep bowl · Freeze · Serve hot · Makes ¹/₂ pt/300 ml/1¹/₄ cups

1 oz/25 g/2 tbsp butter	Melt in a medium saucepan over gentle heat.
1 oz/25 g/¹/₄ cup flour	Stir into the melted butter and cook, stirring continuously, until the mixture is a biscuit colour.
¹/₂ pt/300 ml/1¹/₄ cups Court Bouillon (page 21)	Add all at once to the butter mixture and bring to the boil over moderate heat, stirring continuously until the sauce thickens.
2 tbsp medium white wine	Stir into the sauce, reduce the heat to minimum and cook for a further 10 minutes.
Salt Pepper	Season to taste.

Left: Oyster Sauce *(see page 89)*

Below: Red Cabbage Sauce *(see page 89)*

Opposite: Cocktail Sauce (2) with prawn and crab salad *(see page 89)*

PASTA

Sauces that appear in this section but are not mentioned here either have serving suggestions with the recipe or can be served with anything.
See also the sauces under the following sections:

Bolognese Ragu

Easy to cook · Microwave (see notes page 12) · Freeze · Serve hot ·
Makes 1 pt/600 ml/2½ cups

2 tbsp vegetable oil	Heat in a heavy-based saucepan.
3 oz/75 g streaky bacon, rind removed and diced	Add to pan and fry for 2 minutes.
7 oz/200 g/1½ cups chopped onion 1 medium carrot, scraped and diced ½ stick celery, diced	Add to pan and fry for 4 minutes, stirring occasionally.
3 oz/75 g chicken livers 8 oz/225 g/1 cup raw lean minced or ground beef	Stir into vegetable mixture and fry briskly for 4-5 minutes, stirring constantly.
2 tbsp tomato purée 7 fl oz/200 ml/⅞ cup beef stock 7 fl oz/200 ml ⅞ cup medium red wine ¼ tsp ground nutmeg	Stir into the mixture, reduce heat and simmer gently for 30 minutes or until the sauce is thick.
Salt Freshly ground black pepper	Taste sauce before adding seasoning.

Bolognese Sauce

Easy to cook · Microwave (see notes page 12) · Freeze · Serve hot ·
Makes 1 pt/600 ml/2½ cups

2 oz/50 g streaky bacon, rind removed and diced 1 large onion, peeled and chopped 2 tbsp oil	Stir together in a large frying pan and cook over medium heat for 3 minutes until onion softens.
1 stick celery, finely sliced 1 clove garlic, peeled and crushed	Add to pan and fry for 2 minutes.
12 oz/350 g/1½ cups lean raw minced or ground beef	Stir into pan and fry briskly until brown, stirring continuously.
¼ tsp mixed dried herbs 6 tbsp tomato purée 1 x 8 oz/225 g can tomatoes 1 tsp sugar ¼ pt/150 ml/⅔ cup well-flavoured beef stock ½ tsp freshly ground black pepper	Stir into the beef and simmer gently for 20-30 minutes until the sauce is very thick.
Salt	Add to taste.

Tuna Sauce

Easy to cook · Unattractive on its own but looks good when mixed with pasta · A teaspoon of tomato purée will improve the colour if desired · Do not microwave · Do not freeze · Serve hot · Makes ½ pt/300 ml/1¼ cups

1 x 7 oz/200 g can tuna in oil	Empty into a small saucepan and flake with a fork but do not mash.
2 tbsp fresh chopped parsley ¼ tsp ground white pepper 1 tbsp red wine vinegar	Carefully stir into the tuna and heat gently for 5 minutes.
8 fl oz/250 ml/1 cup light chicken stock 6 anchovy fillets, chopped 1 tbsp chopped capers, drained 2 tbsp fresh lemon juice	Add to the pan, slowly bring to the boil, then simmer until the mixture thickens, about 20 minutes. Add extra seasoning if necessary.

Five Spice Cream Sauce

Requires some care in cooking · Do not microwave · Do not freeze · Serve hot · Makes ¾ pt/450 ml/2 cups

1 pt/600 ml/2½ cups béchamel sauce, pouring consistency 6 tbsp double or heavy cream ½ tsp five spice powder	Stir until thoroughly mixed, then pour into a heavy-based saucepan and cook over minimum heat, stirring continuously, until the sauce boils. Reduce the heat to simmering and continue cooking until the sauce is reduced by half. Strain into a bowl. Place the bowl over a pan half-filled with hot water and set over minimum heat.
2 oz/50 g/¼ cup unsalted butter ¼ tsp fresh lemon juice	Gradually beat small pieces of butter into the sauce and stir in the lemon juice.

Saffron Sauce

Easy to cook · Microwave – thicken on Defrost control · Freeze – liquidize before using · Serve hot · Makes 1¼ pt/750 ml/3 cups

1¼ pt/750 ml/3 cups milk 2-3 strands saffron 1 clove garlic, peeled	Heat together in a saucepan, stirring occasionally, until steaming point is reached, cover and set aside for 30 minutes.
2 oz/50 g/¼ cup butter	Melt in a heavy-based saucepan.
1½ oz/40 g/6 tbsp plain or all-purpose flour	Stir into the melted butter. Cook 1 minute, stirring continuously. Strain in the infused milk gradually, stirring thoroughly to blend. Bring to the boil, stirring continuously until the sauce thickens. Reduce the heat to minimum.
3 tbsp fresh lemon juice Salt Pepper	Beat into the sauce, seasoning to taste, and reheat only until hot enough to serve.

Spaghetti Sauce

Easy to cook · Do not microwave · Freeze · Serve hot · Makes ¾ pt/450 ml/2 cups

1 tbsp oil	Heat in a heavy-based saucepan.
4 oz/100 g mushrooms, finely sliced 1 green pepper, cored, seeded and finely sliced 2 medium onions, peeled and finely sliced 1 clove garlic, crushed	Stir into the oil and fry gently for 10 minutes until the pepper and onions are tender.
1 x 14 oz/400g can tomatoes 2 tbsp tomato purée ½ tsp dried basil	Stir into the vegetables, cover with a lid and simmer for 30 minutes, shaking the pan occasionally.
8 oz/225 g/1 cup cooked minced or ground beef Salt Pepper	Stir into the sauce, adding seasoning to taste. Remove the lid and heat for 5 minutes, stirring continuously.

Clam Sauce

Easy to cook · Microwave · Freeze · Serve hot · Makes 1¼ pt/750 ml/3 cups

1 medium onion, peeled and finely chopped 1 stick celery, scraped and finely chopped 1 clove garlic, peeled and crushed 1 oz/25 g/2 tbsp butter or margarine 1 tsp dried tarragon	Combine in a heavy-based saucepan, cover with a lid and cook over moderate heat, shaking the pan occasionally, until the onion is transparent.
1 x 14 oz/397 g can tomatoes 5 tbsp tomato purée ¼ pt/150 ml/⅔ cup water	Empty the tomatoes and juice and the tomato purée and water into the vegetable mixture, cover and cook gently for 20 minutes until the onion is soft.
Salt Freshly ground black pepper	Add seasoning to taste. Purée the mixture in a liquidizer or blender and return to the saucepan.
4 oz/100 g button mushrooms, sliced 1 x 10 oz/285 g can baby clams	Add to the sauce and cook, covered, over a gentle heat for 15 minutes, stirring frequently. Remove the pan from the heat.
1 tbsp fresh chopped parsley	Stir into the sauce and serve at once. **Note:** You can use any kind of bottled or canned baby clams but you must drain away the brine before using.

Sicilian Sauce

Easy to cook · Economical when using overripe or soft cooking tomatoes · Do not microwave · Freeze · Serve hot or cold · Makes 1½ pt/ 900 ml/3¾ cups

2 lb/1 kg ripe tomatoes, coarsely chopped
1 small onion, peeled and chopped
1 small carrot, scraped and sliced
1 stick celery, finely sliced
1 tbsp fresh chopped parsley
¼ tsp soft brown sugar
1 tsp dried basil
3 tbsp sherry
Salt
Freshly ground black pepper

Combine all the ingredients in a large heavy-based saucepan adding seasoning to taste. Bring to the boil, then reduce to minimum heat. Cover with the lid and cook until the vegetables are tender. Purée in a liquidizer or blender, then press through a sieve. Reheat when required.

Opposite: (left) Pesto *(see page 96)* and *(right)* Saffron Sauce *(see page 93)*

Above: Clam Sauce with spaghetti *(see page 93)*

Right: Sicilian Sauce

Cream Cheese, Parmesan and Nutmeg Sauce (Liquidizer or blender)

Easy to prepare · No cooking required · Do not freeze · Serve cold · Makes 1/2 pt/300 ml/1 1/4 cups

2 egg yolks 1/4 tsp grated nutmeg 1/4 tsp ground pepper 4 tbsp single or light cream 3 tbsp boiling water	Place in the liquidizer and switch on until the mixture is fluffy.
8 oz/225 g/1 cup cream cheese 1/2 oz/15 g/2 tbsp grated Parmesan Cheese	Add a tablespoonful at a time to the liquidizer while the machine is still running.

Sauce Peperonata

Fairly easy to cook and prepare · Do not microwave · Freeze · Serve hot · Makes 3/4 pt/450 ml/2 cups

1 oz/25 g/2 tbsp butter 2 tbsp vegetable oil	Heat in a heavy-based frying pan.
1 Spanish onion, peeled and chopped 1 clove garlic, peeled and crushed	Fry in the melted fat until the onion is brown.
1 lb/450 g ripe tomatoes, skinned and sliced 1 small red pepper, seeded and diced 1 small green pepper, seeded and diced 3-4 basil leaves, chopped	Add to the onion, cover tightly and simmer for 15 minutes. Purée in a liquidizer, then pass through a nylon sieve. Return the sauce to the pan and reheat.
Salt Pepper	Season to taste.

Pesto (Liquidizer)

Easy to prepare · No cooking required · Keeps well in a screw-top jar in the refrigerator · Serve with hot pasta · Makes 1/2 pt/300 ml/1 1/4 cups

4 fl oz/120 ml/1/2 cup olive oil 2 oz/50 g/1/2 cup pine kernels 1 clove garlic, peeled 3 oz/75g basil leaves 1/4 tsp salt 1/2 tsp freshly ground black pepper	Combine in the liquidizer and blend until the mixture is smooth.
2 oz/50 g/1/2 cup grated Parmesan cheese	Add to the liquidizer and blend briefly to mix.

Spinach and Walnut Sauce

Easy to prepare · Microwave · Freezer · Serve hot with any pasta · Makes 3/4 pt/450 ml/2 cups

4 oz/100 g back bacon, rinds removed and chopped 2 tbsp vegetable oil	Combine in a saucepan and cook over moderate heat until the bacon browns.
1 medium onion, skinned and finely chopped 1 clove garlic, peeled and crushed	Stir into the bacon mixture and continue cooking until the onion is soft.
1 lb/450 g spinach leaves, cooked and finely chopped 1/4 pt/150 ml/2/3 cup whipping cream	Stir into the onion mixture and cook gently for 5 minutes.
2 oz/50 g/1/2 cup chopped walnuts	Stir into the hot sauce and serve immediately.

Tomato Sauce (1)

Easy to cook · Suitable for vegetarians · Microwave · Freeze · Serve hot · Makes 1 1/2 pt/900 ml/3 3/4 cups

1 lb/450 g ripe tomatoes, skinned and coarsely chopped 3 sticks celery, coarsely sliced 1 medium onion, peeled and sliced	Purée in a liquidizer or food processor, then place in a medium saucepan.
1/4 pt/150 ml/2/3 cup water	Stir into the tomato mixture. Bring to the boil, then reduce the heat. Place the lid on the pan and simmer for about 20 minutes.
2 tbsp salad oil 2 tbsp wholemeal flour	Mix to a paste in a large saucepan. Gradually stir in the hot tomato mixture.
1 bay leaf 1/2 tsp dried mixed herbs Pinch sugar	Add to the mixture. Cook over moderate heat until the sauce thickens.
Salt Freshly ground black pepper	Season to taste. Continue cooking for 4-5 minutes. Remove the bay leaf.

Lemon Herb Sauce

Fairly easy to cook · Microwave · Freeze · Serve hot · Makes 12 fl oz/ 350 ml/1½ cups

¾ oz/20 g/1½ tbsp butter	Melt in a heavy-based pan.
¾ oz/20 g/3 tbsp plain or all-purpose flour	Stir into melted butter and cook over medium heat for 1 minute, stirring all the time. Do not allow the roux to colour.
½ pt/300ml/1¼ cups jellied fish stock	Stir into the roux and bring to the boil, stirring continuously. Remove the saucepan from the heat.
2 medium lemons, washed	Grate the rind from both lemons and add to the sauce. Squeeze the juice from 1 lemon and add to the sauce. Peel and chop the remaining lemon and set aside.
1 tbsp fresh chopped chives 1 tsp fennel seeds 1 tsp fresh chopped parsley Salt Pepper	Add to the sauce, return to the heat and bring to steaming point but do not boil. Cook over low heat, stirring frequently, for 5 minutes. Adjust seasoning to taste.
½ oz/15 g/1 tbsp butter	Stir into the sauce, remove from the heat and mix the chopped lemon into the sauce.

Tomato Sauce (2)

Easy to cook · The quantity may be halved but this is a very good basic sauce that keeps well · Microwave · Freeze · Serve hot · Makes 1½ pt/ 900 ml/3¾ cups

4 rashers streaky bacon, diced 1 medium onion, peeled and coarsely chopped 1 medium carrot, scraped and finely sliced	Combine together in a heavy-based saucepan and cook over moderate heat until the onion and carrot are cooked.
3 lb/1.5 kg ripe tomatoes	Add to the pan, cover and cook for 5-10 minutes, then crush the tomatoes with a potato masher.
Bouquet garni 1 clove garlic, peeled and crushed 1 tsp sugar 1 tbsp red wine vinegar 1 pt/600 ml/2½ cups light stock ¼ pt/150 ml/⅔ cup tomato purée	Add to the tomatoes in the pan and bring back to the boil. Simmer without a lid until the sauce is reduced by about one-third. Remove the bouquet garni. Purée in several batches in a liquidizer or food processor, then press through a sieve into a large saucepan.
Salt Freshly ground black pepper	Season to taste and reheat the sauce.

Sauce Genoa

Easy to cook but takes 45 minutes · Do not microwave · Freeze · Serve hot · Makes 1 pt/600 ml/2½ cups

1½ oz/40 g/3 tbsp butter	Melt in a heavy-based saucepan.
1 large onion, peeled and finely chopped 1 stick celery, finely chopped	Stir into melted butter and fry gently for 2-3 minutes until the vegetables soften.
1 oz/25 g/¼ cup plain or all-purpose flour	Stir into onion mixture and cook, stirring continuously, until the flour browns. Remove the pan from the heat.
¾ pt/450 ml/2 cups stock 1 beef stock cube, crumbled	Gradually add to the flour mixture, stirring until well blended. Return the pan to the heat.
8 oz/225 g tomatoes, skinned, seeded and chopped 2 oz/50 g mushrooms, finely sliced 6 oz/175 g/¾ cup raw minced or ground pork ⅛ tsp ground juniper berries	Stir into the sauce, bring to the boil, then reduce the heat and simmer for 30-40 minutes until the pork is cooked and the sauce thickens.
Salt Freshly ground black pepper	Season to taste.

Piedmonte Sauce

Easy to cook · Do not microwave · Freeze · Serve hot · Makes 1 pt/ 600 ml/2½ cups

½ oz/15 g/1 tbsp butter 1 tbsp vegetable oil	Heat together in a heavy-based saucepan.
1 medium onion, peeled and finely chopped	Sauté in the hot butter and oil until the onion is just golden.
8 oz/225 g veal, trimmed and finely chopped	Add to the sautéed onion, a handful at a time, and fry, stirring constantly, until the meat browns.
4 oz/100 g chicken livers, rinsed and trimmed	Stir into the fried meat mixture and cook, stirring continuously, for 2-3 minutes.
¼ pt/150 ml/⅔ cup hot water 1 x 14 oz/397 g can tomatoes 1 tbsp tomato purée 1tsp fresh lemon juice ½ tsp dried oregano	Empty the can of tomatoes into the saucepan, then add the remaining ingredients.
Salt Freshly ground black pepper	Season to taste. Bring to the boil over moderate heat, reduce the heat and simmer for 30 minutes or until the mixture thickens.

VEGETABLES

Asparagus

Beurre Fondu
Curried Cream
Microwave
  Hollandaise 2
Mousseuse

Cauliflower

Curd Cheese and
  Mace
Curried Cream

Courgettes (Zucchini)

Hot Cucumber
Tomato 3

Leeks

Microwave
  Hollandaise 2
Parmesan and
  Emmenthal

*Sauces that appear in this section but are not mentioned here either have serving suggestions with the recipe or can be served with anything.
See also the sauces under the following sections:*

Meat

Curry Butter
Garden
Mustard (Hot)
Quick Sweet and
  Sour

Poultry

Paprika and
  Orange Butter

Fish

Beurre Blanc 1
Beurre Blanc 2
Blender Basic
  White
Blender Parsley
Cold Parsley
Hollandaise 1
Hollandaise 2
Microwave
  Hollandaise 1
Jaffa
Lemon
Mushroom 3
Parsley

Pasta

Tomato 3

Aubergine (Eggplant) Cream Sauce

Easy to prepare · Microwave · Do not freeze · Best eaten within 1 day as tends to become bitter · Can also be served as a dip · Serve cold · Makes 1 pt/600 ml/2½ cups

2 x 8 oz/225 g shiny aubergines (eggplant), rinsed and dried	Halve lengthwise, put into a metal colander over a large saucepan one-third full of water. Cover with a lid, bring to the boil, then steam for 30-40 minutes until the flesh is very soft. If necessary, top up the saucepan with boiling water during cooking. Scoop out the soft flesh, then press through a sieve or purée in a food processor or liquidizer. Tip into a cool bowl.
1 tbsp fresh lemon juice 4 tbsp dry white wine ¼ pt/150 ml/⅔ cup double or heavy cream ¼ small onion, finely chopped to a pulp 3 tbsp fresh chopped parsley 3 tbsp fresh chopped chives	Stir into the puréed aubergine.
Salt Freshly ground black pepper	Add to taste. Cover and chill for 2 hours before serving.

Basic Cheese Sauce

Easy to cook · Microwave · Freeze · Serve hot with vegetables or eggs · Makes ½ pt/300 ml/1¼ cups

1 oz/25 g/2 tbsp butter or margarine	Melt in a saucepan over a low heat.
1 oz/25 g/¼ cup flour	Stir into melted fat and cook for 1 minute, stirring continuously. Remove saucepan from heat.
½ pt/300 ml/1¼ cups milk	Gradually stir into flour/butter mixture until smooth. Return the pan to the heat and cook, stirring continuously, until the sauce thickens. Cook for a minute more, still stirring.
2 oz/50 g/½ cup grated Cheddar cheese	Stir into sauce. Immediately remove pan from the heat and stir until the cheese is melted.
Salt Pepper	Season to taste.

Opposite: Aubergine Cream Sauce

Traditional Cheese Sauce

Easy to make · Microwave · Freeze · Serve hot · Makes 1 pt/600 ml/ 2½ cups

1 oz/25 g/2 tbsp butter or margarine	Melt in a heavy-based saucepan over gentle heat.
1 oz/25 g/¼ cup flour	Stir into the melted butter and cook for 1 minute, stirring continuously. Remove the pan from the heat.
1 pt/600 ml/2½ cups cold milk	Gradually mix into the butter paste. Replace the pan on the heat and cook for 3 minutes, stirring continuously, or until the sauce thickens. Remove the pan from the heat.
8 oz/225 g/2 cups grated stale Cheddar cheese	Stir the cheese into the hot sauce until the cheese melts.
Salt Pepper	Season to taste.
	Note: This is a pouring sauce. To make a thicker coating sauce, double the quantity of butter and flour. To make a panada or thick sauce for use in soufflés, etc., use four times as much butter and flour.

Enriched Cheese Sauce

Fairly easy to cook – essential to cook over medium heat · Microwave – use Defrost setting · Do not freeze · Serve hot or warm · Makes ½ pt/ 300 ml/1¼ cups

8 fl oz/250 ml/1 cup cold milk 2 egg yolks 1 oz/25 g/¼ cup plain or all-purpose flour 1½ oz/40 g/3 tbsp butter 2 oz/50 g/½ cup grated stale cheese Salt Pepper	Put all ingredients in a heavy-based saucepan in the order given, beating thoroughly between each addition. Put the pan over minimum heat and stir continuously until the sauce bubbles and becomes thick, creamy and smooth.

Curd Cheese and Mace Sauce

Easy to prepare · No cooking required · Do not freeze · Serve cold · Makes ½ pt/300 ml/1¼ cups

8 oz/225 g/1 cup curd cheese	Beat with an electric whisk.
2 egg yolks, threads removed ¼ tsp ground mace Salt Pepper	Beat into the cheese, seasoning to taste.
4 tbsp milk	Bring to the boil in a small saucepan, and immediately pour into the cheese, whisking all the time. Adjust the seasoning.

Handy Tomato Sauce

Easy to make · Microwave – frequent stirring required · Freeze · Serve hot · Makes ¾ pt/450 ml/2 cups

1 x 14 oz/400 g can tomatoes	Drain, reserving the juice.
1 small onion, peeled and finely chopped	Combine with the tomatoes in a heavy-based saucepan. Bring to the boil over moderate heat.
1 bay leaf 1 tsp mixed dried herbs	Stir into the cooked tomatoes.
1 tbsp cornflour (cornstarch)	Blend in a small bowl with the reserved tomato juice. Pour into the tomatoes. Bring to the boil, lower the heat and simmer, without covering, for 5 minutes until the sauce thickens.

Sauce Poulette

Easy to prepare · Microwave – take care when adding yolk and cream · Do not freeze · Serve hot · Makes 12 fl oz/350 ml/1½ cups

1 oz/25 g/2 tbsp butter	Melt in a heavy-based saucepan.
1 oz/25 g/¼ cup plain or all-purpose flour	Stir into the melted butter. Cook for 1 minute, stirring continuously. Remove the pan from the heat.
½ pt/300 ml/1¼ cups well-flavoured chicken stock	Gradually stir into the flour/butter mixture and cook until the sauce begins to thicken. Remove the pan from the heat.
1 egg yolk 6 tbsp double or heavy cream	Beat together, strain into the sauce and beat thoroughly. Reheat over the lowest possible heat.
¼ tsp paprika 1 tsp fresh lemon juice Salt Freshly ground white pepper	Stir into the sauce, seasoning to taste.

Celery Sauce

Easy to cook · Microwave · Freeze · Serve hot as a hot filling or with croquettes or hot vegetables · Makes ¾ pt/450 ml/2 cups

1 oz/25 g/2 tbsp butter	Melt in a heavy-based saucepan.
4 sticks celery, thinly sliced	Fry gently in the melted butter until soft.
½ oz/15 g/2 tbsp plain or all-purpose flour	Stir into the fried celery and cook for 2 more minutes. Remove the pan from the heat.
¼ pt/150 ml/⅔ cup milk ¼ pt/150 ml/⅔ cup chicken stock 1 tsp fresh chopped parsley	Stir into the celery mixture and, when well blended, place the pan over moderate heat and cook, stirring continuously, for 2-3 minutes until the sauce thickens.
Freshly ground black pepper Salt	Season to taste.

Medium Sweet Wine Sauce

Requires care in cooking · Do not microwave · Do not freeze · Serve hot · Makes ¼ pt/150 ml/⅔ cup

1 small orange	Grate half the rind and squeeze out the juice. Combine in a small bowl.
2 egg yolks, threads removed 1 oz/25 g/2 tbsp butter, softened	Beat into the orange mixture.
6 tbsp medium white wine 1 shallot, peeled and finely chopped	Mix together in a small saucepan and cook over medium heat until only 1 tablespoon of free running liquid remains.
2 tbsp tomato purée	Stir into the wine.
Salt Pepper	Season lightly, remove from the heat and leave to cool. Beat the cooled wine liquid into the creamed egg mixture and place in the top section of a double saucepan. Put 1 in/2.5 cm hot water in the lower section. Place the saucepan over gentle heat.
2 oz/50 g/¼ cup butter, at room temperature	Beat into the sauce a little at a time. Remove the pan from the heat when the sauce is hot.

Tomato Sauce (3)

Easy to cook · Microwave – use only half the quantity of stock · Freeze · Refrigerate · Serve hot · Makes 1 pt/600 ml/2½ cups

2 tbsp vegetable oil	Heat in a heavy-based saucepan.
1 carrot, peeled and finely sliced 1 onion, peeled and finely diced 1 clove garlic, peeled and crushed	Fry gently for 5 minutes until the onion browns.
1¼ lb/550 g very ripe tomatoes, skinned and quartered 1 tsp fresh chopped basil 1 tsp sugar	Add to the saucepan and cook for 5 minutes, stirring continuously.
8 fl oz/250 ml/1 cup well-flavoured beef stock	Stir into the tomato mixture, bring to the boil, then reduce the heat and simmer without covering until the sauce is very thick. Purée in a liquidizer or blender.
Salt Freshly ground black pepper	Season to taste. Reheat before serving.

Window Box Sauce

Easy to cook · Essential to have fresh herbs for this recipe · No milk required, therefore suitable for those on special diets · Microwave · Do not freeze · Serve hot · Makes 1 pt/600 ml/2½ cups

1½ oz/40 g/3 tbsp butter or margarine	Melt in a saucepan over minimum heat.
1½ oz/40 g/6 tbsp flour	Stir into the melted butter and cook, stirring continuously, for 1 minute.
1 pt/600 ml/2½ cups water	Pour all at once into the butter mixture and beat continuously until the sauce boils and thickens. Remove the pan from the heat.
1 tsp tarragon leaves 4 sprigs parsley 10 chives 1 tsp chervil leaves	Stir into the sauce, replace the pan over minimum heat and cook for 5 minutes, stirring continuously. Purée in a liquidizer or blender. Reheat briefly.
Salt Pepper	Season to taste.

Microwave Hollandaise Sauce (2)

Easy to cook · Freeze · Serve warm · Makes ½ pt/300 ml/1¼ cups

5 oz/150 g/⅝ cup unsalted butter	Put into a large bowl and cook on Full Power until melted (about 1 minute).
2 egg yolks, at room temperature ¼ pt/150 ml/⅔ cup double or heavy cream ½ tsp salt ¼ tsp white pepper 2 tbsp lemon juice	Whisk into the melted butter and cook on Full Power, whisking every 15 seconds, until the sauce thickens (about 1 minute). Remove the bowl from the microwave and whisk until the sauce is frothy.
1 tsp butter	Beat into the sauce.

Artichoke Sauce

Very easy to make · Microwave – to help dissolve stock cube · Do not freeze · Serve cold with a tomato salad · Makes ½ pt/300 ml/1¼ cups

1 x 14 oz/400 g can artichoke hearts	Drain, rinse under cold water and then drain again.
½ chicken stock cube ¼ pt/150 ml/⅔ cup water	Combine in a small saucepan. Bring to the boil, stir to dissolve the stock cube, then leave until cool.
4 tbsp double or heavy cream, whipped	Combine with the artichoke hearts and chicken stock in a liquidizer or food processor and purée until smooth.
Salt Freshly ground pepper	Season to taste.

Celeriac and Tuna Sauce

Very easy to cook · Microwave · Freeze · Serve cold with diced cold cooked potatoes · Makes ½ pt/300 ml/1¼ cups

1 x 7 oz/200 g can tuna	Drain, flake and set aside.
8 fl oz/250 ml/1 cup fish stock *3 tbsp fresh chopped parsley* *3 tbsp fresh lemon juice* *⅛ tsp freshly ground black pepper* *¼ tsp celery seed*	Combine in a heavy-based saucepan, bring to the boil, then reduce the heat to minimum and cook for 5 minutes. Leave to cool. Stir in the flaked tuna fish.
4 anchovy fillets, chopped *2 oz/50 g piece peeled celeriac*	Grate into the sauce.

Parmesan and Emmenthal Sauce

Easy to cook · Microwave · Freeze · Serve hot · Makes 1 pt/600 ml/2½ cups

1 oz/25 g/¼ cup plain or all-purpose flour	Put into a heavy-based saucepan and cook over low heat for 5-6 minutes until the flour changes colour. Take care that the flour does not burn.
1½ oz/40 g/3 tbsp butter	Stir into the flour, then remove the saucepan from the heat.
¾ pt/450 ml/2 cups milk	Gradually whisk into the butter and flour mixture until smooth. Bring to the boil over medium heat, stirring continuously until the sauce thickens. Remove the pan from the heat.
1½ oz/40 g/⅜ cup grated Parmesan cheese *1 oz/25 g/¼ cup grated Emmenthal cheese* *1 oz/25 g/2 tbsp butter*	Stir briskly into the hot sauce.

Opposite: Artichoke Sauce *(see page 101)*

Above left: Celeriac and Tuna Sauce on diced cold potatoes

Above right: Parmesan and Emmenthal Sauce on boiled leeks

Beurre Fondu

Easy to prepare · Microwave – only on the lowest setting · Freeze · Serve hot · Makes 4 oz/100 g/½ cup

4 oz/100 g/½ cup butter	Heat in a small heavy-based saucepan until the butter bubbles, then remove the pan from the heat and leave until the sediment settles on the bottom of the pan. Strain through muslin.
¼ tsp fresh lemon juice	Stir into the melted butter. Serve immediately.

Egg Sauce

Easy to cook · Microwave · Do not freeze · Serve hot or cold · Makes 1½ pt/900 ml/3¾ cups

2 oz/50 g/¼ cup butter	Melt in a medium saucepan.
2 oz/50 g/½ cup plain or all-purpose flour	Stir into the melted butter and cook for 1 minute, stirring constantly. Remove from heat.
1¼ pt/750 ml/3 cups milk	Gradually stir into mixture in pan. Stir until mixture is smooth. Cook gently, stirring all the time, until sauce thickens. Remove from heat.
Juice of 1 lemon	Strain and stir into sauce.
2 hard-boiled eggs	Roughly chop and stir into sauce.
Salt Pepper	Add to taste.

Supreme Sauce (2)

Easy to prepare · Requires Chicken Velouté sauce · Microwave · Do not freeze · Serve hot with vegetables · Makes 12 fl oz/350 ml/1½ cups

½ pt/300 ml/1¼ cups Chicken Velouté sauce (page 53)	Place in a heavy-based saucepan.
2 eggs yolks 2 tbsp double or heavy creeam	Beat into the cold sauce. Place the pan over minimum heat and cook until hot but not boiling, stirring continuously.
1 oz/25 g/2 tbsp butter, cut into cubes	Stir into the sauce until melted. Serve at once.

Creamed Tomato Sauce

Easy to cook · Do not microwave · Do not freeze · Serve as a hot filling for pancakes · Makes ¾ pt/450 ml/2 cups

1 oz/25 g/2 tbsp butter or margarine	Melt in a heavy-based saucepan.
1 carrot, peeled and finely chopped	Stir into melted butter and fry gently until soft.
1 small onion, peeled and finely chopped	Stir into carrots and fry for 5 minutes, stirring continuously.
1 lb/450 g ripe tomatoes, coarsely chopped	Stir into the vegetables, cover with a lid and cook over moderate heat for 15-20 minutes until the sauce thickens. Purée in a liquidizer or blender. Return sauce to the pan over minimum heat.
1 oz/25 g/2 tbsp butter ¼ pt/150 ml/⅔ cup double or heavy cream Salt Pepper	Beat into the sauce, seasoning to taste, and immediately remove the pan from the heat.

Cheddar Lemon Sauce

Fairly easy to cook · Microwave · Do not freeze · Serve hot or cold · Makes ¾ pt/450 ml/2 cups

½ tsp mustard powder 2 tsp cold water	Mix, cover and leave to stand for 10 minutes for flavour to develop.
2 oz/50 g/¼ cup butter	Melt in a heavy-based saucepan.
½ oz/15 g/2 tbsp flour	Stir into the butter and cook for 1 minute. Remove pan from heat.
½ pt/300 ml/1¼ cups milk	Stir into the flour mixture, bring to the boil, stirring continuously until the sauce thickens slightly. Remove pan from heat.
3 egg yolks 2 tsp fresh lemon juice	Mix together and stir in 2 tablespoons of the hot sauce. Add the mustard. Pour into the sauce and heat gently for 1 minute, stirring continuously. Remove pan from heat.
3 oz/75 g strong Cheddar cheese, grated Pepper Salt	Stir into sauce until the cheese is melted. Season with pepper and a little salt.

Beginner's Cheese Sauce

*Easy to cook · Microwave · Freeze · Serve hot · Makes ½ pt/300 ml/
1¼ cups*

1 oz/25 g/2 tbsp butter	Place in a heavy-based saucepan and melt over gentle heat.
1 tbsp cornflour (cornstarch)	Stir into the melted butter and remove the pan from the heat.
½ pt/300 ml/1¼ cups milk	Pour into the butter mixture and bring to the boil, stirring continuously. Reduce the heat and simmer for 2 minutes, stirring all the time.
2 oz/50 g/½ cup grated stale Cheddar cheese Pinch mustard powder Pinch cayenne pepper	Stir into the sauce until the cheese has melted. Do not replace the pan on the heat.

Hot Cucumber Sauce

*Fairly easy to prepare and cook but take care when cream is added · Do
not microwave · Do not freeze · Serve hot · Makes ¾ pt/450 ml/2 cups*

1 cucumber, peeled and grated Salt	Place in a colander over a bowl and sprinkle with salt. Leave for 20-30 minutes until the juices begin to run, then strain. Place the grated cucumber in a saucepan.
4 fl oz/120 ml/½ cup soured cream 4 fl oz/120 ml/½ cup single or light cream 1 tsp sugar	Stir into the pan and bring to steaming point. Do not boil. Serve immediately.

Leek Sauce

*Easy to cook · Microwave · Freeze · Serve hot · Suitable for pancake
fillings · Makes 1 pt/600 ml/2½ cups*

1¼ lb/550g firm young leeks, trimmed, sliced and washed ¾ pt/450 ml/2 cups water Salt	Boil the leeks in the lightly salted water until they are soft. Drain, reserving the liquid. Return the liquid to the saucepan and boil until reduced by one-third. Purée the leeks and liquor in a liquidizer or blender.
1 oz/25 g/2 tbsp butter Salt Pepper Pinch bay leaf powder	Place in a saucepan with the puréed leeks and beat thoroughly over low heat.

Mushroom Sauce (3)

*Easy to cook · Can be adapted for vegetarian, fish or meat cookery,
depending upon the stock used · Microwave · Do not freeze · Serve
hot · Makes ¼ pt/150 ml/⅔ cup*

8 oz/225 g mushrooms, coarsely chopped 1 oz/25 g/2 tbsp butter 4 tbsp stock	Combine in a heavy-based saucepan and cook in the covered pan over moderate heat until the mushrooms are soft. Purèe in a liquidizer, then pour back into the saucepan. Bring to the boil, stirring frequently.
5 tbsp Crème Fraîche (page 150)	Stir into the mushroom mixture and simmer for 3-4 minutes, stirring continuously.
Salt Pepper	Add seasoning to taste.
1 tsp lemon juice	Stir into the sauce.

Parsley and Egg Sauce

*Easy to cook · Microwave · Do not freeze · Serve hot · Makes ¾ pt/
450 ml/2 cups*

½ small onion 1 clove	Press clove into onion.
½ pt/300 ml/1¼ cups milk	Place in saucepan and add prepared onion.
½ bay leaf 2 blades mace	Add to milk, bring to steaming point, remove from heat, cover and set aside for 30 minutes.
1 oz/25 g/2 tbsp butter	Melt in a saucepan.
¾ oz/20 g/3 tbsp flour	Stir into butter. Strain the milk into the mixture, beating thoroughly with a wooden spoon. Cook until the sauce thickens.
Salt Pepper	Add to taste.
2 hard-boiled eggs, chopped 4 tbsp fresh chopped parsley	Stir into sauce.

Curried Cream Sauce

Easy to cook · Do not microwave · Freeze – liquidize after reheating · Serve hot · Makes ³⁄₄ pt/450 ml/2 cups

1 oz/25 g/2 tbsp butter	Melt in a heavy-based saucepan.
1 small onion, peeled and finely chopped 2 tsp garam masala	Stir into the melted butter and fry gently until the onion is soft. Remove the pan from the heat.
1 oz/25 g/¹⁄₄ cup plain or all-purpose flour ³⁄₄ pt/450 ml/2 cups hot chicken stock Pinch sugar Pinch garlic powder Pinch ground black pepper Salt	Blend into the onion mixture until smooth, adding salt to taste. Bring to the boil over moderate heat, stirring constantly until the sauce is thick. Cook for a further 2 minutes.

Sauce Mousseuse

Easy to prepare using a liquidizer or blender · Microwave – for heating the butter · Freeze – reconstitute at room temperature or in the microwave oven for a few seconds on the Defrost setting · Serve warm · Makes ³⁄₄ pt/450 ml/2 cups

4 oz/100 g/¹⁄₂ cup butter	Heat in a saucepan until just beginning to bubble.
3 egg yolks 2 tbsp fresh lemon juice ¹⁄₄ tsp salt ¹⁄₄ tsp pepper	Place in the liquidizer and blend until frothy. While the motor is still running, pour in the hot butter in a thin stream and continue blending until the sauce thickens.
¹⁄₄ pt/150 ml/²⁄₃ cup double or heavy cream	Switch on the motor, pour into the liquidizer and blend for 30 seconds.
Salt Pepper	Add extra seasoning if necessary.

Above: (left) Sauce Mousseuse *and (right)* Curried Cream Sauce

Dessert Sauces

Baked Custards

Blackberry
Butterscotch 3
Coffee Caramel
Off-the-shelf
    Raspberry
    Dressing

Fruit

Delta (bananas)
Ginger 1 (pears)
Greengage
    (apples)
Melba 1
Melba 2
Orange Cointreau
    (bananas)
Peach and
    Coconut (fruit
    salad)
Quick Hot
    Strawberry (fruit
    salad)
Raspberry and
    Banana (fruit
    salad)
Stock Syrup (fruit
    salad)
White Rum,
    Lemon and Kiwi
    (bananas)

Ice Cream

Blackcurrant
Butter Mintoe
Butterscotch 1
Butterscotch 2
Chocolate 1 to 6
Fudge
Gooseberry
    (Quick)
Hot Chocolate
Melba 1
Melba 2
Mocha
Peach 1
Peach 2
Pure Raspberry
Ratafia
Toffee and Walnut
Tovarich Butter

Meringues

Chantilly
Crème Fraîche
Melba 1
Melba 2
Mocha
Ratafia
Strawberry Sour

Pancakes and Waffles

Coffee
Dinner Party
    Pudding
Golden Syrup
    Pancake
Lemon Cheese or
    Curd
Marshmallow
Orange and Sweet
    Wine Custard
Peach 1
Sherry and Raisin
    Butter
Strawberry

Pies

Brandy
Caramel Custard
Cherry and
    Almond
Cinnamon
Clear Lemon
Crème Anglaise
Gooseberry 1
Gooseberry 2
Munakermaa
Nutmeg Foam
Sesquiera

Soufflés

Advocaat
Orange Cornflour
    (Cornstarch)
Strawberry

Sponge Puddings or Cakes

Apple 2
Apricot
Blackberry
Blackcurrant
Brandied
    Mousseline
Caramel
    Microwave
Cherry 4
Cherry and
    Almond
Chocolate 1 to 6
Cinnamon
Clear Lemon
Economical
    Lemon
Fluffy Custard
Ginger 2
Hazelnut and
    Date
Honey
Pineapple
Sweet Mousseline
Vanilla 1
Vanilla 2

Steamed Fruit Puddings

Apple and Raisin
Brandy Cream
Custard Powder
    Custard
Fluffy Custard
Hard
Hard Brandy
Orange brandy
    Butter
Rich Almond
    Brandy Butter
Rum Butter
Rum and Brandy
    Vanilla
St. Clements

Wafers or Biscuits

Orange and Sweet
    Wine Custard
Rich Sabayon
Sabayon
Slimmer's Apple

Melted ice cream, warmed syrup or dairy cream, freshly thawed, are the simplest of the dessert sauces, but more exotic and exciting sauces can be easily made in your own kitchen. You may be surprised at how quickly you can cook a dessert sauce and it will certainly taste better than the commercially packaged and often synthetic kinds.

A dessert sauce should complement a dish, so that the flavour and taste of both the sauce and the dish will be even better. Sometimes it is good to have contrasting flavours, such as a bitter sauce with a sweet pudding, and a variation of texture is also a good idea. A smooth sauce containing chopped fresh orange segments will be even more superb when served with a steamed orange-flavoured sponge pudding. A few slices of crystallized ginger in a custard sauce is wonderful with hot ginger cake and a coating of hard chocolate sauce on vanilla ice cream provides you with a home-made choc-ice.

Colour is almost as important as texture or taste because it is the eye that stimulates the salivary glands and makes the mouth water. It is said that food advertisements must appeal to the 'greedy eater' who can hardly wait to rush out and buy the product. Home-made desserts, when sauced beautifully, have much the same effect. Most of the recipes in this chapter can be increased, many can be frozen and nearly all keep in the refrigerator to have a second helping for the next day. Most sauces can be frozen if you intend to serve them cold, but when they are to be reheated, you must take extra care. Single or light cream, soured cream and yogurts tend to curdle on reheating and whipping cream is sometimes unreliable, but double or heavy cream will hardly ever let you down. Egg custards are difficult to thaw and reheat, although in this respect the microwave is surprisingly adept. When reheating, use the same method as the one you initially followed so that, if a sauce was cooked in a double saucepan, warm it up in the same way. You must always be careful when cooking in a double saucepan or in a bowl over a pan of hot water for, if the water boils and touches the base of the upper pan, the sauce is likely to curdle.

The microwave oven is quite brilliant at making sauces, for not only does it avoid lumpiness but it also copes with the delicate sauces. Although microwave techniques have to be acquired, you are hardly likely to go wrong if you cook these critical sauces on a low setting and whisk or stir every 15 or 20 seconds during cooking. The microwave also copes with all chocolate recipes which will not burn, provided the sauce is stirred frequently and never overcooked.

The freezer also has its idiosyncrasies and you will notice that a cold sauce when warmed will taste much sweeter, so do not be tempted to oversweeten when you are preparing sauces for the freezer. Frozen sauces also have the habit of changing texture when thawed and can thicken up quite considerably. Reduce starchy thickeners when preparing the recipe and, if the sauce is to be served hot, you can always thicken it with a little cornflour (cornstarch), arrowroot or flour the next time round. Cornflour (cornstarch) is more stable in the freezer but has twice the thickening power of flour. Arrowroot should be your choice for a crystal clear sauce. However, when using arrowroot as a thickener instead of cornflour (cornstarch), only half as much is required. In the unlikely event of finding that you have a lumpy sauce, it can always be strained but never try to press the lumps through the sieve, which will result in graininess, and you will find that a strained sauce is necessarily thinner. That other remarkable modern appliance, the liquidizer or blender, is an extremely helpful aid in removing lumps. However a really obstinate sauce will even then have to be poured through a strainer. A curdled sauce can often be saved by the addition of 1-2 tablespoons of fast boiling water beaten in vigorously.

There is no limit to the number of sweet sauces that can be made by simply replacing one flavouring with another, adding extra cream or a little liqueur, or both. A pouring sauce becomes a coating sauce when extra thickening is used and a thick sauce can always be thinned down with milk, fruit juice or even water, which should always be boiled even if it is to be added when cool. You can adjust the amount of sweetening to suit your taste and even enhance the colour with a few drops of food colouring.

Always use dessert sauces judiciously and do not serve any dessert in a pond of sauce. It is usually better to serve the sauce from a jug, pouring it over the dessert just before serving. If a sauce has to be left standing, draw a teaspoon of butter over the hot sauce just after cooking – this will form a layer against the drying atmosphere and, when stirred just before serving, the sauce will regain its original glossiness. Alternatively, place a disc of wax or greaseproof paper, well-dampened on the underside, against the surface of the sauce.

Although some suggestions are given below for the type of dessert to be served with any particular sauce, there is no reason at all why you should not mix and match as the fancy takes you.

Coffee Sauce

Easy to cook · Freeze · Microwave · Serve hot · Makes ¼ pt/150 ml/ ⅔ cup

1 tsp cornflour (cornstarch) 1 tbsp caster or superfine sugar	Blend together in a small saucepan
¼ pt/150 ml/⅔ cup cold milk 1 tsp coffee essence	Gradually blend into the sugar and cornflour. Place the pan over moderate heat and bring to the boil, whisking constantly. Remove the pan from the heat.
1 tsp butter or margarine	Whisk into the sauce.

Hard Brandy Sauce

Easy to prepare · No cooking required · Freeze · Serve cold · Makes 6 oz/ 175 g/¾ cup

3 oz/75 g/6 tbsp unsalted butter 3 oz/75 g/6 tbsp caster or superfine sugar	Put into a warmed bowl and beat thoroughly until the mixture is light and fluffy and the sugar crystals are dissolved.
3 tbsp brandy	Beat into the sweetened butter a few drops at a time until all the brandy is incorporated. Pile onto a small serving dish and leave until firm. **Note:** This can be frozen in one piece or in small mounds which make it easier to serve after freezing.

Stock Syrup

Fairly easy to prepare · Do not stir after sugar has come to the boil · Use a large saucepan and wear oven gloves · Microwave – requires a large bowl · No need to freeze as liquid keeps well in a screw-top jar · An essential syrup for use in many sweet recipes · Makes 1/2 pt/300 ml/ 1 1/4 cups, but the recipe may be doubled

8 oz/225 g sugar lumps 1 pt/600 ml/2 1/4 cups water	Place in a large heavy-based saucepan and stir thoroughly over gentle heat. When the sugar has dissolved, raise the heat and bring to the boil. Continue boiling for about 10 minutes or until the sugar thermometer reads 218°F/ 104°C. To test if the syrup is ready, dip a spoon into the syrup and allow to cool for a few moments. Rub between the thumb and forefinger and the syrup should cling to your fingertips.

Rum and Brandy Vanilla Sauce

Requires care in cooking · Do not microwave · Do not freeze · Serve cold · Makes 3/4 pt/450 ml/2 cups

1 oz/25 g/2 tbsp unsalted butter 1 oz/25 g/1/4 cup flour	Beat together until a smooth paste is formed.
12 fl oz/350 ml/1 1/2 cups hot water	Bring to the boil in a heavy-based saucepan, then whisk in the butter mixture a teaspoonful at a time. Cook until the sauce thickens. Remove the pan from the heat.
1 egg yolk	Beat, adding 2 or 3 tablespoons of the cooled sauce. Pour back into the sauce, whisking vigorously. Replace the pan over the lowest possible heat and beat continuously until the sauce thickens further. Remove the pan from the heat.
1 1/2 oz/40 g/3 tbsp unsalted butter	Beat into the sauce a little at a time.
1 tbsp rum 1 tbsp brandy 1/4 tsp vanilla essence	Beat into the sauce.
4 fl oz/120 ml/1/2 cup whipping cream	Half whip.
1 oz/25 g/1/4 cup sifted confectioners' or icing sugar	Beat into the cream. Refrigerate the cream until the custard mixture cools completely. Cover the custard mixture with a damp piece of wax or greaseproof paper to prevent a skin forming during cooling. Beat the cream into the custard mixture.

Golden Syrup Pancake Sauce

Easy to prepare · Microwave – only on the Defrost control · Serve hot · Makes 1/4 pt/150 ml/2/3 cup

7 tbsp golden syrup 1 tbsp fresh lemon juice	Combine in a small saucepan and heat slowly until the syrup is melted and hot but not boiling. Stir thoroughly.

Rich Almond Brandy Butter

Easy to prepare · No cooking required · Freeze · Serve chilled · Makes 8 oz/225 g/1 cup

3 oz/75 g/6 tbsp unsalted butter	Beat until soft.
5 oz/150 g/1 1/4 cups sifted confectioners' or icing sugar	Gradually stir into the creamy butter.
1 oz/25 g/1/4 cup ground almonds	Beat into the butter mixture until light and fluffy.
3 drops almond essence 3 tbsp brandy	Beat into the butter mixture. Put into a small airtight container and freeze if preferred.

Economical Lemon Sauce

Easy to cook · Microwave · Freeze · Serve hot · Makes 1 pt/600 ml/ 2 1/2 cups

2 oz/50 g/1/4 cup soft margarine 2 oz/50 g/1/2 cup plain or all-purpose flour	Place in a saucepan and cook over minimum heat, stirring continuously, until the margarine has melted and blended with the flour.
1 pt/600 ml/2 1/2 cups cold milk	Slowly blend into the butter mixture. Raise the heat and bring to the boil, stirring continuously. Cook for a further 2-3 minutes.
1-2 tbsp caster or superfine sugar Few drops lemon essence	Stir into the sauce until the sugar has dissolved. Taste and add more lemon essence if required.

Crème Anglaise

Requires care in cooking · Nervous cooks should add 1 teaspoon of flour to the cold liquid before placing the pan on the heat · Do not microwave · Do not freeze · Serve cold · Makes 1 pt/600 ml/2 1/2 cups

18 fl oz/500 ml/2 1/4 cups milk 1/2 vanilla pod Pinch salt	Rinse a heavy-based saucepan with cold water, then pour in the milk, adding the vanilla pod and salt. Bring to the boil, remove the pan from the heat, cover and leave to stand for 10 minutes. Remove the vanilla pod.
4 egg yolks 2 oz/50 g/1/4 cup caster or superfine sugar	Beat together in a bowl over a pan of hot water until the mixture is thick and leaves a trail when the back of a spoon is drawn through. Gradually pour the milk onto the mixture, stirring to blend thoroughly. Place the pan containing the water on gentle heat and continue whisking the sauce in the bowl resting above it. When the sauce is thick enough to coat the back of a spoon, pour through a strainer into a jug or bowl, cover with a disc of damp wax or greaseproof paper or plastic cling film and leave until cold. Beat before using.

Advocaat Sauce

Requires care in cooking · Use a double saucepan · Microwave – method is different. Heat milk to lukewarm on Full Power, then reduce setting to Medium Low 35% when adding other ingredients · Requires practice · Do not freeze · Serve cool · Makes 3/4 pt/450 ml/2 cups

2 tbsp caster or superfine sugar 1 tbsp flour Pinch salt	Place in the top half of a double saucepan, putting 1 in/2.5 cm of hot water in the base. Set over gentle heat.
1 egg yolk 1/2 pt/300 ml/11/4 cups milk	Gradually beat into the flour and sugar mixture, and cook until the sauce thickens, stirring frequently during cooking. Remove the pan from the heat.
1/4 tsp ground nutmeg 1 tbsp rum	Stir into the sauce. Cover and leave to cool.
1 egg white 1 tbsp caster or superfine sugar	Whisk together in a grease-free bowl until a soft meringue is formed. Stir into the cooled sauce and serve at once or whisk before serving.

Custard Powder Custard Sauce

Easy to make but must be stirred continuously · Microwave · Refrigerate – add extra liquid and keep covered with a dampened disc of wax or greaseproof paper · Serve warm · Makes 1/2 pt/300 ml/11/4 cups

1/2 pt/300 ml/11/4 cups milk 2 tbsp custard powder 1-2 tbsp sugar	Combine all the ingredients in a saucepan, and bring to the boil over moderate heat, whisking continuously. Continue cooking for 1-2 minutes, still whisking, until the custard is thickened and smooth.

Blackcurrant Sauce

Fairly easy to cook · Microwave · Do not freeze · Refrigerate · Serve warm · Makes 1/4 pt/150 ml/2/3 cup

6 tbsp blackcurrant jam 4 tbsp water	Combine in a heavy-based saucepan and cook over moderate heat, stirring continuously, for 3 minutes. Remove the pan from the heat.
2 tsp arrowroot 2 tbsp cold water 1 tsp lemon juice	Blend together in a small bowl. Pour into the blackcurrant liquid, return the pan to the heat and cook, stirring continuously, until the sauce thickens and clears. Press through a sieve into a clean saucepan and reheat.
1 tsp butter	Stir into the sauce and serve hot.

Apricot Sauce

Easy to prepare provided stock syrup is available · Suitable for use when apricots are plentiful · Microwave · Keeps in the refrigerator for several days · Serve hot or cold · Makes 1 pt/600 ml/21/2 cups

2 lb/1 kg ripe apricots	Peel and stone, then purée the flesh in a food processor or liquidizer.
3/4 pt/450 ml/2 cups Stock Syrup (page 109)	Combine in a large pan with the apricot purée, bring to the boil over low heat, stirring frequently. Skim if necessary. Strain through a nylon sieve.
1 tbsp apricot brandy	Stir into the sauce.

Above left: Advocaat Sauce

Brandied Mousseline Sauce

Requires care and cannot be left during cooking · A whisk is essential · Freeze – must be reconstituted at room temperature or in the microwave oven on Defrost 35% · Serve cold · Makes 1 pt/600 ml/2½ cups

1 egg	Separate the yolk from the white.
Pinch of salt	Beat into the egg yolk.
4 oz/100 g/½ cup butter	Place in a bowl set over a pan of hot water placed over minimum heat until the butter softens.
6 oz/175 g/1⅓ cups sifted confectioners' or icing sugar	Beat gradually into the softened butter until a curdled effect is obtained. Strain in the beaten egg yolk and whisk the mixture until thick and smooth. Remove the pan from the heat.
2 tbsp brandy ¼ pt/150 ml/⅔ cup whipping cream	Fold into the sauce mixture. Whip the cream until thick, then fold into the sauce.
¼ tsp ground mace	Fold into the sauce. Using clean beaters and a grease-free bowl beat the egg white until soft peaks form. Fold into the sauce.

Chocolate Sauce (1)

Easy to make · Fairly sweet · Microwave · Freeze – reconstitutes well · Serve cold · Makes ¼ pt/150 ml/⅔ cup

1 oz/25 g/2 tbsp butter	Place in a saucepan and melt over gentle heat.
½ oz/15 g/2 tbsp sifted cocoa powder 2 oz/50 g/¼ cup caster or superfine sugar	Stir into the melted butter.
1 tsp vanilla essence 1 tbsp freshly-made strong black coffee 4 tbsp milk	Add to the mixture and heat, stirring continuously, until all the ingredients are well blended and the sauce reaches steaming point.
2 tbsp golden syrup	Stir into the sauce, then bring to the boil and cook for 2 minutes.

Chocolate Sauce (2)

Easy to make · Microwave · Freeze – sauce tends to lose its shine when reheated · Serve warm · Makes 7 fl oz/200 ml/⅞ cup

4 oz/100 g/4 squares plain chocolate	Place in a bowl over a pan of hot water, set over low heat and stir until melted.
1 x 6 oz/175 g can evaporated milk 1 tsp cornflour (cornstarch)	Blend together, then gradually beat into the chocolate without removing the pan from the heat. Stir continuously until the sauce thickens.

Opposite right: (top) Apricot Sauce and *(bottom)* Blackcurrant Sauce both on steamed pudding

Above left: Brandied Mousseline Sauce

Above right: Chocolate Sauce (2) on poached pear

Clear Lemon Sauce

Easy to cook · Microwave · Freeze · Serve hot · Makes 8 fl oz/250 ml/ 1 cup

4 tbsp fresh lemon juice Grated rind of 1 large lemon 1/4 pt/150 ml/2/3 cup cold water 2 oz/50 g/1/4 cup caster or superfine sugar	Combine in a saucepan and heat to boiling point. Remove the pan from the heat.
2 tbsp cold water 2 tsp potato flour	Blend together thoroughly. Stir into the lemon liquid, then replace the pan on the heat and bring to the boil, stirring continuously. Remove the pan from the heat.
1 tsp butter	Stir into the lemon sauce.

Cinnamon Sauce

Easy to cook · Microwave – method is slightly different. Cook on Full Power, then reduce to Medium Low 35%, adding the egg beaten with a little of the milk last · Freeze · Serve hot or cold · Makes 3/4 pt/450 ml/ 2 cups

3/4 pt/450 ml/2 cups milk 1 tbsp cornflour (cornstarch)	Blend together in a saucepan.
1 oz/25 g/2 tbsp caster or superfine sugar 1/2 tsp ground cinnamon 1/4 tsp vanilla essence	Stir into the blended milk.
1 egg, lightly beaten	Add to the pan, beating to make sure that no cornflour has settled on the bottom of the pan. Place the pan over moderate heat and cook, stirring constantly, until the sauce thickens.

Cherry and Almond Sauce

Easy to cook · Do not add cherries until cooking is complete · Microwave – stir every 30 seconds · Do not freeze · Serve hot · Makes 1 pt/600 ml/ 2 1/2 cups

1 1/2 oz/40 g/3 tbsp butter or margarine	Melt in a heavy-based saucepan set over gentle heat.
1 oz/25 g/1/4 cup flour	Stir into the melted butter and cook for 1 minute. Remove the pan from the heat.
1 pt/600 ml/2 1/2 cups cold milk	Slowly blend into the butter mixture. Replace pan on the heat, then bring to the boil and cook for 2-3 mintues, stirring continuously. Remove the pan from the heat.
1 tbsp sugar	Stir into the hot sauce.
1/4 tsp almond essence	Stir into the hot sauce.
10 glacé cherries, finely chopped	Stir into the sauce just before serving.

Chantilly Sauce

Easy to cook · Microwave · Freeze · Serve cold · Makes 3/4 pt/450 ml/ 2 cups

1 lb/450 g cooking apples	Peel, core and slice and put into a heavy-based saucepan.
3 tbsp water 1 1/2 oz/40 g/3 tbsp sugar 1 oz/25 g/2 tbsp butter	Stir into the apples, cover with a lid and cook over minimum heat until the apples are soft. Shake the pan two or three times during cooking. Purée in a liquidizer or blender, then rub through a fine nylon sieve. Leave until cool.
1/4 pt/150 ml/2/3 cup double or heavy cream	Whip stiffly, then fold into the apple purée.

Cherry Sauce (4)

Very easy to prepare · Microwave – care required · Do not freeze · Serve warm · Makes 1/2 pt/300 ml/1 1/4 cups

12 fl oz/350 ml/1 1/2 cups water	Put into a saucepan and bring to the boil.
4 oz/100 g/1/3 cup morello cherry jam	Add to the water in spoonfuls, stirring until the mixture boils. Continue boiling for 3 minutes to thicken and reduce the liquid. Strain into another saucepan and remove the pan from the heat.
2 tbsp arrowroot Juice and grated rind of 1 small lemon	Blend together in a small bowl. Pour into the jam liquid and bring to the boil over moderate heat, stirring continuously until the sauce clears. Pour into a serving jug and leave until cool but not cold.

Caramel Sauce (Microwave)

Requires care in cooking · Do not freeze · Refrigerate · Serve hot or cold · Makes 3/4 pt/450 ml/2 cups

3 oz/75 g/6 tbsp granulated sugar 4 tbsp water	Stir together in a large ovenglass bowl until the sugar is partially dissolved. Microwave on Full Power for 5 1/2 minutes, without stirring, until the syrup is mid-brown. Using oven gloves remove the bowl from the microwave oven and put on a dry heatproof surface.
1/2 pt/300 ml/1 1/4 cups milk	Put into a jug and microwave on Full Power for 3 minutes or until steaming. Pour onto the sugar syrup and stir until the caramel is dissolved and well mixed.
3 egg yolks 1 oz/25 g/2 tbsp caster or superfine sugar 1 tsp flour 1/2 tsp vanilla essence	Beat together. Pour into the caramel mixture and beat thoroughly. Reduce the microwave setting to Medium Low 35% and microwave for 6 minutes, whisking once after 2 minutes and then after each minute until the sauce thickens. Strain through a nylon sieve.

Apple Sauce (2)

Fairly easy to cook but take care the sauce does not burn · Microwave – no water necessary · Freeze · Serve hot or cold · Makes 1/2 pt/300 ml/ 1 1/4 cups

1 lb/450 g cooking apples, peeled, cored and sliced 2 tbsp water 1/2 oz/15 g/1 tbsp butter 2 tsp fresh lemon juice 1/2 tsp grated lemon rind 3-4 tbsp granulated sugar	Combine in a large heavy-based pan and bring to the boil. Reduce the heat and cook, stirring constantly, for about 10 minutes until the mixture pulps. Mash thoroughly or purée in a liquidizer or blender.

Apple and Raisin Sauce

Easy to cook · Microwave – take care when reducing the syrup · Freeze · Serve hot with rice or milk puddings · Makes 3/4 pt/450 ml/2 cups

1/2 oz/15 g/1 tbsp butter	Melt in a heavy-based saucepan.
1 lb/450 g cooking apples, peeled, cored and finely sliced Grated rind of 1/2 lemon	Stir into the melted butter, cover and cook over moderate heat until the apples are soft. Purée in a liquidizer or blender.
3 oz/75 g/6 tbsp caster or superfine sugar 1/4 pt/150 ml/2/3 cup water	Stir together in a saucepan until the sugar is dissolved, then bring to the boil and cook for 4 minutes without further stirring until a thick syrup is formed. Stir in the puréed apple.
2 oz/50 g/1/3 cup seedless raisins	Stir into the sauce and simmer uncovered for 3 minutes, stirring occasionally. Leave to stand for at least 2 hours before reheating.

Dinner Party Pudding Sauce

Easy to prepare · No cooking required · Freeze – thaw at room temperature or by microwave on the lowest setting, stirring frequently · Serve cold · Makes 3/4 pt/450 ml/2 cups

1/2 oz/15 g/1 tbsp butter 3 oz/75 g/1/3 cup cream cheese	Soak a basin in boiling water, then immediately wipe dry and put in the butter and cheese. Beat until the mixture is smooth.
1 egg, beaten	Strain into the cheese mixture but do not beat.
4 1/2 oz/125 g/1 cup sifted confectioners' or icing sugar	Add to the bowl, then stir thoroughly until both the icing sugar and the egg are mixed in.
1 tsp fresh lemon juice	Beat in a few drops at a time.
8 fl oz/250 ml/1 cup double or heavy cream 2 tbsp rum	Beat together until soft peaks form. Fold into the cheese mixture.

Caramel Custard Sauce

Fairly easy to cook – a thin sauce reminiscent of rich ice cream · Cook in a double saucepan or in a bowl over a pan part filled with hot water set over moderate heat · Do not microwave · Do not freeze · Serve hot or cold · Makes 1/2 pt/300 ml/1 1/4 cups

1/2 pt/300 ml/1 1/4 cups milk 2 egg yolks 1 tbsp caster or superfine sugar	Beat together in the top section of a double saucepan.
1/2 vanilla pod	Break into three pieces and add to the pan. Cook over gentle heat, stirring continuously, until the sauce is thick enough to coat the back of a spoon. Remove the pan from the heat.
2 oz/50 g/1/4 cup granulated sugar	Place in a small heavy-based pan set over minimum heat and leave until the sugar caramelizes, but be careful not to burn.
5 tbsp warm water	Add to the pan and shake the pan gently, then remove from the heat and continue shaking the pan until the mixture is of an even texture. Pour into the custard, then strain through a nylon sieve and serve as soon as possible. **Note:** The sauce may be kept hot in the top section of the double saucepan but take care that the water in the base is not touching the bottom of the pan or boiling.

Hot Chocolate Sauce

Easy to make · Microwave – ideal for making this but frequent stirring required · Freeze – thaw with care; rum flavour will be more pronounced after thawing · Serve hot · Makes 8 fl oz/250 ml/1 cup

5 oz/150 g/1 cup chocolate cooking drops 2 tbsp soft brown sugar 2 tbsp cold water	Combine in a heavy-based saucepan, place on the lowest possible heat and stir continuously until melted and liquefied.
2 oz/50 g/1/4 cup butter	Without removing the pan from the heat, beat in small quantities into the sauce. Remove the pan from the heat.
1 tbsp rum	Stir into the sauce. Serve at once or keep hot in a double saucepan or in a basin over hot water.

Pure Raspberry Sauce

Easy to cook but make sure that all the juice is extracted · Microwave · Freeze · Serve hot or cold · Makes 1/2 pt/300 ml/1 1/4 cups

1 lb/450 g/3 cups raspberries 2 tbsp water	Put into a heavy-based saucepan over minimum heat and cook until the juice runs freely. Press through a sieve into a bowl and discard the pulp.
Sugar	Sweeten to taste.

Hard Sauce

Easy to prepare · No cooking required but use the microwave to soften the butter if necessary · Freeze · Serve cold · Makes 4 oz/100 g/½ cup

2 oz/50 g/¼ cup unsalted butter	Beat with a wooden spoon until soft.
3 oz/75 g/¾ cup sifted confectioners' or icing sugar	Gradually work into the butter to a creamy consistency.
½ oz/15 g/2 tbsp ground almonds *¼ tsp lemon juice* *1 drop almond essence* *1 drop vanilla essence*	Mix thoroughly into the sweetened butter. Pile into a serving dish and refrigerate until cold.

Orange Brandy Butter

Easy to prepare · No cooking required · Freeze – if taken straight from the freezer, thaw for 30 minutes at room temperature or in the microwave oven for 1-2 minutes on Defrost 35% · Serve cold · Makes 8 oz/225 g/1 cup

3 oz/75 g/⅜ cup unsalted butter	Beat until soft and creamy.
4 oz/100 g/1 cup sifted confectioners' or icing sugar	Gradually beat into the butter.
1 tbsp Grand Marnier *1 tbsp fresh orange juice* *1 tbsp grated orange rind*	Gradually beat into the creamed mixture. Pile into small dishes and chill until firm. To prepare for the freezer, place the mixture in a mound on a sheet of non-stick silicone paper placed on a baking tray or a plate and open freeze. Pack in the usual way when frozen, then place in suitable dishes before thawing or freeze in pats, when no thawing will be required.

Sherry and Raisin Butter

Easy to prepare · No cooking required · Freeze · Serve cool · Makes 6 fl oz/ 175 ml/¾ cup

1 tbsp seedless raisins	Chop finely and place in a bowl.
4 oz/100 g/½ cup caster or superfine sugar	Stir into the raisins.
4 tbsp sweet sherry	Stir into the sugar and raisin mixture and leave until the sugar is dissolved (about 1 hour).
4 oz/100 g/½ cup unsalted butter	Soften in a small bowl set in 1 in/2.5 cm of hot water. Gradually beat the softened butter into the sugar mixture. Leave until set, then stir and spoon into a small dish.

Orange and Sweet Wine Custard

Fairly easy to cook · Use a double saucepan · Microwave – with care on Defrost setting · Do not freeze · Keeps for 4 weeks in the refrigerator · Serve warm or cold · Makes ¾ pt/450 ml/2 cups

3 egg yolks *¼ pt/150 ml/⅔ cup fresh orange juice*	Beat together, then strain into a bowl.
1 oz/25 g/¼ cup plain or all-purpose flour *4 oz/100 g/½ cup caster or superfine sugar*	Stir into the egg mixture.
¼ pt/150 ml/⅔ cup sweet white wine	Put into a medium saucepan and bring to the boil. Pour into the orange mixture and stir thoroughly. Place the bowl over a pan containing 1 in/2.5 cm of hot water and put the pan over moderate heat. Cook, stirring continuously, until the sauce thickens.

Rum Butter

Easy to prepare · No cooking required · Freeze · Makes 6 oz/175 g/ ¾ cup

4 oz/100 g/½ cup dark soft brown sugar *2 oz/50 g/¼ cup unsalted butter* *4 tbsp rum*	Beat with an electric whisk until fluffy. Spoon into a serving dish and chill thoroughly.

Opposite: (top) Orange Brandy Butter, (centre) Hard Sauce and (bottom) Sherry and Raisin Butter

Above: Orange and Sweet Wine Custard on waffles

Butterscotch Sauce (1)

Easy to cook · Microwave – take care and stir frequently · Freeze – melt and reheat gently · Serve hot · Makes ¼ pt/150 ml/⅔ cup

4 oz/100 g butterscotch toffees 4 tbsp water ¼ tsp ground nutmeg ¼ tsp ground cardamom	Combine in a heavy-based saucepan and cook over gentle heat until the toffees are melted, stirring throughout.
1 oz/25 g/¼ cup chopped almonds 2 tbsp single or light cream	Stir into the hot sauce.

Chocolate Sauce (3)

Easy to make · Microwave – can be made in a bowl over a pan of hot water · Freeze – does not reconstitute too well · Serve warm · Can be reheated but beat thoroughly over moderate heat to retain gloss · Makes ¼ pt/150 ml/⅔ cup

½ oz/15 g/1 tbsp butter 4 tbsp golden syrup 2 oz/50 g/2 squares plain dessert chocolate, broken up	Combine in a small suitable bowl or jug and microwave on High for ½ minute. Stir, then microwave on High for a further ½ minute. Give an additional ½ minute if required. Beat until smooth and glossy.

Chocolate Sauce (4)

Easy to cook · Microwave · Freeze – use less cornflour (cornstarch) · Serve hot or cold · Makes ¾ pt/450 ml/2 cups

¾ pt/450 ml/2 cups cold milk 2 tbsp cornflour (cornstarch) 4 tbsp caster or superfine sugar 4 tbsp cocoa powder	Blend all the ingredients together in a saucepan, then place over gentle heat and bring to the boil, whisking continuously. Reduce the heat and simmer for 1 minute. Remove the pan from the heat.
1 oz/25 g/2 tbsp butter or margarine	Stir into the hot sauce. Leave to cool slightly.
2 tbsp single or light cream ¼ tsp vanilla essence	Stir into the warm sauce.

Blackberry Sauce

Quick and easy to make · Frozen berries can be used · Microwave · Freeze · Serve hot or cold · Makes ½ pt/300 ml/1¼ cups

1 lb/450 g/4 cups blackberries, rinsed if necessary	Put the blackberries in a saucepan, cover with water and cook over moderate heat until the fruit is soft. Press through a sieve.
2-3 tbsp clear honey	Stir into the hot purée. Reheat if necessary.

Chocolate Sauce (5)

Easy to cook – a skin forms quickly on the top so cover with a disc of damp wax or greaseproof paper, moist side down · Microwave · Freeze · Serve hot or cold · Makes ¾ pt/450 ml/2 cups

2 tbsp cornflour (cornstarch) 1 tbsp drinking chocolate	Mix together.
¾ pt/450 ml/2 cups cold milk	Add a little of the milk to the cornflour and drinking chocolate. Pour the remaining milk into a saucepan.
2 oz/50 g/2 squares plain chocolate	Add to the milk in the saucepan. Bring to the boil, stirring continuously. Pour onto the chocolate mixture and blend thoroughly. Return the mixture to the saucepan.
1 tbsp sugar ¼ tsp vanilla essence	Stir into the sauce and bring to the boil over moderate heat, stirring continuously. Boil for a further 2 minutes.
1 tbsp double or heavy cream	Stir into the sauce and remove the pan from the heat.

Chocolate Sauce (6)

Easy to cook · Very easy to cook in the microwave oven · Freeze · Serve hot or cold · Makes 3 fl oz/90 ml/⅜ cup

3 oz/75 g/3 squares plain dessert chocolate 2 tbsp cold milk 1 tsp butter or margarine	Put into a bowl over a saucepan part-filled with boiling water. Place the saucepan over minimum heat and beat the chocolate, milk and butter together until the mixture is smooth and glossy. Alternatively, combine the ingredients in a suitable bowl and cook in the microwave oven, beating every 15 seconds.

Brandy Cream Sauce

Fairly easy to prepare · No cooking required · Can be frozen and served partly thawed, but is best served fresh · Makes ½ pt/300 ml/1¼ cups

2 oz/50 g/¼ cup unsalted butter	Beat in a bowl until soft.
4 oz/100 g/⅞ cup confectioners' or icing sugar	Beat into the butter.
2 tbsp brandy	Stir into the cream mixture drop by drop until all the brandy is absorbed.
¼ pt/150 ml/⅔ cup double or heavy cream	Whisk into the creamed mixture.

Crème Fraîche (1)

Requires care in cooking · Use a thermometer to be sure of cooking to the correct temperature · Do not microwave · Do not freeze · Refrigerate – will keep for 1 week · Makes ½ pt/300 ml/1¼ cups

½ pt/300 ml/1¼ cups double or heavy cream 1 tbsp soured cream	Combine in a saucepan and cook over gentle heat until the thermometer registers 85°F/28°C. Remove the pan from the heat, cover and leave to stand at room temperature for 6 hours. Stir thoroughly, then pour into a serving dish.

Brandy Sauce

Easy to prepare · Microwave · Freeze – stir in ½ teaspoon cornflour (cornstarch) after cooking, then bring back to the boil before serving, whisking thoroughly · Serve hot or cold · Makes ½ pt/300 ml/1¼ cups

½ pt/300 ml/1¼ cups milk	Pour about three-quarters of the milk into a saucepan and bring to steaming point.
1 tbsp cornflour (cornstarch) 3 tbsp sugar	Blend together with the remainder of the milk. Pour into the heated milk and bring back to the boil, stirring constantly until the sauce thickens. Continue cooking for a further 2 minutes.
½ oz/15 g/1 tbsp butter 2 tbsp brandy	Stir into the sauce and serve as required.

White Rum, Lemon and Kiwi Sauce

Easy to prepare · Microwave · Do not freeze · Serve hot or cold · Makes ¾ pt/450 ml/2 cups

2 tbsp arrowroot	Place in a heavy-based saucepan.
½ pt/300 ml/1¼ cups cold water	Blend into the arrowroot.
Juice and grated rind of 1 large lemon 2 tbsp white rum	Add to the mixture in a saucepan, stirring thoroughly. Bring to the boil over moderate heat, beating continuously until the sauce thickens.
2-3 tbsp clear honey	Stir into the sauce. Remove the pan from the heat.
1 kiwi fruit	Peel and slice. Put the sauce and kiwi fruit into a liquidizer or blender and blend to a purée. Return the mixture to the saucepan and reheat. Remove the pan from the heat.
Small knob butter	Stir into the hot sauce.

Gooseberry Sauce (1)

Extremely easy to prepare · Microwave – use to melt the butter · Make fresh as needed · Serve hot or cold with bread pudding, or pies or crumbles · Makes ½ pt/300 ml/1¼ cups

1 x 10½ oz/300 g can gooseberries in syrup	Purée in a liquidizer or blender, then strain through a sieve.
1 tsp cornflour (cornstarch)	Stir into the gooseberry purée in a medium saucepan. Bring to the boil, stirring continuously. Remove the pan from the heat.
½ oz/15 g/1 tbsp butter	Stir in.

Lemon Cheese or Curd Sauce

Easy to cook · Microwave – stir frequently · Lemon cheese or curd can be made in the microwave · Freeze · Serve hot with gingerbread · Makes ½ pt/300 ml/1¼ cups

1 tbsp fresh lemon juice ¼ pt/150 ml/⅔ cup sweet white wine ½ oz/15 g/1 tbsp butter 4 oz/100 g/⅔ cup lemon cheese or curd	Combine in a heavy-based saucepan and heat, stirring continuously, until the sauce begins to bubble. Serve at once.

Ratafia Sauce

Requires some care in cooking · Do not microwave · Do not freeze · Serve warm or cold · Makes ¾ pt/450 ml/2 cups

1 egg plus 2 egg yolks	Beat together with a wire whisk, then strain into a larger bowl.
1 oz/25 g/¼ cup plain or all-purpose flour 4 oz/100 g/1 cup sifted confectioners' or icing sugar	Beat into the egg mixture until fluffy.
½ pt/300 ml/1¼ cups milk	Bring to steaming point in a medium saucepan.
Pinch salt 3-4 drops almond essence	Stir into the milk to taste. Pour the flavoured milk into the egg mixture, pour back into the saucepan, then pour once more into the bowl and beat thoroughly. Part-fill the saucepan with hot water and set the bowl on top making sure that the water does not touch the bottom of the bowl. Set over moderate heat and stir continuously until the sauce is thick and smooth. Remove the bowl from the heat.
1 oz/25 g/2 tbsp unsalted butter 2 tbsp crushed ratafias	Mix into the sauce. **Note:** If not using immediately, cover the sauce with a piece of wax or greaseproof paper dampened on the underside.

Delta Sauce

Easy to cook but remember to stir all the time to prevent sticking · Do not microwave · Do not freeze · Serve hot with baked or fried bananas · Makes ³/₄ pt/450 ml/2 cups

1 oz/25 g/2 tbsp butter or margarine	Place in a heavy-based saucepan and melt over gentle heat.
2 tsp grated lemon rind 3 tbsp fresh lemon juice ¹/₄ pt/150 ml/²/₃ cup Stock Syrup (page 109)	Stir into the melted butter.
2 tsp arrowroot 4 tbsp double or heavy cream ¹/₄ pt/150 ml/²/₃ cup cold water	Blend together in a jug, pour into the mixture in the saucepan. Place the saucepan over gentle heat and bring to the boil, stirring continuously until the sauce thickens.

Fudge Sauce

Fairly easy to cook · Do not microwave · Freeze · Serve hot · Makes 1 pt/ 600 ml/2¹/₂ cups

1 x 14 oz/400 g can evaporated milk 1 lb/450 g/2 cups caster or superfine sugar 3 oz/75 g/3 squares plain dessert chocolate	Combine in a heavy-based saucepan, bring to the boil over moderate heat, stirring continuously. Cook for a further 5 minutes, still stirring, or until the chocolate is fully melted. Remove the pan from the heat.
1 tsp vanilla essence	Add to the sauce and beat with a whisk or electric beater for 1 minute. Strain.

Coffee Caramel Sauce

Requires some skill · Essential to have a heavy-based saucepan · Do not microwave · Do not freeze · Serve warm · Makes 6 fl oz/175 ml/³/₄ cup

8 oz/225 g/1 cup caster or superfine sugar	Put into a heavy-based pan over minimum heat and cook until the sugar dissolves and begins to brown. Remove the pan from the heat.
¹/₂ pt/300 ml/1¹/₄ cups freshly-made hot strong coffee	Slowly stir into the sugar and boil rapidly for 4-5 minutes until syrupy. Leave to cool slightly before serving.

Quick Hot Strawberry Sauce

Easy to make using convenience foods · Microwave – use with care · Freeze – sauce will not harden · Reheat and stir thoroughly to avoid lumpiness · Serve hot · Makes ³/₄ pt/450 ml/2 cups

1 x 15 oz/425 g can strawberries in syrup	Strain over a bowl.
1 tbsp arrowroot	Blend into the syrup. Pour into a saucepan and bring to the boil over moderate heat, stirring continuously. Cook for a minute more until the mixture thickens and clears. Remove the pan from the heat. Stir in the strawberries.

Above left: Delta Sauce with baked bananas

Above right: Coffee Caramel Sauce on baked custard

Pineapple Sauce

Easy to cook · Microwave · Freeze – Serve hot or cold · Makes ¹/₂ pt/ 300 ml/1¹/₄ cups

¹/₄ pt/150 ml/ ²/₃ cup water *4 tbsp sugar*	Combine in a heavy-based saucepan and stir until the sugar is almost dissolved.
2 tbsp fresh lemon juice *1 thick slice fresh, frozen or canned pineapple, finely chopped*	Stir into the melted sugar. Bring to the boil over gentle heat, stirring occasionally. Remove the pan from the heat.
2 tsp cornflour (cornstarch) *2 tbsp cold water* *2 drops yellow food colouring*	Blend together. Pour into the sauce in the pan, then bring to the boil, stirring contiuously.

Gooseberry Sauce (Quick)

A quick and easy recipe to cook · Microwave · Do not freeze · Serve cold or hot · Makes ³/₄ pt/450 ml/2 cups

1 x 14 oz/400 g can gooseberries in syrup	Drain the juice into a saucepan and set the fruit aside.
1 tbsp lemon juice *1 tbsp arrowroot*	Blend together, then stir into the gooseberry juice. Place the pan over moderate heat and bring to the boil, stirring continuously. Cook for 1-2 minutes until the syrup clears. Fold in the gooseberries.
1-2 drops green food colouring	Stir in to give additional colour if preferred.

Low Calorie Egg Custard

Requires care in cooking · Microwave – only on the lowest setting · Do not freeze · Serve hot or cold – ideal for invalids · Makes 12 fl oz/350 ml/ 1¹/₂ cups

1 oz/25 g/¹/₃ cup low fat dried milk granules *¹/₂ pt/300 ml/1¹/₄ cups water*	Combine in a saucepan and heat until lukewarm. Remove the pan from the heat.
2 eggs, lighlty beaten	Beat into the milk, then cook over the lowest possible heat, stirring continuously, until the mixture thickens. The mixture must not boil.
Sweetener or sugar	Add to taste.

Fluffy Custard Sauce

Fairly easy to prepare but use a double saucepan · Microwave – with care on the Low or Defrost setting · Do not freeze · Serve hot with pies or hot puddings or on its own · Makes 1 pt/600 ml/2¹/₂ cups

¹/₂ pt/300 ml/1¹/₄ cups milk *1 tbsp caster or superfine sugar* *¹/₄ tsp vanilla essence*	Combine in the top section of a double saucepan and put 1 in/2.5 cm of hot water in the base. Stir.
1 large egg	Separate and stir the yolk into the milk mixture. Put the saucepan over moderate heat and cook, stirring continuously, until the sauce is thick enough to coat the back of the spoon. Remove the pan from the heat and cover with a lid. Using clean beaters in a grease-free bowl, beat the egg white until stiff. Off the heat stir in 1 tablespoon of the egg white, then add the remainder and whisk vigorously until the sauce is frothy.

Butter Mintoe Sauce

Easy to prepare · Microwave · Do not freeze · Serve hot · Makes ¹/₂ pt/ 300 ml/1¹/₄ cups

1 × 6 oz/175 g packet butter mintoes *2 oz/50 g/¹/₄ cup butter*	Place in a small heavy-based saucepan set over gentle heat and stir until melted.
¹/₄ pt/150 ml/²/₃ cup milk	Add to the pan and stir until the mixture boils. Serve immediately.

Above: Fluffy Custard Sauce with poached orange slices

Greengage Sauce

Easy to prepare but measuring jug required · Microwave · Freeze · Serve hot or cold with stewed apples · Makes 1 pt/600 ml/2½ cups

2 lb/1 kg greengages Water	Rinse, then remove the stones. Weigh the fruit and add ½ pt/300 ml/1¼ cups water for every 1 lb/450 g soft fruit.
2-3 oz/50-75 g/4-6 tbsp granulated sugar	Stir into the pan.
4 or 5 strips lemon peel	Add to the pan. Cover and cook over the lowest possible heat, shaking the pan occasionally, until the fruit is pulpy (about 45 minutes). Remove the lemon peel, purée the sauce in a liquidizer or blender.
2 tbsp double or heavy cream	Stir into the fruit purée.

Melba Sauce (1)

Easy to prepare · No cooking required · Useful as an instant summer sauce · Makes 7 fl oz/200 ml/⅞ cup

8 oz/225 g/1½ cups prepared raspberries, fresh or thawed	Blend in a liquidizer or blender, then press through a sieve into a bowl.
4 tbsp sifted confectioners' or icing sugar	Gradually stir into the raspberry purée.

Mocha Sauce

Easy to cook · Microwave · Freeze · Serve hot · Makes ¾ pt/450 ml/ 2 cups

1 oz/25 g/2 tbsp butter 1 oz/25 g/¼ cup flour ¾ pt/450 ml/2 cups milk	Place in a saucepan over the lowest possible heat and whisk thoroughly until the ingredients are blended. Raise the heat, bring the mixture to the boil, whisking continuously. Remove the pan from the heat.
1 oz/25 g/⅙ cup chocolate cooking drops 2 tsp coffee essence	Add to the pan, replace over the heat and stir continuously until the sauce boils. Cook for a further 2 minutes, stirring continuously.

Gooseberry Sauce (2)

Easy to cook · Microwave – stir frequently · Freeze · Serve hot or cold with bread pudding, or pies or crumbles · Makes 12 fl oz/350 ml/ 1½ cups

1 lb/450 g frozen gooseberries, topped and tailed ¼ pt/150 ml/⅔ cup water	Place in a saucepan, bring to the boil, then simmer until the gooseberries are soft. Rub through a nylon sieve into a saucepan.
3 oz/75 g/6 tbsp sugar	Stir into the purée and heat gently until the sugar is dissolved.
½ oz/15 g/1 tbsp butter	Stir into the sauce. Remove from the heat

Marshmallow Sauce

Fairly easy to cook · Microwave · Do not freeze · Serve hot or cold · Makes ¾ pt/450 ml/2 cups

4 oz/100 g/½ cup caster or superfine sugar Pinch salt 3 tbsp water	Combine in a heavy-based saucepan and cook over minimum heat, stirring continuously, until the sugar dissolves. Raise the heat and bring to the boil, then continue boiling, without stirring, for 2 minutes.
6 large marshmallows ½ tsp vanilla essence	Add to the boiling syrup, reduce the heat and cook until the marshmallows melt, about 2 minutes. Remove the pan from the heat.
1 egg white	Beat until the mixture stiffens, add to the marshmallow syrup and beat thoroughly.
1-2 drops red food colouring 8 oz/225 g/2 cups blackberries, puréed	Stir into the sauce. Stir thoroughly before serving.

Off-the-shelf Raspberry Dressing

Easy to prepare · No cooking required · Do not freeze · Refrigerate · Serve cold · Makes ¾ pt/450 ml/2 cups

4 tbsp raspberry jam	Melt in a large bowl over a pan of hot water but do not heat the pan. Remove the bowl from the pan.
½ pt/300 ml/1¼ cups raspberry-flavoured yogurt 4 tbsp soured cream	Pour into the bowl and mix thoroughly.
2 egg whites	Beat in a grease-free bowl until stiff peaks form. Stir 1 tablespoon of beaten egg white into the raspberry mixture then fold in the remainder.

Nutmeg Foam Sauce

Fairly easy to cook · Do not microwave · Freeze – must be reconstituted in microwave · Serve hot · Makes 12 fl oz/350 ml/1½ cups

4 oz/100 g/½ cup unsalted butter	Beat until soft and creamy.
4 oz/100 g/1 cup sifted confectioners' or icing sugar ½ tsp grated nutmeg	Beat into the butter until fluffy.
1 egg, beaten 1 tsp vanilla essence 1 tsp grated lemon rind	Gradually beat into the butter mixture. Put the bowl over a pan of hot water set over low heat and cook, stirring continuously, for 3 minutes. Remove the pan from the heat. Leave to cool.
¼ pt/150 ml/⅔ cup double or heavy cream, whipped	Fold into the cooled sauce.

Orange Cointreau Sauce

Easy to prepare · Be sure that sugar has dissolved before heating · Microwave – with care · Do not freeze · Serve hot · Makes ½ pt/ 300 ml/1¼ cups

2 oz/50 g/¼ cup sugar 6 tbsp water	Combine in a saucepan.
2 oranges	Grate the rind and squeeze the juice. Add the rind to the sugar mixture and stir until the sugar is dissolved. Bring to the boil and simmer for 5 minutes without stirring.
2 oz/50 g/¼ cup unsalted butter	Stir into the sauce with the orange juice until dissolved. Remove the pan from the heat.
2 tbsp Cointreau	Stir into the sauce. Serve at once.

Honey Sauce

Easy to make · Do not microwave · Do not freeze · Refrigerate · Serve hot · Makes ¼ pt/150 ml/⅔ cup

2 oz/50 g/¼ cup butter	Melt in a heavy-based small saucepan.
2 tsp cornflour (cornstarch)	Stir into the melted butter.
4 oz/100 g/½ cup clear honey	Stir into the pan, then bring to the boil over moderate heat, stirring continuously. Cook for a further minute.

Melba Sauce (2)

Easy to cook · Microwave · Do not freeze · Serve hot or cold · Makes ½ pt/300 ml/1¼ cups

4 tbsp redcurrant jelly 3 oz/75 g/6 tbsp caster or superfine sugar 8 oz/225 g/1½ cups raspberries	Combine in a saucepan and bring to the boil, stirring continuously.
2 tsp arrowroot 1 tbsp cold water	Blend thoroughly together, pour into the raspberry mixture, then bring back to the boil, stirring continuously until the sauce clears. Strain through a nylon sieve, pressing the fruit through thoroughly so that only the pips are discarded. Serve at once or leave to cool.

Slimmer's Apple Sauce

Easy to prepare · Microwave · Freeze · Serve hot or cold · Makes ½ pt/ 300 ml/1¼ cups

1 lb/450 g cooking apples, peeled, cored and quartered 1 oz/25 g/2 tbsp low calorie margarine	Combine in a heavy-based saucepan and stir over low heat until the apples are well coated with the margarine and begin to soften. Cover with a lid and simmer until soft. Purée in a liquidizer or blender.
Sweetener	Sweeten to taste.

Orange Cornflour (Cornstarch) Sauce

Easy to prepare · Microwave · Freeze – add ½ teaspoon of cornflour (cornstarch) before freezing, then bring the sauce back to the boil before serving · Serve hot or cold · Makes ½ pt/300 ml/1¼ cups

1 tbsp cornflour (cornstarch) Grated rind of 1 orange 3 tbsp sugar	Blend together in a saucepan away from the heat.
¼ pt/150 ml/⅔ cup milk	Whisk into the cornflour mixture, place the pan over moderate heat and bring to the boil, beating all the time until a thick sauce is formed.
Juice of 2 large oranges	Beat into the sauce, then reheat but do not boil.
Small knob butter	Stir in and remove the sauce from the heat. **Note:** When reheating some of the Vitamin C will be destroyed.

Butterscotch Sauce (2)

Easy to cook · Do not overboil or the sauce will become too thick · Microwave – care required · Freeze · Serve hot · Makes 3 fl oz/90 ml/ ⅜ cup

4 oz/100 g/½ cup soft dark brown sugar ¼ pt/150 ml/⅔ cup water	Stir together in a heavy-based saucepan and place over gentle heat, stirring frequently until the sugar dissolves.
½ oz/15 g/1 tbsp butter or margarine	Stir into the dissolved sugar, raise the heat and bring to the boil. Continue cooking for 4-5 minutes without stirring until the mixture is syrupy. Remove the pan from the heat.
1 tsp arrowroot 1 tbsp cold water	Blend together in a small bowl.
¼ tsp vanilla essence	Stir into the arrowroot paste. Pour the mixture into the hot syrup and bring to the boil, stirring continuously.

Butterscotch Sauce (3)

Easy to cook · For best results maple syrup should be used but golden syrup may be substituted, although the finished sauce will taste slightly different · Do not microwave · Do not freeze · Serve hot · Makes 12 fl oz/ 350 ml/1½ cups

3 oz/75 g/6 tbsp soft light brown sugar ¼ pt/150 ml/⅔ cup maple syrup 1½ oz/40 g/3 tbsp butter or margarine Pinch salt	Combine in a heavy-based saucepan, bring to the boil over moderate heat. Stir once, then cook without further stirring for 3 minutes until a thick syrup is formed.
¼ pt/150 ml/⅔ cup single or light cream	Stir into the syrup, raise the heat and bring back to the boil. Immediately remove the pan from the heat.
2 tsp vanilla essence	Add to the sauce. Leave to cool for a few minutes and stir before using.

Peach and Coconut Sauce

Very easy to prepare · Use a food processor or liquidizer · No cooking required · Can be stored in the refrigerator for a few hours · Makes 1 pt/ 600 ml/2½ cups

½ pt/300 ml/1¼ cups natural yogurt *3 tbsp double or heavy cream* *Grated ring of 1 orange* *4 tbsp confectioners' or icing sugar* *1 tbsp desiccated or shredded coconut.*	Purée in the liquidizer or food processor. Leave in the machine.
2 fresh peaches	Skin, stone and cut into quarters. Add to the liquidizer or processor and switch on until the peaches are chopped but not puréed.

Sweet Mousseline Sauce

Tricky to cook · Microwave – can only be cooked on the lowest setting · Freeze – must be reconstituted by microwave on lowest setting · Serve warm · Makes ½ pt/300 ml/1¼ cups

3 egg yolks *2 egg whites* *5 tbsp double or heavy cream* *1½ oz/40 g/3 tbsp caster or superfine sugar* *1 tbsp sweet sherry*	Combine in a bowl and beat thoroughly. Place the bowl over a pan of hot water, but make sure that the water does not touch the bottom of the bowl. Set over low heat and cook, whisking continuously, until the sauce thickens sufficiently to coat the back of a spoon.

Above: Peach and Coconut Sauce with fruit salad

Strawberry Sour

Easy to prepare in a liquidizer or blender · No cooking required ·
Freeze · Serve cold · Makes 1 pt/600 ml/2½ cups

8 oz/225 g/1½ cups strawberries, fresh or thawed *½ pt/300 ml/1¼ cups soured cream*	Purée in the liquidizer or blender, then press through a nylon sieve to remove the strawberry pips. Return the mixture to the liquidizer.
6 oz/175 g/¾ cup caster or superfine sugar *4 tbsp brandy* *Pinch ground nutmeg*	Add to the liquidizer and purée until smooth.

Munakermaa

Fairly easy to cook but take care not to overheat when thickening · Do
not microwave · Do not freeze · Serve cold · Makes ¾ pt/450 ml/2 cups

2 egg yolks *1 egg white* *1 oz/25 g/2 tbsp caster or superfine sugar* *¼ tsp ground cardamom*	Combine in a bowl and beat thoroughly until the mixture is foaming.
¾ pt/450 ml/2 cups milk	Put into a saucepan and bring to the boil. Pour into the egg mixture, beating vigorously. Return the mixture to the pan, reduce the heat to minimum and cook, stirring continuously, until the sauce thickens.

Above: Strawberry Sour with meringue and cream

Peach Sauce (1)

Fairly easy to prepare · Use a stainless steel fork for crushing · Microwave · Freeze · Serve warm or cold · Makes ½ pt/300 ml/1¼ cups

4 large ripe peaches	Skin, remove the stones and crush the flesh with a stainless steel fork. Purée in a liquidizer or blender, then press through a nylon sieve.
1 tbsp Jamaica rum 1 tsp Maraschino 4 tbsp confectioners' or icing sugar	Combine in an enamelled or non-stick pan with the peach purée and warm over gentle heat, but do not boil.

Peach Sauce (2)

Easy to prepare · No cooking required · Freeze · Serve cold · Makes ½ pt/300 ml/1¼ cups

4 large ripe peaches	Peel, halve, remove the stones, then coarsely chop and press through a sieve into a bowl.
4 oz/100 g/1 cup sifted confectioners' or icing sugar 1 tbsp fresh lemon juice	Stir into the puréed peaches until the sugar is dissolved.

St Clements Sauce

Easy to cook · Microwave – requires care · Freeze · Serve hot · Makes ½ pt/300 ml/1¼ cups

4 oz/100 g/½ cup butter 4 oz/100 g/½ cup sugar	Blend together in a saucepan. Place the pan over gentle heat and stir until the sugar is melted and froth appears on the surface.
Juice and grated rind of 1 large orange Juice and grated rind of 1 lemon 2 tsp cornflour (cornstarch)	Blend together in a small bowl. Pour into the melted mixture, then bring to the boil, stirring continuously until the sauce thickens.

Swiss Muesli Sauce

Very easy to prepare · Requires food processor or liquidizer · No cooking required · Do not freeze · Serve cold on its own · Makes 1 pt/600 ml/ 2½ cups

½ pt/300 ml/1¼ cups natural yogurt 3 tbsp muesli 3 large bananas, peeled and cut into chunks ¼ pt/150 ml/⅔ cups single or light cream	Blend all the ingredients together in the liquidizer or food processor. Do not strain.

Strawberry Sauce

Easy to prepare · No cooking required · Freeze · Serve cold · Makes ½ pt/300 ml/1¼ cups

6 oz/175 g/¾ cup caster or superfine sugar 2 tbsp fresh lemon juice 1 tsp Dubonnet	Combine in a large bowl and stir until the sugar is dissolved.
1 lb/450 g/3 cups fresh strawberries	Hull, rinse and dry. Purée in a liquidizer or blender and then press through a nylon sieve into the sugar mixture. Stir thoroughly.
Few drops red food colouring (optional)	Add to the sauce to improve the colour.

Raspberry and Banana Sauce

Easy to prepare · No cooking required · Do not freeze · Refrigerate – short time only · Serve cold · Makes ½ pt/300 ml/1¼ cups

1 large banana Juice of ½ lemon 3 tbsp single or light cream 2 tbsp caster or superfine sugar	Peel the banana, cut into chunks, then mash with the lemon juice, cream and sugar. Beat with a whisk until frothy.
8 oz/225 g/1½ cups raspberries, fresh or thawed	Mash, press through a nylon sieve to remove the pips, then mix the purée into the banana mixture.

Sesquiera Sauce

Requires care in cooking · Do not microwave · Do not freeze · Serve hot · Makes ¼ pt/150 ml/⅔ cup

3 oz/75 g/6 tbsp caster or superfine sugar 1 tbsp cornflour (cornstarch) ¼ tsp salt 4 tbsp cold water	Blend together in a saucepan.
¼ pt/150 ml/⅔ cup boiling water Grated rind of ½ lemon	Whisk into the sugar mixture and bring to the boil over moderate heat, beating continuously. Cook for a further 5-6 minutes until the sauce has thickened slightly.
1 egg yolk 6 tbsp fresh lemon juice ¼ tsp ground mace	Blend together thoroughly in a small bowl. Add 2 or 3 tablespoons of the hot sauce, then pour back into the pan and cook over minimum heat, stirring continuously, for 1 minute. Strain into a warmed bowl.
1 oz/25 g/2 tbsp butter, soft	Immediately stir into the sauce until melted.

Sabayon Sauce

Some expertise required when preparing the sugar syrup · Microwave – take care as above · Freeze – reconstitute carefully at room temperature or in microwave on 10% · Refrigerate – do not keep for longer than 24 hours · Serve warm or cold · This sauce is very rich · Makes ½ pt/300 ml/ 1¼ cups

2 egg yolks	Remove the threads with a fork, then beat the egg yolks with a whisk until thick.
2 oz/50 g/¼ cup caster or superfine sugar 4 tbsp water	Put into a small saucepan and stir until the sugar is dissolved. Bring to the boil over moderate heat, raise the heat to fast boiling and cook until the thermometer registers 225°F/ 107°C – a teaspoon of the syrup when dropped from a height onto a dish forms a fine thin thread. Immediately pour the syrup onto the beaten yolks, whisking briskly until the mixture fluffs up.
1 tsp grated lemon rind 1 tbsp lemon juice 1 tbsp sweet sherry	Fold into the sauce.
2 tbsp double or heavy cream	Lightly whip and fold into the sauce. Serve warm or chilled.

Toffee and Walnut Sauce

Easy to cook but take care that the sauce does not darken too much · Microwave – with care · Do not freeze · Serve hot or cold · Makes 8 fl oz/ 250 ml/1 cup

2 tbsp demerara sugar 1 tbsp golden syrup ½ oz/15 g/1 tbsp butter or margarine	Combine in a heavy-based saucepan set over minimum heat and cook, stirring occasionally, until the sugar has dissolved. Bring to the boil, then cook rapidly, without stirring, until the mixture is a rich golden colour. Immediately remove the pan from the heat.
¼ pt/150 ml/⅔ cup warm water	Add to the caramel mixture and shake the pan until the liquid is an even texture.
1 tbsp custard powder 2 tbsp cold water	Blend together in a large bowl, pour the caramel syrup into the custard, stir thoroughly and return to the pan. Replace the pan over moderate heat and bring to the boil, stirring continuously.
1 tsp fresh lemon juice 2 tbsp chopped blanched, skinned walnuts 2 tbsp double or heavy cream	Stir into the hot sauce.

Tovarich Butter Sauce

Easy to prepare · No cooking required · Freeze · Serve cold · Makes 8 fl oz/250 ml/1 cup

5 canned pitted red cherries	Slice into rings.
3 tbsp vodka	Mix with the cherries in a small bowl and cover tightly. Leave to stand 1 hour, shaking the bowl occasionally.
4 oz/100 g/½ cup unsalted butter	Beat until soft and fluffy.
3 oz/75 g/¾ cup sifted confectioners' or icing sugar	Gradually beat into the softened butter. Drain the vodka into the sweetened butter, beating thoroughly, then fold in the sliced cherries.

Vanilla Sauce (1)

Requires some care · Microwave – use to heat the milk but complete the recipe conventionally in a saucepan · Do not freeze · Serve hot · Makes ½ pt/300 ml/1¼ cups

8 fl oz/250 ml/1 cup milk 1 vanilla pod, broken in half	Put in a heavy-based saucepan, bring to the boil, then reduce the heat to minimum. Cover with the lid and cook for 10 minutes. Inspect frequently to make sure that the milk is not boiling over.
3 egg yolks 2½ oz/65 g/⅔ cup granulated sugar	Beat together with an electric whisk until the mixture lightens and thickens so that a spoon handle, when drawn through the mixture, will leave a channel. Remove the vanilla pod from the milk and while beating, pour the milk into the egg mixture. Strain through a nylon sieve back into the saucepan. Cook over minimum heat, stirring continuously, until the sauce is thick enough to coat the back of a spoon. The sauce must not boil or the mixture will curdle.

Vanilla Sauce (2)

Very easy to cook · Microwave · Freeze · Serve hot · Makes 1 pt/600 ml/ 2½ cups

1 pt/600 ml/2½ cups milk	Place in a saucepan.
1 vanilla pod, split lengthwise and then cut in half	Put the small pieces of the vanilla pod into the milk and bring to steaming but not boiling point. Cover and set aside for 30 minutes.
1½ oz/40 g/3 tbsp butter or margarine	Melt in a heavy-based saucepan over minimum heat.
1½ oz/40 g/6 tbsp flour	Stir into the melted butter and cook for 1 minute, stirring continuously. Remove the pan from the heat. Slowly strain in the milk (rinse and dry the vanilla pod for future use). Bring the sauce to the boil, stirring continuously until thick.
2-3 tbsp caster or superfine sugar	Add to taste. Continue boiling for 2-3 minutes, stirring constantly.

Rich Sabayon Sauce

Requires some care · Cook in a double saucepan · Have the ice cubes ready · Microwave · Freeze – becomes thinner; reconstitute carefully at room temperature · Serve cold · Recipe can be halved · Makes 1½ pt/ 900 ml/3¾ cups

6 oz/175 g/¾ cup caster or superfine sugar 4 egg yolks, threads removed	Beat together until thick and aerated.
¼ pt/150 ml/⅔ cup sweet white wine	Place in the top section of a double saucepan, place 1 in/2.5 cm of hot water in the base and set over moderate heat. Heat until the wine is warm. Pour the egg mixture into the wine, increase the heat under the base pan and beat vigorously until the sauce thickens slightly.
Bowl of ice cubes	Remove the pan from the heat and place the top half in the bowl of ice. Using an electric beater, whip until the sauce is cold.
½ pt/300 ml/1¼ cups double or heavy cream	Lightly whip, then fold into the cool sauce.

Hazelnut and Date Sauce

Easy to cook but hazelnuts must be roasted or toasted · Microwave – hazelnuts may be browned in the microwave but take care that they do not burn inside · Freeze · Serve warm · Makes ¾ pt/450 ml/2 cups

1 oz/25 g/¼ cup shelled hazelnuts	Toast or roast until the skins are dry, then rub in a dry cloth to remove the skins. Chop the hazelnuts finely.
1 oz/25 g/⅛ cup stoned dates	Chop finely.
4 oz/100 g/½ cup sugar 1 tbsp cornflour (cornstarch) ½ pt/300 ml/1¼ cups cold water Pinch salt	Combine in a heavy-based saucepan, then place over moderate heat and stir continuously until the sauce thickens.
½ oz/15 g/1 tbsp butter	Stir into the hot sauce.
2 tbsp fresh lemon juice 1 tbsp fresh orange juice	Stir into the sauce. Remove from the heat, then add the dates and nuts.
	Note: It is sometimes easier to chop the dates and hazelnuts together to lessen the possibility of the dates sticking to the knife.

Ginger Sauce (1)

Easy to cook · Microwave – stir frequently · Freeze – reheat gradually · Serve hot with baked pears · Makes 14 fl oz/400 ml/1¾ cups

4 oz/100 g/½ cup caster or superfine sugar 2 tsp cornflour (cornstarch) ½ tsp ground ginger Pinch salt	Combine together in a saucepan.
½ pt/300 ml/1¼ cups cold water	Stir into the mixture. Place over moderate heat and cook, stirring constantly, until the sauce clears and thickens slightly. Remove the pan from the heat.
½ oz/15 g/1 tbsp butter 1 tsp fresh lemon juice	Stir into the sauce.

Ginger Sauce (2)

Very easy to prepare · No cooking required · Freeze · Refrigerate · Serve cold · Makes ½ pt/300 ml/1¼ cups

¼ pt/150 ml/⅔ cup whipping cream	Whip stiffly.
2 tbsp ginger syrup (from jar of stem ginger) 1 tbsp brandy	Fold into the whipped cream.

Opposite: Rich Sabayon Sauce

Above: (left) Hazelnut and Date Sauce and *(right)* Ginger Sauce (2)

Herbs and Spices

Spice	Description	Flavour
ALLSPICE	*Ground or whole*	Fragrant blend of cinnamon, nutmeg and cloves – looks like a black pepper.
ANISEED	*Whole*	Liquorice flavour with mint overtones.
BASIL	*Leaf or ground*	Mildly sweet and pungent.
BAY LEAVES	*Leaf or ground*	Sweet in a delicate manner.
BORAGE	*Leaf*	Has the flavour of cucumber.
BOUQUET GARNI	*Sachet*	Mixture of bay leaf, parsley and thyme in a muslin sachet, or can be made up in the kitchen.
CARAWAY	*Whole*	Pungent and slightly sharp.
CARDAMOM	*Whole green or brown pods containing seeds or ground seeds*	Sweet and slightly perfumed.
CAYENNE	*Ground*	Pungent, orangey red in colour.
CELERY SEED	*Usually ground and mixed with salt*	Tastes like fresh celery.
CHERVIL	*Whole or dried*	Similar to parsley.
CHILLI	*Whole or crushed*	Ground – very very hot so must be used sparingly. Powder (sometimes known as chilli compound powder, also contains other ingredients, such as oregano and cumin) – hot or medium in intensity according to the contents as shown on the label.
CHIVES	*Fresh or dried*	Similar to onion.
CINNAMON	*Ground or sticks*	Aromatic bark with a slightly sweet, dry taste.
CLOVES	*Whole or ground*	Powerful in a sweet manner.
CORIANDER	*Whole or ground*	Combination of lemon peel and sage.

Spice	Description	Flavour
CUMIN	*Whole or ground*	Looks like caraway seed but tastes like pungent savory.
CURRY	*Ground*	Blend of various spices, including cumin, ground peppers, ginger and turmeric, which can be hot or mild according to title.
DILL	*Weed or seed*	Similar to parsley or fennel with mild aniseed taste. Seeds are stronger than weed.
FENNEL	*Leaves or seed*	Liquorice taste, also from parsley family – the tops of the fennel vegetable are used.
FENUGREEK	*Seeds*	Square-shaped, slightly bitter like burnt sugar.
FIVE SPICE	*Ground*	Chinese mixture of anise, star anise, cassia, cinnamon, cloves and fennel – liquorice flavour.
GARAM MASALA	*Ground*	Mixture of cardamom, cinnamon, clove, cumin and peppercorns. Garam means hot, masala means spice.
GARLIC	*Whole, ground, flakes or mixed with salt*	One clove is a pod from the head and, once peeled, can be crushed, sliced or chopped. Keep in a covered container away from other foods. A tiny quantity is subtle and highly effective; a large quantity can be overpowering and ruin a dish.
GINGER	*Fresh or ground, crystallized, preserved*	Hot and rich. Flavour not impaired by freezing.
HORSERADISH	*Fresh or ground*	Grate the root before use. Potent and hot.
JUNIPER BERRIES	*Whole*	Like large peppercorns. Bruise before use. Flavour of gin.
LEMON THYME	*Leaf or chopped*	Lemony scent.

Spice	Description	Flavour
LEMON VERBENA	Leaf	Lemony-lime flavour.
LOVAGE	Seeds or chopped leaf	Strong aromatic taste with overtones of celery.
MACE	Sliced or ground	Very expensive outside of the nutmeg.
MARJORAM	Leaf	Grey-green, from mint family.
MINT	Fresh or dried, chopped	Various flavours exist, the commonest having the taste of spearmint. After freezing it is very soft and of poor appearance but the flavour remains.
MIXED HERBS	Ground	Pleasant aromatic blend of seven herbs.
MIXED SPICES	Ground	Blend of spices often including cinnamon, nutmeg and allspice.
MONOSODIUM GLUTAMATE	Finely ground crystals	White crystalline powder derived from vegetable protein. No flavour of own but enhances savoury dishes and is slightly salty.
MUSTARD	Seed or ground	Black, brown, white or yellow seeds. Best made in a conventional manner.
NUTMEG	Whole, grated or ground	Inside of the mace, slightly sweet and delicate
OREGANO	Leaves	Aromatic herb not dissimilar to marjoram.
PAPRIKA	Powder	Can be sweet or hot – many varieties emanating from the many red peppers.
PARSLEY	Fresh or dried, whole or flakes	Mild – use only in savouries.
PEPERANDER	Seeds	Proprietary mixture of black and white peppercorns with coriander seeds – consequently adds these flavours readily.

Spice	Description	Flavour
PEPPERCORNS	Whole or powder (white or black)	Black are milder than white but richer in flavour and are white peppercorns before they become ripe. The white peppercorns are left on the trees longer and are hotter because they are more mature, although there is some disagreement about this.
POPPY SEEDS	Seeds	Blue-black with nut-like sweetish taste. These do not come from the narcotic variety of flower.
QUATRE-ÉPICES	Powder	Mixture of ground peppercorns, cloves, nutmeg and cinnamon but sometimes also ginger – can be mixture of any four.
ROSEMARY	Fresh or dry leaves or powder	Sweet, has sharp spiky leaves.
SAFFRON	Strands or powder	The most expensive of all, as 60,000 flower stamens are needed for 1lb/450g. Usually comes from Spain and is slightly sweet.
SAGE	Leaves	Member of the mint family often used with onion.
SAVORY	Leaves or ground	Winter, which is more aromatic, or summer varieties. Member of the mint family.
SESAME	Seeds	Roasted or unroasted, hence black or white – rich nut-like flavour and, when crushed, turns into an oil.
SORREL	Leaves	Sharp vinegary flavour.
TARRAGON	Leaves	Should be used in savoury dishes only and particularly for flavouring vinegar.
THYME	Leaf or chopped	Member of the mint family.
TURMERIC	Powder	Aromatic root from the ginger family, bright yellow in colour and hence good for colouring savoury dishes.
VANILLA	Pods or liquid essence	Pods can be used several times. Vanilla extract is pure; vanilla flavouring is much weaker as it comes from vanillan.

Marinades and Vinegars

The word 'marinate' means to pickle and has a connection with the sea, as it derives from the same root as the words 'marine' and 'maritime'. It was an early form of preserving that was especially important for meat and game, which would otherwise have gone bad, as there was no refrigeration. Brine was also used to pickle fish before it was cooked but is now used to flavour and soften prior to cooking.

A marinade is a strongly-flavoured liquid which may contain oil, lemon juice, vinegar, red or white wine, cider or other acid ingredients, or it can be a combination of oil and an acid ingredient—nowadays, yogurt is often used as a marinade. The acid ingredient is used to impregnate and tenderize the food, while the oil is used for its softening powers. Marinades are usually flavoured with carrots and onions, garlic, bay leaves, herbs and spices and can be either cooked or uncooked.

Allowing food to marinate for a length of time serves two purposes: one to tenderize; two to improve the flavour – although some recipes include a marinade solely for flavour. After the marinated food is removed, the remaining marinade is often reduced over medium heat in a saucepan to form the basis of a sauce to complement the food when it is cooked. However, some marinades are not consumed at all, such as the brine in which pickles are steeped.

Because of the long soaking period, dried herbs and vegetable flakes, such as onion or celery, can be used, as they reconstitute during the soaking. Ground spices are suitable for use in cold marinades because they spread through the mixture more evenly, whereas the flavour of whole spices is brought out by heating.

The kind of spices and the length of marinating time depends upon the food selected. Use robust flavours for meat and game, such as cloves or caraway seeds, and choose more subtle spices to flavour veal, poultry and fish. Herbs are more frequently used in fish marinades than spices and celery and fennel are outstandingly good with fish. Vegetables are frequently marinated using basil, tarragon, marjoram or parsley flakes. Wine and vinegar are usually used for meat, poultry and seafood but wine is rarely used in vegetable marinades. Lemon juice is suitable for all marinades. To produce slower absorption use a greater quantity of oil.

Choose a container to fit the food you are marinating and you will then require less marinade. Put the food into the dish before pouring the marinade over and baste occasionally. Keep the bowl in a cool place and cover tightly to keep in the strong flavours.

When the marinades are to be left standing for a long time, reduce the amount of the acid in the ingredients because evaporation will cause it to become more concentrated and thus have a stronger effect. Heating the marinade also helps to concentrate the flavours and once the flavours of the spices have been released they will continue to emit flavour to the cold marinade as long as they are left in it. Whole spices have the advantage that they are easy to remove and this is particularly useful if the marinade is then going to be used for making a sauce. However, these whole spices do release their flavour more slowly and are therefore most effective when used for long-term marination. Herbs may be used on the sprig; there is no need to remove the leaves or to chop fresh herbs.

When marinating a whole cut of meat, pierce the flesh well with a skewer before treating, weight the meat down and turn it over occasionally. Long thin cuts will marinate more successfully than short wide cuts because the marinade does not need to penetrate so far. The larger the pieces of meat, the longer the marinating time will be and large cuts of meat should be marinated overnight. Small pieces will only take a few hours but these should not be pierced too much before inserting into the soaking liquid. Overtenderization produces a very poor texture in cubed meat. Chops, steaks and thin slices of meat will require only one to two hours. On the other hand, game such as venison requires a marinating time of several days.

A cooked marinade will keep for about one week and it is best to use glass or earthenware containers so that any acid ingredients do not damage the surface of your bowl. Do not use a metal spoon when cooking vinegars as it will turn green. If the food is to be kept for long, the marinade must be reboiled every two days and then left to cool before replacing the meat. When preparing pâtés it is a good idea to marinate the meat or fish first, as the flavour will then be at its best.

Not all meat that is marinated requires tenderizing. For example, tender pieces of lamb for a kebab are only marinated to produce a characteristic flavour. The same applies to seafood and vegetables and also to tender poultry, so these should have marinades that complement their flavours. Madeira, sherry or brandy are ideal for use with steaks, and in Provence a little orange rind is added to the basis for braised beef.

Marinating has enormous potential and it is a great pity that so few people think of using marinades except for basic meat cookery. Fruit prepared in a marinade can taste quite different: for example, mango marinated in lemon juice, pineapple soaked in Kirsch, fresh strawberries in brandy, etc. Whenever you are looking for some new way of cooking, think about marinades. They are very easy to prepare and highly effective. Most of the recipes in the chapter are interchangeable, which gives you even greater scope for experimenting.

Sherry Marinade

Easy to prepare · No cooking required · After marinating, use as a basis for a sauce · Makes 7 fl oz/200 ml/⁷⁄₈ cup

4 fl oz/120 ml/¹⁄₂ cup medium sherry
3 tbsp soy sauce
1 tsp lemon juice
6 spring onions or scallions, finely sliced
2 tbsp soft light brown sugar
¹⁄₂ tsp salt
¹⁄₂ tsp ground ginger

Combine in a bowl and stir thoroughly until the sugar has dissolved. Use as required.

To thicken, combine 1 or 2 teaspoons of cornflour (cornstarch) with 1 or 2 tablespoons of cold water. Mix into the marinade, then bring to the boil, stirring continuously.

Dry White Wine Marinade

Easy to prepare · No cooking required · Use for diced chicken or fish · Makes ¹⁄₄ pt/150 ml/²⁄₃ cup

5 tbsp dry white wine
4 tbsp olive oil
2 tbsp fresh chopped parsley
1 small onion, quartered
2 bay leaves, roughly torn
Salt
Freshly ground black pepper

Combine all the ingredients, seasoning to taste with salt and pepper.
Leave overnight, then strain through a fine nylon sieve before use.

Chilli Marinade for Lamb

Easy to prepare · Has a strong flavour · No cooking required · Marinade will keep in a screw-top jar for several weeks · Makes ³⁄₄ pt/450 ml/2 cups

1 small onion, peeled and finely chopped *1 clove garlic, peeled and crushed* *2 tbsp vegetable oil* *Juice of 2 large oranges* *Grated rind of 1 orange* *4 fl oz/120 ml/¹⁄₂ cup medium red wine* *4 fl oz/120 ml/¹⁄₂ cup bottled chilli sauce* *1 tbsp sugar* *2 tsp chilli compound powder* *2 tsp dried basil* *2 tsp salt*	Thoroughly mix together in a large bowl, cover and leave overnight. Strain. Leave lamb to soak for 24 hours in the marinade before using.

Cognac Marinade

Easy to prepare · No cooking required · Will keep for a few days in the refrigerator · Expensive but gives a wonderful flavour to fillet steaks · Makes ³⁄₄ pt/450 ml/2 cups

4 tbsp cheap brandy *8 fl oz/250 ml/1 cup dry white wine* *2 tbsp olive oil* *2 oz/50 g button mushrooms, finely sliced* *2 shallots, peeled and finely chopped* *¹⁄₄ tsp dried thyme* *¹⁄₄ tsp bay leaf powder* *1 small clove garlic, peeled and crushed* *10 peppercorns, crushed* *1 tsp salt*	Combine all the ingredients together and use as required.

Above left: Chilli Marinade for Lamb

Above right: Cognac Marinade

Marinade Lapin

Fairly easy to prepare · No cooking required · Marinate rabbit pieces for 2-3 days in the refrigerator · Remove the rabbit, strain the marinade and use in sauces for rabbit, chicken or other game · Makes 8 fl oz/250 ml/ 1 cup

1 lemon	Squeeze out the juice and finely grate the peel. Place in a large bowl.
2 large onions, peeled and finely sliced 2 medium carrots, peeled and finely sliced 2 cloves garlic, peeled and bruised 2 bay leaves 1 tsp rosemary leaves $1/4$ tsp fennel seeds $1/2$ tsp salt 5 tbsp vegetable oil	Add to the lemon in the bowl, stir thoroughly and use as required.

Brandy Marinade

Easy to prepare · No cooking required · Instead of soaking the poultry or fish, arrange in layers and sprinkle with the marinade · Only a small quantity is usually required. · Makes 4 fl oz/120 ml/$1/2$ cup

6 tbsp brandy $1/2$ tsp salt $1/4$ tsp ground white pepper 2 tsp coarsely cut fresh chervil leaves	Combine in a screw-top jar.
1 small onion, peeled	Mince or chop finely and strain the juice into the marinade, discarding the pulp. Screw the top on the jar to prevent evaporation and leave for 24 hours before using.

Tarragon Marinade

Easy to prepare · No cooking required · Do not freeze · Keeps well in the refrigerator for a few days · Makes enough to marinate 2 lb/1 kg meat

4 fl oz/120 ml/$1/2$ cup dry red wine 3 tbsp tarragon vinegar 8 fl oz/250 ml/1 cup olive oil 1 medium onion, peeled and finely sliced 1 bay leaf $1/2$ tsp mustard powder 2 cloves garlic, peeled and crushed	Combine together in a glass or pottery bowl.
1 lemon	Squeeze the juice, pare the rind and cut into strips. Stir into the marinade.
$1/2$ tsp salt $1/4$ tsp freshly ground black pepper	Stir in, adding extra seasoning if preferred, and use as required.

Barbecue Marinade

Easy to cook · Requires several easy-to-obtain ingredients · Microwave · Keeps in a screw-top jar or corked bottle for several weeks · Makes $1/2$ pt/ 300 ml//$1 1/4$ cups

6 tbsp fresh lemon juice 2 tbsp fresh orange juice Grated rind of $1/2$ lemon Grated rind of $1/2$ orange $1/4$ pt/150 ml/$2/3$ cup strong beef stock 2 tbsp cider vinegar 1 tsp Tabasco sauce 1 tbsp mustard powder 1 tbsp salt 3 bay leaves 1 clove garlic, peeled and crushed 2 tbsp soft dark brown sugar $1/4$ tsp chilli powder 6 fl oz/175 ml/$3/4$ cup salad oil 2 pickled onions, finely chopped 1 tsp freshly ground black pepper	Stir all the ingredients together in a large heavy-based saucepan and bring to the boil over a moderate heat. Reduce to simmering and cook without a lid for 20 minutes. Remove the pan from the heat, leave the sauce to cool, then bottle and use as required. Shake before use.

Baster Sauce

Easy to prepare · No cooking required · Tenderizes and brings out the flavour of tougher cuts of meat · Makes $3/4$ pt/450 ml/2 cups

$1/4$ pt/150 ml/$2/3$ cup olive oil 6 tbsp vinegar 6 tbsp fresh lemon juice 3 tbsp soy sauce $1/4$ tsp papaya powder (meat tenderizing powder) $1/2$ tsp monosodium glutamate (MSG) $1/2$ tsp salt $1/2$ tsp pepper $1/4$ tsp mustard powder	Combine all the ingredients together in a jar or bowl and use as a marinade or brush over steaks or chops at least 30 minutes before cooking. Brush once more during cooking.

Cardamom Marinade

Fairly easy to prepare but take care that the seeds do not scatter when fried · Do not microwave · Do not freeze · Do not refrigerate · Serve cold · Makes ½ pt/300ml/1¼ cups

1 tbsp oil	Heat in a heavy-based pan.
1 tbsp cardamom seeds	Fry gently in the oil.
1 small onion, peeled and finely chopped	Stir into the oil and continue cooking.
1 x 8 oz/225 g can tomatoes	Empty into the mixture. Crush with a potato masher or fork.
1 tsp salt ⅛ tsp chilli powder	Add to the marinade, bring to the boil, then place a lid on the pan. Remove from the heat and leave to cool. Use as required.

Escabèche Marinade

Easy to prepare · Microwave · No need to freeze · Use as a marinade for raw fish before frying or strain before use and use as part of the liquid in a batter for frying · Makes ½ pt/300 ml/1¼ cups

2 medium onions, peeled and thinly sliced 4 tbsp olive oil 2 cloves garlic, peeled and crushed	Combine in a heavy-based saucepan and cook gently until the onions are soft. Remove the pan from the heat.
4 tbsp white wine vinegar ¼ tsp bay leaf powder ¼ tsp salt ¼ tsp white pepper	Stir into the onion mixture. Pour into a bowl and use as required.

Pineapple Marinade

Easy to prepare · No cooking required · Makes ½ pt/300 ml/1¼ cups

4 tbsp fresh pineapple juice 2 tbsp salad oil 4 tbsp fresh orange juice ½ tsp grated orange peel 1 tbsp brown sugar 2 tsp lemon juice 1-in/2.5-cm slice fresh pineapple, finely chopped ¼ tsp salt ¼ tsp pepper	Combine all ingredients together, leave to stand for 2 hours, then purée in a liquidizer or blender. Use as required. Strain through a sieve if using for vegetables.

Rechauffé Marinade

Fairly easy to prepare · Microwave · Freeze – flavours intensify · Use as a marinade or as part of a sauce or gravy when cooking cooked meats · Makes ½ pt/300 ml/1¼ cups

2 tbsp redcurrant jelly	Put in a bowl over a saucepan half-filled with hot water and placed over moderate heat.
6 tbsp tomato purée 6 tbsp port 6 tbsp red wine vinegar 1 tbsp soft dark brown sugar 1 tsp ground allspice 1 tsp lemon thyme leaves 1 tsp dried oregano 1 medium onion, peeled and very finely chopped	Stir into the melted jelly. Remove the bowl from the heat and cover until required.

Paw-Paw Marinade

Easy to prepare using a liquidizer or food processor · No cooking required · Freeze · Refrigerate – will keep 24 hours only · Makes ¾ pt/450 ml/2 cups

1 ripe paw-paw ½ lime	Cut open the paw-paw and remove all of the seeds. Squeeze the juice from the lime. Scoop out the paw-paw flesh and add to the liquidizer with the lime juice.
2½ tbsp medium white wine 5 tbsp salad oil ½ small onion, peeled and coarsely chopped ½ small carrot, scraped and sliced ½ clove garlic, peeled Pinch chilli compound powder Pinch mustard powder ½ tsp caster or superfine sugar ¼ tsp salt	Add to the liquidizer and blend until the ingredients are well mixed. Use as required.

Lime Marinade

Easy to prepare · No cooking required · Will keep in the refrigerator for a few days · Makes 6 fl oz/175 ml/¾ cup

Juice of 4 limes Thinly pared peel of 2 limes, cut into strips 2 tsp salt 3 tbsp vegetable oil 12 white peppercorns, bruised	Mix thoroughly in a bowl, cover and leave for 6-8 hours. Strain before using.

Marinade For Fish

*Easy to prepare · No cooking required · Do not freeze – garlic odour will
be too powerful · Fish should soak in the marinade for several hours
before using · Makes 8 fl oz/250 ml/1 cup*

¹/₄ pt/150 ml/²/₃ cup white wine vinegar *1 tsp fresh lemon juice* *¹/₂ tsp salt* *¹/₄ tsp ground white pepper* *¹/₄ tsp ground coriander* *2 tbsp tomato ketchup* *2 tbsp fresh chopped parsley* *1 large clove garlic, crushed*	Combine together in a glass mixing bowl.
3 strands saffron *2 tbsp boiling water*	Combine in a small bowl, then cover and leave to stand for ¹/₂ hour. Remove the saffron strands and pour the liquid into the marinade. Cover and use as required.

Green Bean Marinade

*Easy to prepare · No cooking required · Keeps for a few days only · Use
for green beans or other cooked vegetables that can be used in salads,
e.g. cauliflower, carrots, etc. You only need a few tablespoons · Makes
¹/₂ pt/300 ml/1¹/₄ cups*

¹/₄ pt/150 ml/²/₃ cup salad oil *3¹/₂ fl oz/100 ml/7 tbsp cider vinegar* *3 tbsp fresh lemon juice* *1 clove garlic, peeled and crushed* *2 tsp chopped chives* *2 tsp dried marjoram* *¹/₂ tsp salt* *1 tsp freshly ground black pepper*	Mix thoroughly together. Stir in drained hot vegetables and leave to marinate for at least 2 hours. Drain.

Above left: Marinade for Fish

Above right: Green Bean Marinade

Hawaiian Island Marinade

Very easy to prepare · No cooking required · Do not freeze · Do not refrigerate · Makes ³/₄ pt/450 ml/2 cups

¹/₂ pt/300 ml/1¹/₄ cups vegetable oil Juice of 2 large lemons 6 tbsp soy sauce 1 clove garlic, crushed 1 tsp ground ginger ¹/₂ tsp dried marjoram ¹/₂ tsp salt 1 tsp sweet paprika Few drops Tabasco ¹/₂ tsp monosodium glutamate (optional)	Stir together until well combined. Use as required. Store in a screw-top jar, putting a waxed disc or plastic cling film over the surface before screwing on the metal top. To use, remove the waxed disc and shake, provided the jar can be vigorously shaken without mishap.

Wine Marinade and Baster Sauce

Easy to prepare · No cooking required but the marinade can be reduced for use as a basting sauce · Makes 8 fl oz/250 ml/1 cup

8 tbsp medium red wine 2 cloves garlic, peeled and crushed 2 slices onion, finely chopped until the juices run free 1 tsp salt 1 tsp black pepper 2 tbsp Worcestershire sauce	Combine all the ingredients together thoroughly, then add the meat or poultry to be marinated. After use as a marinade, strain the liquid into a large heavy-based saucepan. Cook until reduced to a few tablespoons, strain and use to flavour meat sauces.

Orange Herb Marinade

Easy to prepare · No cooking required · No need to freeze · Can also be used as foundation for a sauce · Makes ¹/₂ pt/300 ml/1¹/₄ cups

¹/₄ pt/150 ml/²/₃ cup dry white wine 3 tbsp olive oil Juice of 2 large oranges 1 tsp fresh rosemary leaves 1 tsp dried marjoram 1 tsp dried thyme ¹/₂ tsp salt ¹/₄ tsp pepper 1 clove garlic, crushed	Mix together in a bowl or screw-top jar and use as required.

Above left: (left) Hawaiian Island Marinade and (right) Orange Herb Marinade

Above right: Wine Marinade and Baster Sauce

3-2-1 Barbecue Marinade

Easy to make · Microwave – the flavour is less sharp · Keeps well in a screw-top jar · Makes ¾ pt/450 ml/2 cups

3 tbsp soy sauce 3 tbsp caster or superfine sugar 2 tbsp red wine vinegar 2 tbsp tomato ketchup 2 tbsp cold water 1 tbsp dry sherry	Combine in a saucepan.
1 tbsp cornflour (cornstarch)	Sprinkle over the surface of the liquid, then whisk in until well blended.
1 x 8 oz/227 g can crushed pineapple	Stir into the cold mixture in the saucepan, place the pan over moderate heat and bring to the boil, stirring continuously until the sauce thickens slightly. Leave to cool for a few minutes, then purée in a liquidizer or blender.

Vegetable Marinade

Easy to prepare · No cooking required · Can be stored in a screw-top jar · Makes ½ pt/300 ml/1¼ cups

6 fl oz/175 ml/¾ cup tarragon vinegar 3 fl oz/90 ml/⅜ cup olive oil 1 clove garlic, peeled and crushed ¼ tsp salt 1 tsp French mustard 2 tbsp fresh chopped parsley 1 tsp dried oregano 1 tsp paprika 2 tbsp granulated sugar	Combine in a large jar, screw the lid on carefully and shake thoroughly.

Jamaican Marinade

Easy to prepare · No cooking required · Expensive but can be used as a basis for a sauce or gravy · Makes 6 fl oz/175 ml/¾ cup

¼ pt/150 ml/⅔ cup light rum 1 tsp ground allspice 1 large onion, finely chopped 1 sprig thyme 1 bay leaf 2 tsp fresh chopped parsley 2 tbsp olive oil Salt Pepper	Combine all the ingredients together, seasoning to taste. Use as required.

Lemon Verbena Marinade

Easy to prepare · Store in a screw-top jar · Use for diced rabbit or turkey · Makes 7 fl oz/200 ml/⅞ cup

¼ pt/150 ml/⅔ cup medium red wine 2 tbsp chicken stock 1 small onion, sliced 1 tsp dried lemon verbena leaves	Combine in a saucepan, bring to the boil, then remove the pan from the heat. Cover and leave until cold.
2 tbsp olive oil Salt Pepper	Stir into the cold marinade and use as required.

No Oil Barbecue Sauce

Easy to prepare · Microwave · Strong but can be diluted · Useful for poultry as no oil in recipe, so preventing too much softening · Use as a marinade or to baste · Makes 12 fl oz/350 ml/1½ cups

8 fl oz/250 ml/1 cup soy sauce 4 tbsp red wine vinegar 3 tbsp mustard powder 1 tsp salt ½ tsp pepper 1 small onion, peeled and finely chopped 1 clove garlic, bruised 6 tbsp fresh chopped chives 4 tbsp muscavado sugar	Combine all the ingredients in a heavy-based saucepan and bring to the boil over moderate heat, stirring continuously until all the sugar is dissolved. Use as required.

Venison Marinade

Easy to cook but odour in kitchen can be pungent · Microwave · Keeps well in a screw-top jar · Makes ¾ pt/450 ml/2 cups

1 bottle Beaujolais ¼ pt/150 ml/⅔ cup cider vinegar 1 large onion, peeled and finely chopped 1 large carrot, peeled and finely chopped 8 black peppercorns, bruised 8 juniper berries, bruised 2 bay leaves, coarsely torn Handful sprigs fresh herbs, including parsley, thyme, borage and chervil	Combine together in an enamel or non-stick saucepan and, without covering, bring to the boil. Simmer for 30-45 minutes until the mixture is reduced by half.
2 tbsp olive oil Salt Pepper	Stir in and season to taste. Cover and leave until cold before using.

Orange Barbecue Sauce

Easy to prepare using convenience foods · No cooking required · Use as a marinade and also to brush over meat towards the end of barbecuing · Makes ¾ pt/450 ml/2 cups

½ pt/300 ml/1¼ cups canned orange juice, frozen or liquid 2 oz/50 g/¼ cup demerara sugar 2 tbsp tomato ketchup 2 tbsp fresh lemon juice 3 spring onions or scallions, thinly sliced, or 2 tsp dried onion flakes ¼ tsp garlic salt ½ tsp ground white pepper	Combine all ingredients in a bowl, beat thoroughly, then cover and leave for 2 hours before using. During this time the frozen orange juice will thaw and the dried onion flakes will reconstitute.

Marinade Marie Brizzard

Easy to prepare · No cooking required · Keep covered tightly to prevent the aniseed odour from permeating other foods nearby · Use for white fish · Makes ¼ pt/150 ml/⅔ cup

4 tbsp salad oil 2 tbsp Pernod 2 tbsp fresh lemon juice 1 tsp fennel seeds ¼ tsp salt ¼ tsp black pepper	Combine all the ingredients together in a bowl, jug or bottle. Cover securely and use as required.

Herb Vinegar

Easy to prepare · Use cider, malt or wine vinegar and add herbs according to taste · Will keep in a well-corked bottle for 6 months to 1 year · Leave to stand 1 month in a cool place before using · Makes 1 pt/600 ml/2½ cups

2 tbsp dried or 6 tbsp fresh herbs, including tarragon, basil, chervil, thyme, chives, fennel, dill, marjoram	Place in a bottle or jar.
1 pt/600 ml/2½ cups white vinegar	Heat in a saucepan to steaming point, pour gradually onto the herbs.
1-2 cloves garlic, peeled	Add to the vinegar and herbs. Cork securely, leave for 1 month, then strain and rebottle.

Raspberry Vinegar

Fairly easy to make · Do not microwave · Do not freeze · Do not refrigerate · Serve at room temperature · Makes 1 pt/600 ml/2½ cups

8 oz/225 g/1½ cups raspberries, cleaned 1 pt/600 ml/2½ cups red wine vinegar	Combine with the raspberries in a glass bowl, cover and leave to stand for 1 week. Strain through a nylon sieve but do not apply pressure to the raspberries.
4 oz/100 g/½ cup granulated sugar	Stir into liquid and pour into an enamel or non-metallic-lined saucepan. Bring to the boil, reduce the heat and simmer for 6-7 minutes. Leave to cool, then pour into a jar or wine bottle and seal or cork. Store for 4 weeks before using.

Spiced Vinegar

Easy to prepare · Microwave · Keeps well in a screw-top jar but the metal lid must be separated from the vinegar by plastic cling film or a wax disc · Makes ¹/₂ pt/300 ml/1¹/₄ cups

¹/₂ pt/300 ml/1¹/₄ cups malt vinegar 4 cloves ¹/₂-in/1-cm piece cinnamon stick 4 whole allspice 6 peppercorns	Combine all the ingredients in an enamel or glass saucepan. Bring to the boil, remove the pan from the heat, cover with the lid and set aside for 3 hours. Strain and store in a jar or corked bottle.

Tarragon Vinegar (1)

Easy to prepare · Requires fresh leaves · No cooking required · Do not freeze · Do not refrigerate · Store in a well-corked bottle · Keep for 4 weeks before using · Makes 1 pt/600 ml/2¹/₂ cups

2 oz/50 g tarragon leaves	Rinse and dry the leaves, place on a wooden board, cover with a piece of plastic cling film and beat lightly with a rolling pin.
1 pt/600 ml/2¹/₂ cups white malt vinegar	Mix together in a jar, cover the top with plastic cling film and then screw on the lid. Store for 4-6 weeks, strain through a nylon sieve and rebottle.

Tarragon Vinegar (2)

Easy to prepare · No cooking required · Do not freeze · Do not refrigerate · Serve at room temperature · Makes 1 pt/600 ml/2¹/₂ cups

4 well-endowed stalks tarragon	Insert into a used wine bottle, cutting the stalks to reach about two-thirds up the bottle.
1 pt/600 ml/2¹/₂ cups white malt vinegar	Put into an enamel or non-metallic saucepan and bring to the boil. Using a lipped jug or funnel, pour into the wine bottle. Cork, label and store for 6 weeks before using. Do not remove the tarragon from the bottle.

Above: (left) Tarragon Vinegar (2), (centre) Spiced Vinegar and (right) Raspberry Vinegar (see page 137)

Salad Dressings

A good salad dressing should be piquant but not strong. It should refresh the palate, enhance but not mask the flavours and be a complement to the main dish. The most popular salad dressing is the simple French vinaigrette or dressing but good quality ingredients must be used. (French dressing and vinaigrette are really the same, but in America the French dressing has strongly-flavoured additives.)

Mayonnaise though not categorized as a salad dressing is nevertheless understood to be one. Other salad dressings may be made with yogurt, cream or fruit juices and, although some may be cooked initially, they are always served cold.

The prime ingredients in all salad dressings are oil and vinegar, so it is worth experimenting with all the different varieties. Olive oil, which may come from Italy, Spain, Greece or France, has a very definite flavour that depends upon the area of growth and also from which pressing it comes. The first pressing is the finest grade and has the most distinctive flavour.

Sunflower and safflower oil are high in polyunsaturates, very thin and light in colour and have little flavour of their own. So if they are used, they reduce the richness of the mayonnaise.

Peanut oil has a distinctive flavour and is light in colour. Sesame and walnut oils are expensive and they too have a flavour of their own. A little walnut oil mixed in with corn or another ground nut oil will add flavour to the salad dressing and, when added in a small proportion, will not make the dressing appreciably more expensive.

Soya oil, made from the soya bean, is becoming increasingly available and compares very favourably in price with the other vegetable oils. It is completely neutral in taste and so is suitable for use in dressings that are highly seasoned.

Sesame seed oil has its special nutty flavour and mustard seed oil naturally has overtones of mustard.

Vinegar has as much effect upon the flavour as oil and considerably influences the tartness of a dressing. Plain white vinegar may be derived from malt, rye or barley and these are rather rough on the palate. Cider vinegar is less sharp and slightly sweet, while red and white wine vinegars are only marginally different in flavour; the red usually being milder than the white. However, you may prefer a rosy glow to your dressing, in which case you would use the red. Lemon juice may always be substituted for vinegar and it is better to dilute malt vinegar with an equal quantity of water.

The proportion of oil to vinegar or lemon juice may be 2:1, 3:1 or 4:1, depending on how oily you like dressings to be. The flavour of the vinaigrette is determined mostly by the oil, but also by the vinegar so that flavoured vinegars save the trouble of adding extra herbs and spices – the herbs generally used are parsley, tarragon, chervil and chives, plus, of course, salt and pepper. About 4 tablespoons of salad dressing will coat a salad for four to six people.

Both vinaigrette and mayonnaise dressings have good keeping qualities. Mayonnaise can be kept in the refrigerator for about two weeks but it should be allowed to breathe at room temperature for two hours before use. If when you take it from the refrigerator it seems to be curdled, just add a tablespoon of boiling water and whisk thoroughly.

Always keep bottles of oil and vinegar well sealed – this is particularly important with olive oil, which otherwise will start to become rancid and will darken in colour. For successful mayonnaise, always use a sufficient volume of egg for it to be foamy before the oil is added and make sure that there is enough liquid for the oil to mix with.

When vegetables such as coleslaw and potato salad are prepared in advance, it is more usual to mix the ingredients with the salad dressing, a green salad should be tossed in the dressing just before serving.

Although there are some very good commercial salad dressings available, they tend to have a strong flavour and there is very little variation in the taste, so it is best to make your own.

Avocado Dressing

Easy to prepare · Liquidizer or blender needed · No cooking required · Do not freeze · Serve cold as a dressing with mixed salads or as a dip for fresh vegetables · Makes ½ pt/300 ml/1¼ cups

1 tbsp freshly squeezed lime juice 1 tbsp freshly squeezed lemon juice 1 thin slice onion ¼ clove garlic, peeled and crushed 1 tsp salt	Put into the liquidizer and purée briefly.
2 ripe avocados	Peel, remove the stone and cut up the flesh. Add to the ingredients in the liquidizer and purée.
1 ripe tomato	Peel, quarter, remove the seeds and add to the liquidizer.
1 bottled or blanched green chilli	Cut through the middle lengthwise and remove the seeds. Cut into six pieces and add to the liquidizer. Switch on until puréed. Pour the avocado dressing into a bowl.
Freshly ground white pepper	Season to taste.

Above: Avocado Dressing

Basic Mayonnaise

Requires care when adding the oil · Microwave – use to slightly warm the oil and vinegar · Do not freeze · Serve cold · Makes 6 fl oz/175 ml/ ³/₄ cup

1 egg yolk Pinch mustard powder Salt Pepper	Beat together with a wooden spoon or whisk until the egg yolk is fluffy.
¹/₄ pt/150 ml/²/₃ cup salad oil	Add drop by drop until the mayonnaise thickens, beating in between each addition. Add the remainder of the oil in a steady stream, beating continuously.
1-2 tbsp vinegar or lemon juice	Stir in to taste and to thin down the mayonnaise.

Banana Dressing

Easy to prepare · No cooking required · Do not freeze · Serve cold as a dressing for fruit starters · Makes ¹/₂ pt/300 ml/1¹/₄ cups

2 large bananas	Peel and thoroughly mash.
¹/₄ pt/150 ml/²/₃ cup double or heavy cream	Whip until thick.
2 tbsp clear honey 1 tbsp fresh lemon juice 2 tbsp sunflower oil Pinch salt	Blend together thoroughly, then mix with the bananas. Fold in the cream.

Beetroot Sauce

Easy to prepare · No cooking required · Liquidizer or blender needed · Do not freeze · Serve cold as a dressing for green salads · Makes ¹/₂ pt/300 ml/1¹/₄ cups

1-in/2.5-cm slice cooked peeled beetroot or beet ¹/₂ pt/300 ml/1¹/₄ cups soured cream 2 tsp fresh lemon juice Pinch salt Pinch sugar	Liquidize all the ingredients together.

Lemon and Paprika Dressing

Easy to prepare · No cooking required · Do not freeze · Keeps well in a screw-top jar · Serve cold with a sliced tomato and red pepper salad · Makes 7 fl oz/200 ml/⁷/₈ cup

1 tbsp muscavado sugar ¹/₄ tsp paprika ¹/₄ tsp salt	Stir together thoroughly.
4 tbsp fresh lemon juice 4 fl oz/120 ml/¹/₂ cup corn oil	Work in the lemon juice and then mix in the oil gradually.

Beetroot and Horseradish Sauce

Easy to prepare · No cooking required · Do not freeze · Refrigerate · Serve cold · Makes ³/₄ pt/450 ml/2 cups

¹/₂ pt/300 ml/1¹/₄ cups double or heavy cream	Beat until soft peaks form.
2-3 oz/50-75 g freshly cooked beetroot or beet	Grate coarsely.
1 tbsp creamed horseradish ¹/₄ tsp caster or superfine sugar 2 tsp vinegar	Fold into the cream, adding the beetroot.
Salt Freshly ground pepper	Add seasoning to taste.

Cream Cheese and Lemon Dressing

Easy to prepare · No cooking required · Do not freeze · Serve with diced apple and Cheddar cheese salad or green salad · Makes ¹/₄ pt/150 ml/ ²/₃ cup

2 oz/50 g/¹/₄ cup cream cheese 1 tbsp soft light brown sugar Pinch salt Pinch pepper A little garlic powder	Beat together until the sugar has dissolved.
2 tbsp fresh lemon juice	Gradually beat into the cheese mixture.
1-2 tbsp milk	Beat into the dressing to the desired consistency.

Blender Mayonnaise

Easy to prepare · Do not freeze · Makes ¹/₂ pt/300 ml/1¹/₄ cups

1 egg	Break into the blender or liquidizer.
Pinch mustard powder ¹/₄ tsp salt ¹/₄ tsp white pepper 1 tbsp white wine vinegar	Add to the egg and blend until the mixture is fluffy.
¹/₂ pt/300 ml/1¹/₄ cups salad oil	Switch on the blender to Maximum and pour in the oil in a thin but steady stream and blend until the mayonnaise thickens.

Chinese Dressing

Easy to prepare but requires fresh root ginger · No cooking required ·
Will keep in refrigerator for 2 days · Makes 8 fl oz/250 ml/1 cup

½-in/1-cm slice fresh root ginger	Chop finely, then press the juice through a strainer.
1 tbsp fresh lemon juice *2 tbsp soy sauce* *1 tsp dry sherry* *6 fl oz/175 ml/¾ cup mayonnaise*	Blend with the ginger juice.
Salt *Pepper*	Add seasoning if required.

Convenient Sharp Green Sauce

Easy to prepare using store cupboard ingredients · No cooking required · Do not freeze · Leave to stand 1 hour before using · Serve cold · Makes ¼ pt/150 ml/⅔ cup

1 tbsp dried parsley *½ tsp dried tarragon* *4 cocktail gherkins, chopped* *1 tbsp chopped capers* *5 tbsp bottled mayonnaise*	Stir thoroughly in a salad bowl, cover and leave to stand at room temperature until required.

Cooked Mayonnaise

Fairly easy to cook · Microwave – reduce the setting to Defrost when adding the egg · Do not freeze · Serve cold with white fish, poultry or hard-boiled eggs · Makes ½ pt/300 ml/1¼ cups

1 tbsp flour *1 tbsp caster or superfine sugar* *1 tsp salt* *1 tsp mustard powder*	Blend together in a small saucepan.
3 tbsp lemon juice *5 tbsp cold water*	Stir into the mixture in the saucepan and cook over gentle heat for 5 minutes, stirring constantly.
½ oz/15 g/1 tbsp butter	Stir into the mixture.
1 egg	Beat with 2 tablespoons of the hot liquid. Pour back into the saucepan and beat thoroughly. Immediately remove the pan from the heat. Leave until cold.
4-6 tbsp single or light cream	Stir into the sauce.

Aïoli (Liquidizer or blender)

Easy to prepare · No cooking required · Do not freeze · Serve cold · Makes 12 fl oz/350 ml/1¾ cups

4 cloves garlic, peeled *1 whole egg* *1 egg yolk, strained* *¼ tsp salt*	Place in liquidizer and blend at high speed until thick.
½ pt/300 ml/1¼ cups vegetable oil	Put into a jug. Switch on the liquidizer or blender and pour in the oil through the feed tube drop by drop until the mixture is thick, then add in a steady stream until all the oil is thoroughly blended. Switch off.
1 tsp hot water *2 tsp fresh lemon juice*	Add to the sauce while the motor is running at high speed.
Salt *Pepper*	Season to taste.

Cheddar and Yogurt Dressing

Easy to prepare · No cooking required · Do not freeze · Refrigerate · Makes ½ pt/300 ml/1¼ cups

½ pt/300 ml/1¼ cups natural yogurt *1½ oz/40 g/6 tbsp finely grated stale Cheddar cheese* *2 tsp tomato purée* *¼ tsp salt* *Pinch cayenne pepper*	Mix thoroughly together. Serve chilled.

Lemon Processor Mayonnaise

Easy to prepare · No cooking required · Ingredients for mayonnaise must be at the same temperature. The processor causes a rise in the temperature of the eggs so the oil must be warmed slightly. Put the oil in a jug standing in a pan of very hot water or briefly in a microwave oven · Do not freeze · Store for a few days only in the refrigerator, leave at room temperature for 1 hour before use and stir just before serving · Serve cold · Makes 1 pt/600 ml/2½ cups

2 large eggs *1 tbsp French mustard* *Pinch sugar* *Salt* *Pepper*	Switch on the food processor and add the eggs and other ingredients while the motor is running.
¾ pt/450 ml/2 cups salad oil	Switch the processor to Maximum and pour the oil slowly through the feed tube directing the oil onto the blades and process until the mayonnaise thickens slightly.
2 tbsp fresh lemon juice	Add to the processor bowl a teaspoon at a time, blending briefly between each addition. Taste and add additional salt and pepper if required.

Note: This is a thin mayonnaise.

Apple, Celery and Sunflower Relish (Liquidizer or food processor)

Easy to prepare · No cooking required · Serve cold · Makes ³/4 pt/450 ml/ 2 cups

2 large green dessert apples	Wash, dry and quarter but do not peel. Remove cores. Place in liquidizer or processor bowl.
1 stick celery, roughly cut into slices ¹/2 small onion 3 tbsp clear honey 3 tbsp cider vinegar	Add to the liquidizer or processor and blend until smooth. Turn into a bowl.
Salt Pepper	Season to taste.
2 oz/50 g/¹/2 cup sunflower seeds	Fold into the mixture. Keep covered until required or pot and seal.

Mayonnaise Nantua

Requires some care · No cooking required · Do not freeze · Refrigerate – 24 hours only · Serve cold · Makes ³/4 pt/450 ml/2 cups

4 oz/100 g cooked prawns (shrimp) in their shells	Remove the shells and set the peeled prawns aside.
¹/2 pt/300 ml/1¹/4 cups olive oil 1 tsp paprika	Mix in the blender with the prawn shells and process until the shells are pulverised. Set aside for 30 minutes. Strain through a nylon sieve into a jug.
3 egg yolks ¹/4 tsp salt ¹/4 tsp ground white pepper	Beat together in a bowl, then beat in the strained oil drop by drop until the mixture thickens. Add the rest of the oil in a steady stream still beating vigorously.
1 tbsp white wine vinegar	Stir into the mayonnaise. Chop the shelled prawns finely and stir into the mayonnaise. Taste and adjust the seasoning.

Above: (top) Carolina Relish *(see page 32), (centre)* Home-made Tomato Ketchup *(see page 150) and (bottom)* Apple, Celery and Sunflower Relish

Above: (top) Mayonnaise Nantua, *(centre)* Sauce Vincent and *(bottom)* Aioli *(see page 141)*

Sauce Vincent

Easy to make but requires fresh herbs · Microwave · Do not freeze · Keeps 1 week in the refrigerator · Serve cold · Makes ¹/₂ pt/300 ml/1¹/₄ cups

2 eggs	Hard-boil, separate the yolks from the whites. Sieve the yolks and chop the whites finely.
¹/₂ oz/15 g spinach leaves ¹/₂ oz/15 g watercress leaves ¹/₄ oz/7 g sprigs parsley ¹/₄ oz/7 g chervil leaves ¹/₄ oz/7 g tarragon leaves 6 chives, chopped ¹/₄ oz/7 g sorrel leaves, coarsely shredded	Put into a saucepan, just cover with cold water, bring to the boil, then, without covering, simmer for 2 minutes. Pour into a strainer and cool under cold running water. Drain thoroughly. Chop finely, then press through a sieve.
¹/₄ pt/150 ml/²/₃ cup thick mayonnaise 1 tsp Worcestershire sauce	Combine with the herbs and eggs.

Bagna Calda

Fairly easy to cook · Do not microwave · Do not freeze · Serve warm · English translation – Hot Bath. An anchovy sauce to serve as a light dip for bite-size pieces of raw cauliflower, cabbage, celery, endive, sweet peppers, etc · Makes ¹/₂ pt/300 ml/1¹/₄ cups

¹/₂ pt/300 ml/1¹/₄ cups first grade olive oil 1¹/₂ oz/40 g/3 tbsp unsalted butter	Place in small heavy-based saucepan and heat gently until the butter is melted.
3 large cloves garlic, peeled 8 anchovy fillets	In a small bowl, pound together to a smooth paste. Add to oil in pan and cook over gentle heat for 6 minutes or until the sauce is golden. Remove from the heat, place the saucepan in a roasting dish of boiling water to keep warm for serving. Do not overheat or overcook the sauce or the anchovy fillets will become dark and begin to burn.

Above: Bagna Calda

Cucumber-flavoured Piquant Salad Dressing

Easy to cook · Do not microwave · Do not freeze · Refrigerate · Serve cold · Makes ½ pt/300 ml/1¼ cups

½ cucumber	Peel, halve lengthwise, remove the seeds and slice the flesh thinly. Set aside.
5 tbsp caster or superfine sugar 3 tbsp white wine vinegar 2 tbsp soy sauce ½ tsp salt	Place in a heavy-based saucepan over the lowest possible heat and stir until the sugar is dissolved. Add the cucumber, remove from the heat, cool and leave to refrigerate for 1 hour.
6 fl oz/175 ml/¾ cup water 1 tbsp cornflour (cornstarch)	Blend together in a small saucepan. Strain the cucumber liquid into the pan. Bring to the boil slowly, stirring continuously, to thicken the sauce. Remove the pan from the heat.
2 tbsp medium sherry	Stir into the sauce. Chill.
	Note: The reserved cucumber can be used in salads with other ingredients.

Pumpkin Seed Dressing

Easy to prepare using a liquidizer or blender · No cooking required · Store in a screw-top jar or corked bottle · Makes 7 fl oz/200 ml/⅞ cup

1 egg white Pinch salt Pinch sugar Pinch mustard powder Pinch pepper	Place in the liquidizer and blend until the mixture is frothy.
1 tbsp pumpkin seeds	Add through the feed tube while the motor is running.
7 tbsp sunflower oil	Add a teaspoonful at a time to the liquidizer while the motor is running until 3 tablespoons have been used.
1 tbsp white wine vinegar 1 tbsp fresh lemon juice	Mix together and add alternate teaspoons and the remaining oil to the liquidizer while the motor is still running. Season with additional salt and pepper, if required, and store in a screw-top jar or corked bottle. Shake before use.

Quick Horseradish Dressing

Easy to prepare · Do not freeze · Serve cold · Particularly good with chicory or endive salad · Makes 6 fl oz/175 ml/¾ cup

3 tbsp creamed horseradish ¼ pt/150 ml/⅔ cup soured cream	Mix thoroughly together.
Salt Pepper	Season to taste.

Celery Seed Dressing

Easy to prepare · No cooking required · Do not freeze · Serve as a dressing for fruit cocktail starters · Makes 7 fl oz/200 ml/⅞ cup

½ tsp mustard powder ½ tsp salt ½ tsp paprika Pinch freshly ground black pepper 1 slice onion, finely chopped 2 oz/50 g/¼ cup caster or superfine sugar 2 tbsp red wine vinegar	Combine together in a bowl.
4 fl oz/120 ml/½ cup sunflower oil	Add to the vinegar mixture a teaspoon at a time, beating in between each addition.
2 tsp celery seeds	Stir into the sauce.
1-2 drops red food colouring (optional)	Stir in to deepen the colour, if you wish.

Glow Dressing

Easy to prepare · No cooking required · Do not freeze · Serve cold · Makes 12 fl oz/350 ml/1½ cups

¼ pt/150 ml/⅔ cup thick mayonnaise 3 tbsp double or heavy cream 1 tbsp fresh lemon juice 1 tsp tomato ketchup ¼ tsp paprika Pinch chilli powder 1 tsp chopped chives 1 small shallot, peeled and finely chopped 1 oz/25g cooked ham, finely chopped	Stir all the ingredients together until well blended.
Salt Freshly ground black pepper	Add seasoning to taste.

Green Yogurt Dressing

Easy to prepare · No cooking required · Do not freeze · Refrigerate – for 2-3 days only · Serve cold · Makes 6 fl oz/175 ml/¾ cup

¼ pt/150 ml/⅔ cup natural yogurt ½ tsp lime juice cordial ½ tsp fresh lemon juice 1 tsp finely chopped fresh mint	Beat together thoroughly.
Green food colouring	Add a drop at a time to achieve a cool pale green.

Honey, Orange and Lemon Dressing

Easy to prepare · No cooking required · Do not freeze · Serve cold as a dressing for fruit salad starters or grated beetroot salad · Makes ¹/₂ pt/ 300 ml/1¹/₄ cups

5 tbsp fresh lemon juice *¹/₄ pt/150 ml/²/₃ cup sunflower oil* *Juice and grated rind of 1 medium orange* *¹/₂ tsp salt* *Pinch mustard powder* *Pinch freshly ground black pepper*	Mix all the ingredients together thoroughly in a bowl.
2 tbsp clear honey	Stir into the orange mixture until dissolved. Pour into a screw-top jar or corked bottle and shake thoroughly before using.

Honey and Yogurt Dressing

Very easy to prepare · No cooking required · Prepare freshly · Serve with sliced banana salad · Makes ¹/₄ pt/150 ml/²/₃ cup

¹/₄ pt/150 ml/²/₃ cup natural yogurt *1 tbsp clear honey* *¹/₂ tsp fresh lemon juice* *1 tsp grated lemon rind*	Combine all the ingredients together, stirring until the honey is dissolved.

Horseradish Sauce

Fairly easy to prepare · No cooking required · Do not freeze · Serve cold · Makes 1 pt/600 ml/2¹/₂ cups

¹/₄ pt/150 ml/²/₃ cup evaporated milk	Chill for 1 hour, then whip until thick and mousse-like.
2 oz/50 g piece horseradish	Peel and finely grate. Stir into the milk.
1 tbsp white vinegar *Pinch cayenne pepper* *Pinch sugar*	Stir into the sauce.
Salt *Pepper*	Add seasoning to taste.

Watercress Yogurt Dressing

Easy to prepare · No cooking required · Keeps in refrigerator for a few days · Makes ¹/₄ pt/150 ml/²/₃ cup

¹/₄ pt/150 ml/²/₃ cup natural yogurt *1 tsp lemon juice* *1 tsp clear honey* *1 tsp olive oil*	Combine together in a bowl.
6 sprigs watercress	Remove the stalks, chop the leaves and stir into the dressing.

Larnaca Vinaigrette

Easy to prepare · No cooking required · Can be stored in a corked bottle for a few months · Remember to stir before serving · Makes ¹/₂ pt/300 ml/ 1¹/₄ cups

4 cloves garlic, peeled and crushed *¹/₄ pt/150 ml/²/₃ cup first grade olive oil* *1 tsp mustard powder* *Juice of 2 fresh lemons* *2 tsp grated lemon rind* *2 tbsp fresh chopped parsley* *Salt* *Freshly ground black pepper*	Beat all the ingredients together or combine in a screw-top jar and shake thoroughly. Season to taste with salt and pepper.

Lemon Vinaigrette

Very easy to prepare · No cooking required · The quantity may be increased · About ¹/₂ lemon should be sufficient · Do not freeze · Keeps well in a small screw-top jar · Makes about 5 tablespoons

2 tbsp fresh lemon juice *2 tbsp corn oil* *¹/₂ tsp salt* *¹/₂ tsp pepper* *¹/₂ tsp sugar* *¹/₂ tsp made English mustard*	Combine all the ingredients together in a screw-top jar and shake thoroughly before use.

Quick Salad Dressing

Easy to prepare · Microwave – reduce to lowest setting when boils, then stir every 15 seconds. Freeze – thaw at room temperature or in the microwave oven set on Low · Mix warm, eat cold · Makes 12 fl oz/ 350 ml/1¹/₂ cups

1 oz/25 g/2 tbsp butter or margarine	Melt in a saucepan over minimum heat.
1 oz/25 g/¹/₄ cup flour	Stir into the melted butter. Cook for 1 minute, stirring continuously.
¹/₄ pt/150 ml/²/₃ cup milk *¹/₄ pt/150 ml/²/₃ cup water*	Gradually mix into the flour and butter paste, raise the heat and bring to the boil, stirring continuously.
¹/₂ tsp dried basil *Salt* *Pepper*	Stir into the sauce, seasoning to taste. Remove the pan from the heat.
1 egg yolk *2 tbsp fresh lemon juice*	Beat together in a small bowl, add 2 tablespoons of the hot sauce, then pour into the sauce. Return the pan to the heat, whisking continuously until hot. The sauce must not boil. Leave to cool before using as a dressing.

Carrot and Peanut Dressing

Fairly easy to prepare · Liquidizer or blender needed · No cooking required · Serve with green salad or cold roast meats · Makes 6 fl oz/ 175 ml/³⁄₄ cup

1 tbsp roasted unsalted peanuts	Put into a small saucepan over medium heat and shake the pan vigorously for 1 minute to loosen the skins. Rub the skins away between sheets of kitchen paper towel.
1 small carrot, scraped and sliced 1 tbsp fresh lemon juice 2 tbsp salad oil 1 tsp soy sauce	Place in the liquidizer with the peanuts and blend at full speed.
5 tbsp natural yogurt	Pour into the liquidizer with the other ingredients and process until well mixed.
Salt Pepper	Season to taste.

Cottage Cheese and Chive Dressing

Easy to prepare · Can be made in a liquidizer or blender · No cooking required · Do not freeze · Refrigerate · Serve with baked potatoes or Jerusalem artichokes · Makes 6 fl oz/175 ml/³⁄₄ cup

4 oz/100 g/¹⁄₂ cup cottage cheese	Press through a sieve into a large bowl.
4 tbsp top of the milk 1 tbsp salad oil ¹⁄₂ tsp French mustard 1 tbsp fresh lemon juice 1 tsp white wine vinegar 2 tbsp fresh chopped chives	Add and beat thoroughly.
Salt Pepper	Season to taste. Use immediately or cover and refrigerate for a few hours until required. Stir before serving.

Blue Cheese Dressing

Easy to prepare · No cooking required · Do not freeze · Serve cold as a dressing for green salads or cold fish salads · Makes ¹⁄₄ pt/150 ml/²⁄₃ cup

2 oz/50 g/¹⁄₂ cup Danish Blue cheese	Beat carefully with a fork until creamy.
3 tbsp mayonnaise	Work in gradually to a smooth consistency.

Above left: (top) Carrot and Peanut Dressing *and (bottom)* Celery Seed Dressing *(see page 144)*

Above right: Cottage Cheese and Chive Dressing on baked jacket potato

Opposite: Blue Cheese Dressing on mixed green salad

French Dressing (1)

Easy to prepare · No cooking required · Store in a screw-top jar and shake before using · Makes 1 pt/600 ml/2½ cups

¼ pt/150 ml/²⁄₃ cup white malt vinegar ¾ pt/450 ml/2 cups corn oil 2 tsp caster or superfine sugar 2 tsp salt ¼ tsp freshly ground black pepper 2 tsp French mustard	Combine all the ingredients in a screw-top jar or well-corked bottle and shake vigorously.

Thousand Island Dressing

Easy to prepare · No cooking required · Best eaten within 24 hours of preparation · Serve cold · Makes 1 pt/600 ml/2½ cups

½ pt/300 ml/1¼ cups mayonnaise 3 tbsp bottled chilli sauce	Stir together until well blended.
1 hard-boiled egg, shelled and finely chopped ¼ green pepper, finely diced ½ stick celery finely sliced ½ bottled pimiento, finely chopped 2 tbsp fresh chopped chives	Stir into the chilli mayonnaise.
Salt Pepper	Add seasoning to taste.

Curd Cheese and Yogurt Dressing

Easy to prepare · No cooking required · Do not freeze · Serve cold as a dressing for green salads · Makes ¼ pt/150 ml/²⁄₃ cup

4 oz/100 g/½ cup curd cheese 1 tbsp corn oil 1 tbsp fresh lemon juice	Beat together until smooth.
6 tbsp natural yogurt	Mix into the cheese.
Salt Pepper	Season to taste.

Tomato Ketchup Dressing

Very easy to prepare · No cooking required · Keeps for 2 weeks in a screw-top jar · Makes ¼ pt/150 ml/²⁄₃ cup

1 medium tomato	Skin and chop.
4 tbsp tomato ketchup ¼ tsp Worcestershire sauce Juice of 1 fresh lemon 4 tbsp light salad oil ½ tsp dried basil	Add to the chopped tomato, stirring to blend.

Salsa Verde

Easy to prepare using food processor, but can be prepared by hand · No cooking required · Refrigerate – will keep for a few days but allow to stand for 1 hour at room temperature and stir before serving · Makes ¼ pt/150 ml/²⁄₃ cup

1 oz/25 g/½ cup sprigs parsley	Chop in the food processor using the double-bladed knife.
1 slice wholemeal bread, crusts removed	Break into pieces, place in the processor bowl, then blend with the parsley to fine crumbs.
1 tbsp capers 1 clove garlic, peeled and sliced 1 anchovy fillet	Add to the processor bowl and blend.
4 tbsp olive oil	Switch on the machine and pour the oil gradually through the feed tube until it is all incorporated.
1-1½ tbsp fresh lemon juice ¼ tsp freshly ground black pepper	Add to the bowl and process briefly.

Russian Dressing

Easy to prepare · No cooking required · Do not freeze · Refrigerate · Makes ¾ pt/450 ml/2 cups

1 bottled green chilli ½ green pepper 1 stick celery 1 slice cooked beetroot or beet	Mince or finely chop.
1 tbsp bottled chilli sauce	Stir into the mixture.
½ pt/300 ml/1¼ cups mayonnaise	Fold into the chopped vegetables.
Salt Freshly ground black pepper	Add seasoning to taste. Chill before serving.

Swedish Dressing

Easy to prepare · Microwave · Keep in a corked bottle · Suitable for dieters as no oil in the recipe · Makes 3 fl oz/90 ml/³/₈ cup

¼ pt/150 ml/²/₃ cup water	Place in a small saucepan.
1 tbsp caraway seeds	Stir into the water, then bring to the boil over moderate heat. Reduce the heat and simmer until the liquid is reduced by half.
1 tsp salt 1 tbsp malt vinegar 1 tsp caster or superfine sugar	Stir into the hot liquid until the sugar has dissolved. Cool before using.

Tarragon Mousseline Dressing

Easy to prepare · No cooking required · Do not freeze · Refrigerate · Makes ¼ pt/150 ml/²/₃ cup

5 tbsp double or heavy cream	Whip to soft peaks.
1 tbsp tarragon vinegar 1 tsp fresh lemon juice Pinch cayenne pepper ¼ tsp salt Pinch sugar	Fold into the cream.
1 egg white	Beat with grease-free beaters until soft peaks form. Fold the beaten egg white into the creamy mixture and serve as soon as possible to maintain the lightest texture.

Onion and Gherkin Vinaigrette

Easy to prepare · No cooking required · Can be stored in a screw-top bottle or jar for a few months · Stir before serving · Makes ¼ pt/150 ml/²/₃ cup

4 sprigs fresh parsley 1 cocktail gherkin 1 slice onion	Chop finely.
4 tbsp salad oil 2 tbsp white wine vinegar	Stir into the chopped vegetables.
Salt Freshly ground black pepper	Season to taste and stir thoroughly.

Pineapple Mayonnaise

Easy to prepare · No cooking required but must be allowed to infuse for minimum of 2 hours · Do not freeze · Refrigerate · Serve cold · Makes 1 pt/600 ml/2½ cups

1 x 8½ oz/234 g can pineapple chunks in syrup 1 tbsp white wine vinegar ½ tsp dried fennel leaves	Combine together in a glass bowl, cover tightly and set aside for 2 hours. Strain, discarding the liquid.
2 tbsp sweet chutney	Stir into the pineapple pieces.
½ pt/300 ml/1¼ cups mayonnaise	Blend into the pineapple mixture.
Salt Pepper	Season to taste.

Rémoulade

Easy to prepare · No cooking required · Do not freeze · Serve cold · Makes ¾ pt/450 ml/2 cups

½ pt/300 ml/1¼ cups thick mayonnaise 1 tbsp French mustard 2 tbsp double or heavy cream ¼ tsp anchovy essence	Stir together until well blended.
1 tbsp finely chopped gherkins 1 tsp fresh chopped parsley 1 tsp chopped chives 1 tsp chopped chervil leaves	Fold into the sauce.

French Dressing (2)

Easy to prepare · No cooking required · Do not freeze · No need to refrigerate · Store in a screw-top jar or well-corked bottle and shake vigorously before using · Keeps well for several months · Makes ¼ pt/150 ml/²/₃ cup

6 tbsp olive oil 1 tbsp white wine vinegar 2 tbsp fresh lemon juice ¼ tsp mustard powder ½ tsp salt Pinch pepper	Beat all the ingredients thoroughly together and mix well before using.

Home-made Ingredients

Coral Butter

Easy to prepare · No cooking required · Freeze · Serve cold · Makes 1 oz/ 25 g/2 tbsp

½ oz/15 g/1 tbsp cooked lobster coral	Place in a small bowl and mash.
1 oz/25 g/2 tbsp butter	Leave to stand at room temperature, then add little by little to the lobster coral, beating thoroughly. Press through a small sieve or clean tea strainer.
Salt White pepper	Add seasoning to taste.

Crème Fraîche (2)

Easy to prepare · No cooking required but a warm atmosphere necessary · Do not freeze · Refrigerate – keeps up to 1 week · Use as required to enrich sauces or as a cream topping for desserts or savouries · Makes ½ pt/300 ml/1¼ cups

½ pt/300 ml/1¼ cups double or heavy cream 1 tbsp buttermilk	Combine in a screw-top jar and shake vigorously for 2 minutes. Stand the jar in a bowl of hot water for 5 minutes, then remove from the water. Dry the outside of the jar and shake it for 2 minutes. Leave to stand at room temperature for 24 hours until thick. Use as required.

Coconut Milk

Easy to make · Use freshly grated or desiccated coconut · Microwave · Prepare as needed · Makes ½ pt/300 ml/1¼ cups

6 oz/175 g/1¾ cups shredded fresh or desiccated coconut ½ pt/300 ml/1¼ cups water	Mix together in a saucepan and bring to the boil. Remove the pan from the heat, cover and leave to infuse for 30 minutes. Strain into a jug or bowl through a clean kitchen cloth, twisting the top and squeezing until all the milk comes through and the coconut is left in the cloth. Use as required. **Note:** The coconut need not be thrown away. It can be dried and browned either in the microwave oven or on a baking tray under a medium grill. Stir frequently during drying.

Demi-glace (Simple)

Easy to cook · Do not microwave · Freeze · Use hot to enrich a brown sauce · Makes ½ pt/300 ml/1¼ cups

½ oz/15 g/1 tbsp butter	Heat in a heavy-based saucepan.
3 shallots, peeled and finely chopped 1 rasher bacon, diced	Fry gently in the melted butter until golden brown.
1 carrot, peeled and grated	Stir into bacon mixture and fry for 2 minutes until the carrot changes colour.
1 tbsp flour	Mix into fried ingredients, cook gently, stirring continuously, until the flour changes colour. Remove the pan from the heat.
2 tsp tomato purée 1 mushroom, finely chopped ¾ pt/450 ml/2 cups beef stock Salt Freshly ground black pepper 2 sprigs parsley 1 small bay leaf	Gradually stir into mixture in the pan. Bring to the boil, then lower the heat and simmer for 15 minutes, stirring frequently. Taste and adjust the seasoning. Strain and discard pulp.

Home-made Tomato Ketchup

Easy to prepare · Keeps well, so can be made up in large quantities and stored in screw-top jars or corked bottles · Serve with cold meats or fried fish, or use in other recipes · Makes 1 pt/600 ml/2½ cups

4 lb/2 kg ripe tomatoes 3 medium onions, peeled and thinly sliced 1 large red pepper, cored, seeded and finely sliced 1 clove garlic, peeled and crushed	Cut up the tomatoes and put with the other ingredients in a large heavy-based saucepan. Just cover with cold water, bring to the boil over moderate heat, then reduce the heat. Place the lid on the pan and simmer until the vegetables are soft. Stir occasionally during cooking to prevent burning. Liquidize the mixture in batches and strain into another large saucepan.
8 fl oz/250 ml/1 cup red wine vinegar 4 oz/100 g/½ cup dark soft brown sugar 1 tsp salt ½ tsp freshly ground black pepper	Stir into the vegetable purée.
½ cinnamon stick 3 bay leaves 1 tsp celery seeds 2 tsp mustard seeds 1 small dried red pepper	Add to the mixture, then bring to the boil and simmer, stirring continuously, until the mixture is thick. Strain through a nylon sieve to remove the seeds, pepper and bay leaves. Leave to cool, then pot or bottle and use as required.

Liquid Caramel

Fairly easy to cook but take care not to burn · Do not microwave · Store in a screw-top jar or bottle · Keeps for up to 6 months · Use to add flavour and colour to gravies and sauces · Makes ¼ pt/150 ml/⅔ cup

4 oz/100 g/½ cup granulated sugar	Place in a deep heavy-based saucepan.
4 tbsp water	Stir into the sugar and bring to the boil without stirring but gently shaking the pan occasionally. Continue boiling until a thick deep brown syrup is formed. Move the pan away from the heat. Switch off the heat.
2 tbsp warm water	Taking great care, pour into the saucepan and shake the pan until the water is incorporated. (This prevents the caramel from blackening and burning.) Return the pan to the heat until the syrup comes back to the boil. Remove from the heat.
½ tsp glycerine or salad oil	Stir in, then leave to cool. Store in a screw-top jar or bottle. Shake before use.

Redcurrant Jelly

Time-consuming to make but useful if bottled jelly is difficult to obtain · Microwave · Store in a screw-top jar · Makes 8 oz/225 g/1 cup

1 lb/450 g/4 cups redcurrants	Pick over – some stems may be left on. Wash and drain. Put into a large pan and crush with a potato masher.
¼ pt/150 ml/⅔ cup water	Add to pan and simmer until the colour drains from the redcurrants. Strain through muslin or a jelly bag (takes overnight). Measure juice.
Sugar	Stir in 8 oz/225 g/1 cup to each ½ pt/300 ml/ 1¼ cups juice. Stir until sugar is dissolved, then boil rapidly until setting point is reached and a few drops set when dropped onto a cold plate.

Sautéed Onion Purée

Easy to cook · Use food processor · Microwave · Freeze · Makes 8 oz/ 225 g/1 cup

8 oz/225 g onions, peeled and chopped 2 oz/50 g/¼ cup butter	Place in a heavy-based saucepan and cook over moderate heat, stirring continuously, until the onions are golden brown. Purée in the food processor or blender.
Salt Pepper	Add seasoning to taste. Pot in a small jar, cover and seal. Use as required in any recipe requiring sautéed onions.

Tomato Coulis

Easy to prepare · Use less garlic if preferred · Do not microwave · Freeze · Use as filling for pancakes or to add flavour to other dishes · Makes 8 fl oz/250 ml/1 cup

12 oz/350 g ripe tomatoes, coarsely chopped 1 tsp thyme leaves 1 tsp tarragon leaves 10 chives 2 cloves garlic, sliced	Combine in a heavy-based saucepan, bring to the boil, then reduce the heat to minimum and cook until the mixture pulps. Press through a sieve. Return the purée to the pan.
4 tbsp vegetable oil	Stir into the puréed tomato and serve hot or cold. **Note:** This may be stored in covered jars in the refrigerator for a few days.

Tomato Purée

Easy to prepare · Microwave · Freeze · Refrigerate – keeps only a few days · Use as a base for other sauces · Makes ½ pt/300 ml/1¼ cups

1 lb/450 g ripe tomatoes	Cut up and purée in a liquidizer or food processor. Press through a sieve into a saucepan.
¼ pt/150 ml/⅔ cup water 4 basil leaves ¼ tsp salt ¼ tsp freshly ground black pepper	Add to the tomato purée and bring to the boil. Reduce the heat to minimum, half cover the saucepan with a lid and cook until the purée is thick. Stir frequently during cooking to prevent sticking.

Combination Dishes

Boeuf Bourguignon

Easy to prepare but cooking time 3-4 hours · Do not microwave · Freeze · Serves 4

4 oz/100 g bacon	Remove the rind and cut the bacon into thin strips. Place half the strips in an ovenproof casserole.
8 oz/225 g carrots, scraped and sliced 1 large onion, peeled and finely sliced 1 clove garlic, peeled and crushed	Arrange half of the vegetables on top of the bacon.
1 lb/450 g topside or lean round of beef, thinly sliced	Arrange on the bed of vegetables.
Salt Freshly ground black pepper	Season to taste with salt and pepper. Cover the meat with the remaining vegetables.
1/2 pt/300 ml/1 1/4 cups red Burgundy wine 1/2 pt/300 ml/1 1/4 cups hot beef stock	Pour into the casserole and cover the meat with the remaining bacon. Cover with the lid and cook in a slow oven, 300°F/150°C/Gas Mark 2, for 3-4 hours or until the meat is tender. Add additional seasoning if required.

Shrimp and Tomato Cocktail Sauce

Fairly easy to prepare · No cooking required · Do not freeze · Refrigerate · Serve cold · Makes 3/4 pt/450 ml/2 cups

4 tbsp double or heavy cream	Whip until fairly stiff.
2 tomatoes, skinned, seeded and finely chopped 6 tbsp tomato purée 1/2 tsp fresh lemon juice 1/2 tsp Worcestershire sauce	Stir into the cream.
8 oz/225 g/1 cup peeled shrimps	Chop finely and fold into the cream mixture.
Salt Freshly ground white pepper	Season to taste.

Boeuf en Daube

Fairly easy to cook · Take care when browning the flour · Do not microwave · Freeze · Serves 4

1 oz/25 g/1/4 cup plain or all-purpose flour	Put into a deep heavy-based frying pan and cook, stirring continuously, over minimum heat until the flour is a nut-brown colour. Remove the pan from the heat and tip the browned flour onto a plate.
1 oz/25 g/2 tbsp butter or margarine	Place in the frying pan, replace the frying pan on the heat.
1 1/2 lb/750 g well-trimmed chuck steak	Cut into eight large pieces, add to the sizzling butter and fry briskly, turning the pieces until the juices are sealed in and the meat is a golden colour. Transfer the meat to a casserole.
Salt Freshly ground black pepper	Season the meat to taste.
2 rashers streaky bacon, rinds removed and finely chopped 1 medium onion, peeled and finely chopped 1 stick celery, scraped and finely sliced	Add to the frying pan and cook, stirring continuously, until the onion is soft. Stir in the browned flour and cook for 1 minute.
1/4 pt/150 ml/2/3 cup hot water 1/4 pt/150 ml/2/3 cup medium red wine	Stir into the vegetable mixture, then bring to the boil over moderate heat, stirring continuously until the sauce thickens.
1 large carrot, scraped and finely sliced 1 leek, trimmed, washed and finely sliced 1 Bouquet garni 6 pitted black olives, sliced 1/2 tsp sugar 1/4 tsp ground cloves 1/4 tsp bay leaf powder	Stir into the sauce, pour over the meat, cover the casserole with the lid and bake in a very moderate oven, 325°F/160°C/Gas Mark 3, for 2-2 1/2 hours until the meat is tender. If the sauce is too thin, blend 1 tablespoon of cornflour (cornstarch) with 2 tablespoons of water. Add 3 or 4 tablespoons of the sauce, combine in a small saucepan and bring to the boil, stirring continuously until very thick. Stir into the meat mixture.
2 tbsp fresh chopped parsley	Sprinkle over the meat just before serving.

Osso Buco

*Easy to prepare provided the butcher agrees to cut up the meat ·
Traditionally uses knuckle of veal but stewing veal may be
substituted · Can be adapted for microwave – the veal will be less
tender · Freeze · Serves 4*

1 oz/25 g/2 tbsp butter or margarine	Place in a large heavy-based saucepan or heatproof casserole and melt over moderate heat.
2 onions, peeled and finely chopped 2 carrots, scraped and finely chopped 2 sticks celery, finely sliced 1 leek, washed, trimmed and finely sliced	Add to the melted butter and sauté for 5 minutes, stirring frequently, until the vegetables are tender but not brown.
2 bay leaves 1 tsp thyme leaves 2 tbsp fresh chopped parsley	Stir into the vegetable mixture.
Salt Pepper	Season to taste.
2 lb/1 kg shin of veal, cut through the bone into 1-in/2.5-cm slices 1 oz/25 g/¼ cup flour	Dip the meat in the flour, then place the meat over the vegetables in the pan.
4 strips lemon peel 1 tbsp fresh lemon juice 3 tbsp tomato purée ¼ pt/150 ml/²/₃ cup dry Italian white wine ¾ pt/450 ml/2 cups hot veal stock	Stir into the meat and vegetable mixture and bring to the boil. Reduce to simmering point and cook in the covered pan for 1 hour. Reduce the heat to minimum and continue cooking for a further 1-1½ hours until the meat is tender and is bathed in a thick sauce. If the sauce is too thin, blend the remaining flour left over after coating the meat with 1 tablespoon of cold water, stir into the mixture, then raise the heat to boiling point and stir frequently until the sauce thickens. Remove the bay leaf and the lemon strips, and adjust seasoning if necessary.

Huitres Sauce Parfumée

*Easy to cook but requires care · Do not microwave · Do not freeze · Serve
hot · Serves 2*

12 fresh oysters	Open the oysters over a fine sieve over a bowl. Set oysters aside. Put the liquor into a small saucepan.
Pinch ground mace Strip lemon peel	Stir into oyster liquid, bring to the boil, then reduce the heat and cook for 5 minutes.
½ oz/15 g/1 tbsp butter 1 tsp plain or all-purpose flour	Stir together in a small bowl until a smooth paste is formed. Beat into the liquor in teaspoonfuls and remove from the heat as soon as the sauce thickens.
Pepper	Season to taste. Grill or broil oysters lightly, then mix with the sauce.

Coq au Vin

*Easy to cook but requires attention · Do not microwave · Do not
freeze · Serves 4*

½ oz/15 g/1 tbsp butter 1 tbsp olive oil	Heat in a heavy-based pan over gentle heat.
4 oz/100 g unsmoked bacon, rind removed and diced	Add to saucepan and fry gently for 4 minutes or until the bacon is golden.
6 oz/175 g button mushrooms 12 tiny onions, peeled	Add to pan and fry for 3 minutes until the onions are brown. Remove the bacon, mushrooms and onions from the pan with a slotted spoon.
3-3½ lb/1.5 kg oven-ready chicken, cut into 8 pieces 3 tbsp flour	Dip the chicken pieces in the flour, then fry in the fat remaining in the pan for 8-10 minutes until the chicken is golden brown. Transfer the chicken pieces to an ovenproof casserole and add the cooked onions, mushrooms and bacon.
¾ pt/450 ml/2 cups full-bodied red wine ¼ pt/150 ml/²/₃ cup chicken stock 2 tsp sugar 1 clove garlic, crushed 2 sprigs parsley 1 sprig thyme 2 bay leaves Salt Freshly ground black pepper	Gradually stir into the juices left in the saucepan, bring to the boil, stirring continuously, until the sauce thickens. Pour into the casserole and mix gently. Cover the casserole tightly and bake at 325°F/160°C/ Gas Mark 3 for 30-40 minutes until the chicken is tender. Remove the casserole from the oven and take off the lid.
4 tbsp brandy	Pour into metal soup ladle and warm gently well above the flames or heat. Pour into the casserole and using a lighted taper ignite the sauce. Allow flames to die down, then serve at once.

Fish Fillets in Sherry and Mushroom Sauce

*Very easy to cook using convenience foods · Microwave – takes about 5
minutes · Do not freeze · Serves 3*

3 fillets of plaice or any white fish, fresh or thawed	Fold in half crosswise and place in a single layer in a shallow casserole.
1 x 10 oz/285 g/1¼ cup can condensed mushroom soup 4 tbsp dry sherry 3 tbsp fresh chopped parsley 4 tbsp water	Blend together in a saucepan, then heat until boiling. Pour over the fish fillets, cover and bake at 325°F/160°C/Gas Mark 3 for 20-25 minutes until the fish is cooked.

Turkey Casserole

Very easy to cook if you use a casserole that can be used on the hob and also in the oven · Can be adapted for microwave – do not fry the turkey pieces · Freeze · Serves 4

1 oz/25 g/2 tbsp butter	Place in a suitable casserole or large frying pan and melt over moderate heat.
1 lb/450 g raw turkey, cut into bite-size pieces	Raise the heat under the pan, then brown the turkey pieces in the sizzling butter, tossing them so that all sides are equally browned. Remove the turkey with a slotted spoon and set aside.
4 oz/100 g onions, peeled and finely chopped *1 clove garlic, peeled and crushed*	Add to the butter remaining in the pan and cook over moderate heat until the onion is soft.
4 oz/100 g mushrooms, sliced *1 x 14 oz/397 g can tomatoes*	Stir mushrooms, tomatoes and the juice into the onion mixture.
1 chicken stock cube, crumbled *2 tsp dried oregano*	Stir into the vegetables and continue cooking for 3-4 minutes, stirring continuously.
Salt *Pepper*	Season to taste. Place the sauce and the turkey pieces into the casserole, cover with the lid and bake in a very moderate oven, 325°F/160°/Gas Mark 3, for 1-1¼ hours or until the turkey is tender.

Pork Smetana

Easy to cook · Can be adapted for microwave – cook on Defrost 35% · Do not freeze · Refrigerate – the dish is tastier after 24 hours · Reheat carefully and thoroughly for at least 30 minutes · Serves 4

4 well-trimmed pork chops	Slice each chop horizontally from the rounded outside part to the bone to make a pocket.
Salt *Pepper*	Season to taste inside the chops.
1 small onion, peeled and finely chopped *2 tbsp fresh chopped parsley* *¼ tsp dried rosemary* *2 oz/50 g mushrooms, finely chopped*	Combine together and spread a teaspoon of the mixture inside the cavity of the chops. Press the chops well down to seal, inserting a wooden cocktail stick in each to secure it.
1 oz/25 g/2 tbsp butter or margarine	Place in a frying pan. Heat until the butter is sizzling, then seal the chops on both sides, frying until they are golden brown. Transfer the pork chops to a casserole. Stir the remaining vegetable mixture into the juices in the frying pan and sauté for 2 minutes, stirring continuously.
1 oz/25 g/¼ cup flour	Stir into the vegetable mixture.
½ pt/300 ml/1¼ cups veal or bone stock *3 tbsp fresh lemon juice* *Pinch sugar*	Stir into the vegetable mixture and bring to the boil, stirring continuously until the sauce thickens. Remove the pan from the heat.
4 tbsp soured cream	Stir into the sauce, pour the sauce into the casserole, cover with the lid and bake in a moderately hot oven, 375°F/190°C/Gas Mark 5, for 1 hour or until the meat is tender. Add extra stock if the sauce seems to be drying up during cooking.
4 tbsp soured cream	Spoon over the chops at the moment of serving.

Poached Sole in Soured Cream Sauce

Easy to cook · Can be adapted for microwave · Do not freeze · Serve hot · Serves 4

4-6 x 6 oz/175 g fillets of sole or lemon sole	Halve the fillets and roll up tail to head. Place in an ovenproof dish. Set oven at 350°F/180°C/Gas Mark 4.
1 medium onion, peeled and finely chopped *4 oz/100 g cooked ham, diced* *4 oz/100 g/¾ cup grated Edam cheese* *½ pt/300 ml/1¼ cups soured cream* *10 tarragon leaves* *Salt* *Pepper*	Combine all ingredients, pour over the fish and bake for 15-20 minutes until the flesh flakes easily.

Above: Pork Smetana

Opposite: Poached Sole in Soured Cream Sauce

Curried Kidneys

Easy and quick to cook · Can be adapted for microwave · Freeze · Serves 4

1 tbsp vegetable oil	Place in a heavy-based frying pan.
1 lb/450 g lamb or veal kidneys, rinsed, trimmed and sliced	Dry on kitchen paper towel, heat the oil in the frying pan, then add the kidney slices. Cook over moderate heat, stirring frequently, until the kidneys are opaque. Remove the kidneys and their juice and set aside.
1 oz/25 g/2 tbsp butter	Melt in the frying pan.
1 tbsp flour	Stir into the melted butter and cook over moderate heat, stirring continuously, until the flour browns.
2 tsp curry powder	Stir into the browned flour.
³/₄ pt/450 ml/2 cups hot water	Stir into the curry mixture and bring to the boil, stirring continuously.
1 beef stock cube	Crumble into the sauce and continue cooking, still stirring, for about 3 minutes. Stir in the cooked kidneys and their juice, reduce the heat and simmer for 5 minutes, stirring frequently.
Salt Freshly ground black pepper	Season to taste.
4 oz/100 g/1¹/₄ cups long grain rice, freshly cooked (weight before cooking)	Arrange in a border on a hot serving dish and pour the curry sauce into the centre.

Liver and Onion Casserole

Easy to cook · Can be adapted for microwave – seal the liver in a frying pan first · Freeze · Serves 4

1¹/₂ lb/750 g ox liver	Wash, slice, trim and pat dry on kitchen paper towel.
3 tbsp flour ¹/₂ tsp salt ¹/₄ tsp freshly ground black pepper	Combine together on a plate or piece of wax or greaseproof paper. Add the slices of liver and coat thoroughly. Reserve excess flour.
4 oz/100 g streaky bacon, rind removed and sliced into strips 1 medium onion, peeled and finely chopped	Combine in a frying pan over moderate heat and fry until the bacon is opaque and the onion is soft. Raise the heat and quickly brown the liver on both sides. Remove the liver, onion and bacon with a slotted spoon and place in a large casserole. Stir the reserved seasoned flour into the fat left in the pan and cook over moderate heat, stirring continuously, until the flour browns slightly.
1 pt/600 ml/2¹/₂ cups beef stock	Pour into the frying pan and bring to the boil, stirring continuously until the sauce thickens slightly.
2 tbsp tomato purée 1 tsp Liquid Caramel (page 151)	Add to the sauce and cook for a further 2 minutes. Pour the sauce over the liver and bacon, cover the casserole with the lid and bake in a very moderate oven, 325°F/160°C/Gas Mark 3, for 40-50 minutes until the liver is tender.

Sole Bonne Femme

Easy to cook · Can be adapted for microwave · Do not freeze · Serves 4

4 sole or Dover sole, skinned and filleted Squeeze fresh lemon juice Salt Freshly ground black pepper	Squeeze the lemon juice over the fish, season with salt and pepper and place the fish fillets in a greased casserole dish.
8 oz/225 g button mushrooms, finely sliced 2 tbsp fresh chopped parsley	Spread over the fish.
¹/₂ pt/300 ml/1¹/₄ cups dry white wine ¹/₄ pt/150 ml/²/₃ cup water	Blend together, then pour over the fish. Cover with the lid and bake in a moderate oven, 375°F/190°C/Gas Mark 5, for 30 minutes or until the fish is cooked. Spoon the liquid into a saucepan, replace the lid on the casserole, switch off the heat and leave in the oven while finishing the sauce. Boil the liquid until it is reduced by half.
1 tbsp butter 1 tbsp flour	Blend together in a small bowl. Add to the hot liquid in small pieces, whisking continuously until the sauce thickens.
¹/₄ pt/150 ml/²/₃ cup double or heavy cream 1 egg yolk	Beat together, stir in 1 tablespoon of the hot sauce, then pour back into the sauce and immediately remove the pan from the heat.
2 oz/50 g/¹/₄ cup butter	Beat into the sauce in small pieces. Adjust the seasoning, then pour the sauce over the hot fish fillets.

Beef in Stroganoff Sauce

Easy to prepare using convenience foods · Can be adapted for microwave – the meat must be tenderized first · Freeze · Serves 4

1 lb/450 g tender lean beef	Cut into strips about 2 in/5 cm long.
2 tbsp flour Salt Pepper	Season the flour with the salt and pepper, then dip the meat strips into the mixture, shaking away the surplus flour.
1¹/₂ oz/40 g/3 tbsp butter or margarine	Place in a frying pan and heat until the butter sizzles. Add a handful of the meat to the sizzling butter and cook, stirring continuously, until the meat is brown. Transfer the meat to an ovenproof casserole, continue cooking the remainder of the meat, adding that to the casserole.
1 x 7¹/₂ oz/215 g can sliced mushrooms 1 x 10 oz/285 g/1¹/₄ cup can condensed mushroom soup ¹/₂ pt/300 ml/1¹/₄ cups boiling water 1 beef stock cube, crumbled 4 tbsp medium sherry	Stir all the ingredients, including the juice from the can of mushrooms, into the beef. Add seasoning to taste. Cover the casserole with the lid and bake in a moderate oven, 350°F/180°C/Gas Mark 4, for 35-45 minutes or until the beef is soft.
¹/₄ pt/150 ml/²/₃ cup soured cream	Stir into the meat.

Index

Ancient Indian Massage

Traditional Massage Techniques Based on the Ayurveda

HARISH JOHARI

Munshiram Manoharlal
Publishers Pvt. Ltd.

ISBN 81-215-0008-7
This edition 2000
© 1984 **Johari**, Pratibha

Printed and published by
Munshiram Manoharlal Publishers Pvt. Ltd.,
Post Box 5715, 54 Rani Jhansi Road,
New Delhi 110 055.